Ports of Trade, Al Mina and Geometric Greek Pottery in the Levant

Joanna Luke

BAR International Series 1100
2003

Published in 2016 by
BAR Publishing, Oxford

BAR International Series 1100

Ports of Trade, Al Mina and Geometric Greek Pottery in the Levant

ISBN 978 1 84171 478 3

Typesetting and layout: Jerko Darko

BAR Publishing is the trading name of British Archaeological Reports (Oxford) Ltd.
British Archaeological Reports was first incorporated in 1974 to publish the BAR
Series, International and British. In 1992 Hadrian Books Ltd became part of the BAR
group. This volume was originally published by Archaeopress in conjunction with
British Archaeological Reports (Oxford) Ltd / Hadrian Books Ltd, the Series principal
publisher, in 2003. This present volume is published by BAR Publishing, 2016.

Printed in England

BAR
PUBLISHING

BAR titles are available from:

BAR Publishing
122 Banbury Rd, Oxford, OX2 7BP, UK
EMAIL   info@barpublishing.com
PHONE   +44 (0)1865 310431
FAX   +44 (0)1865 316916
www.barpublishing.com

Contents

Illustrations

Figures

Plates

Maps

Tables

Abbreviations

CC	Concentric Circle
cm	Centimetre
EG	Early Geometric
EPC	Early Protocorinthian
EPG	Early Protogeometric
LG	Late Geometric
LPG	Late Protogeometric
m	Metre
MG	Middle Geometric
MPC	Middle Protocorinthian
MPG	Middle Protogeometric
PC	Protocorinthian
PG	Protogeometric
PSC	Pendent Semicircle
SG	Subgeometric
SPG	SubProtogeometric
SM	SubMycenaean

Preface and acknowledgements

This monograph has its roots in a thesis written between 1989 and 1993 at the Faculty of Classics, Cambridge University (Luke 1994a), although it has been updated to take account of more recent material and all "thesis-speak" has, I hope, been excised.

Restrictions of time and circumstances have given rise to some sins of omission, one particularly large one best confessed here. References to Cilicia, assuredly in receipt of Geometric Greek pots, have been removed; it seemed kinder to do this than do present an unimproved version. Here then, the "Levant" starts from the imposing Amanus montains and stops at Philistia, with a brief excursus to Cyprus.

Some will doubtless detect an element of Hellenocentricity, perhaps in the very selection of study material, and certainly in the conclusions, which favour the Euboeans with the capacity to sail beyond their own shores eastwards as well as westwards. But it is not an "either…or" situation: Phoenicians, Cypriots and north Syrians may well have been active in the same waters at the same time. On a related note, studies in ethnicity have much to offer our understanding of cross-cultural relations in the past, and how ethnic identity (whatever that it is, in each case) can be seen in the material record. As a result, current conceptions of (to cite a recent example) "Phoenicians, Cypriots and north Syrians" are likely to be modified.

Initial research was funded by the British Academy, and both Christ's College and the Faculty of Classics at Cambridge eased the financial burden.

Many scholars have given their time and expertise, and it is a pleasure to be able to thank them here: Professor John Cherry, who bravely supervised the doctoral thesis; Professor Anthony Snodgrass for his continuing support and practical help well beyond the call of duty (and his own retirement); Professor Nicolas Coldstream for his stimulating comments on paper and in person, mainly during enjoyable discussions at UCL. Both examiners, Professor Nicholas Postgate and Dr Susan Sherratt, provided constructive criticism of which I have made much use. The late Professor Robert Cook waded through early drafts of the thesis and made helpful observations. Professor John Boardman has been an ever-courteous source of criticism and fresh ideas (and photographs). Sally-Anne Ashton and Alexandra Villing gave gracious assistance with access to the Al Mina database and the unpublished material in the British Museum. Many others have provided support, encouragement and information at various times, including: Professor Sue Alcock, Professor Robin Osborne, Ina Berg and Tamar Hodos.

Scholars whom I have never met have also been generous with their own unpublished research and with their ideas and criticisms, from which I have profited hugely. Among these are: Dr Gunnar Lehmann (Ben-Gurion University of the Negev); Professor Elizier Oren (Ben-Gurion University); Professor Guenter Kopcke (New York University); Professor Jane Waldbaum (University of Wisconsin-Milwaukee); David Ridgway (Edinburgh University); Dominik Bonatz (University of Freiburg); Professor Seymour Gitin (W.F. Albright Institute of Archaeological Research).

Museums, publishers and individuals have been generous in their supply of images for reproduction and of copyright permissions; they are individually acknowledged in the captions. David Davison has patiently fielded many queries.

I should also thank Ed for his babysitting stints, Dad for his proofreading skills and Mum and close friends for sustained if bemused support while I tried to work this strange obsession out of my system; but most of all I should thank my son Joseph, without whose obliging afternoon naps this monograph would never have seen the light of day.

The sins of commission will be many, but they are all my own work.

Chapter 1

Ports of trade: behavioural and material characteristics

Through this harbour of Goa was always the principal passsage to the kingdom of Narsinga and of Daquem; and for this reason it contained much merchandise, and large caravans of merchants came from the interior country in quest of it, and bought other commodities in exchange.

Alboquerque
(cited Leeds 1961: 34)

Al Mina, lady of many guises

This study begins with Al Mina (Map 1), a site that has long dominated discussions of Greek-Levantine relations in the Geometric Period. Her primacy in the secondary literature is due to a number of factors. First and foremost, she was the first Levantine site with an abundance of Greek pottery to be excavated and published. Second, she remains the findspot of the greatest quantity of Greek Geometric pottery in the Levant—about 1500 sherds (p.44). Lastly, her excavator's interpretation propelled it into Classical Archaeology textbooks as a Greek colony. But despite her long pedigree, interpretations of the site have been many and varied; if ever there was a cautionary tale against letting published artefacts speak for themselves, Al Mina is it.

Interpretations of Al Mina

Sir Leonard Woolley excavated Al Mina in 1936-7. Woolley was an Orientalist seeking the connection between the Bronze Age civilisations of the Near East and the Aegean (Woolley 1938: 1). He considered Al Mina the likely port of Bronze Age Alalakh. Hence the presence of large quantities of not Bronze Age but Iron Age material was problematic. But by identifying this otherwise 'irrelevant' site as Posideum, a legendary Greek city founded by Amphilochus after the Trojan War (Herodotus 3.91), Woolley bestowed on Al Mina an intrinsic importance of its own.[1]

Woolley's identification of Al Mina as Posideum dominated the publication timetable of the kept finds. The Greek material, exclusively ceramic, was the focus of the preliminary publication, and was studied in some detail almost two decades before the non-Greek pottery was published (Robertson 1940; Taylor 1959). Many non-ceramic (non-Greek) finds were published, but mainly in catalogue form. Hence the notion of Greek residence at the site was the inevitable result of its initial identification: Posideum was a Greek colony, the most fully studied and presented finds at Al Mina were Greek, so Al Mina was a Greek colony.

Dunbabin, then the foremost authority on Greek colonisation, ushered Al Mina into Greek colonial history with the remark that "there is nothing to differentiate the place from one of the many Greek colonies in Italy or Sicily" (1957: 25), a view still held today (e.g. Boardman 1999b: 155). For some, Al Mina remains a Greek settlement (e.g. Kearsley 1999: 128), and constitutes a satisfying balance to the perceived Euboean dominance of the central Italian coastal trade and the settlement of Pithekoussai in the late eighth century BCE.

More recently, the Levantine characteristics of many artefacts at the site have been acknowledged. As a result, some have removed Al Mina from Greek control, making the site an independent port of multiple *enoikismoi* and hinterlands, a "great international emporium" (e.g. Ridgway 1992: 108), Aubet's "free port" where Euboeans and Phoenicians cohabited (2001: 63).

Others have re-rooted Al Mina in its native north Syrian context. Perreault regards Al Mina as a fundamentally domestic site founded and inhabited by Levantines (1993: 68), and Saltz argued that Al Mina was a port of an inland power (1978: 40, 42). The idea that Al Mina may have had a native hinterland for which it acted as a port, as opposed to a solely Greek one to which it passed Orientalia, has gained currency (e.g. Braun 1982: 11-12; Boardman 1990b: 172).

As a result, most Classical Archaeologists have quantitatively modified Greek involvement at Al Mina, with Greeks, whose presence is supposedly attested by the large quantity of Greek

---

[1] That the historicity of a site was an important element in decisions to excavate is clear from Woolley's introduction to the account of the entire campaign, *A Forgotten Kingdom*, which, he explains, is an "apologia" for having taken the unusual step of excavating a site unattested in Classical literature.

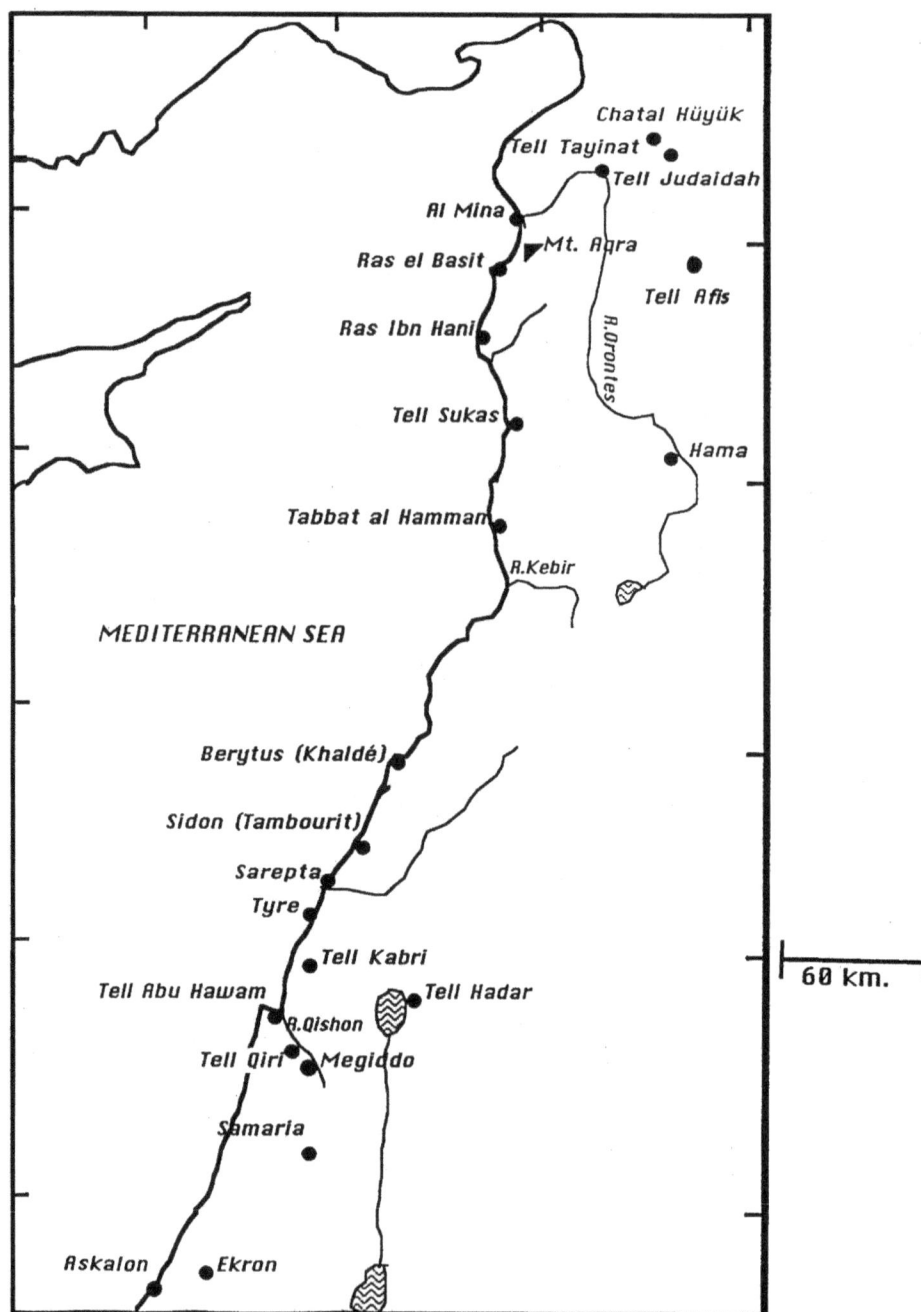

Map 1. Findspots of Greek Geometric pottery along the Levantine littoral (excl. Babylon and Nineveh)

pottery at the site, inhabiting a (usually dominant) enclave. Elayi (1987: 249-250, n. 3) lists popular epithets of the site, such as "Greek emporion", "comptoir grec", "Greek harbour town", which are all in accord with Boardman's classic estimation of Al Mina that it "only assumed real importance as an emporium when the Greeks began to visit the port and established a small community there" (1999a: 43). Its primary *raison d'être* is Levantine-Greek/Cypriot trade (*idem* 1999b: 154-5).

"Emporion" is the modern term usually applied to sites whose principal function is believed to be trade, such as Pithekoussai and Naukratis, both sites where Greeks are known to have settled (e.g. Bresson and Rouillard 1993). In ancient Greek literature, *emporion* was applied to any locus of exchange (Hind 1969, Appendix III: 18). Its myriad mental associations embroiled "emporion" in the primitivist-modernist

terminological debates (for which see e.g. Finley 1979; Austin and Vidal-Nacquet 1980; Möller 2000).

In the search for a neutral terminology, Finley (1962: 34) briefly referred to the term "Port of Trade", a concept developed by Karl Polanyi, founder of substantivism, to describe loci of cross-cultural exchange. Together with his colleagues in the Economic History Department of Columbia University, Polanyi argued, like Bucher, that pre-modern economies were embedded in socio-political structures and should not be analysed using the terms and concepts of formal economic theory, and he developed a set of alternative terms (Polanyi *et al.* 1957; Polanyi 1963). One of these was "port of trade", a politically neutral institution which sponsors safe and reliable trading relations between strangers. Polanyi used Al Mina as a type-site in this concept, along with, among many others, 15th-16th century Aztec-Mayan settlements and

18th century Whydah in East Africa. In Polanyi's analysis, Al Mina was an independent Bronze Age principality feeding imports to a thalassophobic hinterland empire (1963: 33).[2]

Ports of trade in the ancient world

While Al Mina has no demonstrable Bronze Age existence, its characterisation as a port of trade is potentially useful. There is no reason to suppose that ancient Greeks were unique either in their need to maintain cross-cultural trading relations or in the ways in which they went about doing so. Indeed, "port of trade" has made the occasional foray into Classical scholarship (e.g. Humphreys 1978: 57; Austin and Vidal-Nacquet 1980; Casson 1989: 279; Möller 2000).

Strictly speaking, the term "port of trade" does not necessarily apply to the place where the actual exchange occurs, but to the place providing facilities for traders and their goods, where the initial break of bulk occurs.[3] This is important from an archaeological perspective, since the behavioural processes by which the port's material record is formed include ones beyond the purely economic sphere—in particular residence of foreigners—which can be easier to identify on the ground than the mere point of exchange.

The port of trade's potential for archaeological detection has led to its exploration by non-Classical archaeologists, such as archaeologists of the Medieval world (e.g. Hodges 1978a; Þorláksson 1978). Chapman's study of Aztec-Mayan ports of trade has been extended by archaeologists working on the Mesoamerican island of Cozumel (e.g. Chapman 1957; Rathje and Sabloff 1973; Sabloff and Rathje 1975a; Sabloff and Freidel 1975; Freidel and Sabloff 1984).

Models in Classical Archaeology

Overall, the "port of trade" concept has been largely ignored in Classical Archaeology, the most traditional branch of 'Traditional Archaeology'. Classical Archaeology has generally dismissed model-building, preferring to adopt a particularistic historical approach and to spurn the cross-disciplinary methodologies of the 'New Archaeology' (e.g. Renfrew 1980; Dyson 1981; 1993; Snodgrass 1985).

Greek colonial archaeology exemplifies all of the particularistic tendencies of Traditional Archaeology. The classic, invaluable, commentaries, such as Boardman's *The Greeks Overseas* and the *Cambridge Ancient History*, tackle colonisation as a narrative, focusing on the respective regions to present a history of the topic. Themes (such as colony relations with natives or with the mother community) are considered solely in terms of the 'evidence', preferably of the literary variety. In sum, the approach is inductive in the extreme. Cross-cultural generalisations and ideas from ethno-history are not considered. Indeed, the impression is that Classical Archaeology has no need of models, there is so much data: better to leave such practices to those who need to 'fill out' their meagre and unimpressive material and literary records.

Where they are acknowledged, models are treated with suspicion. For example, Boardman warns of the "unwillingness to treat them (*sc.* material artefacts) on their own terms rather than on the terms dictated by modern typologies and models" (1999a: 10; *idem* 2001: 34; Coldstream 1996: 137). But models are still used, in order to establish precisely what the own terms of the artefacts are: (arte)facts are not absolute, but are contingent upon interpretation, as the history of interpretation of Al Mina amply testifies. So models are employed, but usually unconsciously. This is particularly true of those of an (instinctively if not avowedly) 'modernist' frame of mind, who use concepts like export trades, bulking points, balance of payments etc. in their interpretations of early Greek trade and colonisation, a tendency perhaps best expressed in variations on the expression 'Trade before the Flag' (e.g. Blakeway 1932-1933: 202; Boardman 1999b: 162).

Yet, despite the inherent dangers of over-simplification, models can accommodate, explain and utilise information from a range of material and literary sources in ways that entrenched inductive interpretations of the individual sources cannot.[4] Certainly, impressive recent material discoveries from Sardinia to the Levant have not been accompanied by similar progress in the great debates of Greek colonial archaeology.

Nonetheless, there have been a few conscious efforts to use models to distinguish certain types of Greek colonial settlement. The most frequently perceived distinction has been that between *apoikiai* (residential settlements away from home) and *emporia* (e.g. Austin and Vidal-Nacquet 1980: 61; Graham 1983: 4-5). The 1960's and 1970's witnessed a concerted effort to distinguish such sites on the ground, mainly by way of models inspired by spatial analysis. Trading colonies (called *type Phocéen* after the most enthusiastic founders of such settlements) possessed little territory, had fortifications focusing upon the port facilities, good transportation routes, and enjoyed *ententes* with the native hosts; settlement colonies had extensive well-defended territory, and a strong sense of territoriality that often resulted in bloodshed between Greeks and natives (Martin 1973).

Such model building implicitly recognised the validity of seeking predictable patterns in the material record, and attempted to include a wide range of material evidence in the identification of type-sites.

---

[2] Polanyi's distinctions between state vs. private trade, treaty vs. market etc tend to over-compartmentalise ancient trade and depend on a mutual exclusivity between types of trade that does not seem borne out by more recent evidence. Cf. Möller 2000: 21, who insists on the importance of administered trade (here confined mainly to type A ports of trade).

[3] This distinction has caused confusion. For example, Torrence (1978: 108-109) takes issue with Hodges' (1978a: 97; 1978b: 115) locational use of Renfrew's "middleman trading" model, pointing out that this location may simply be the place where traders were based, not the place where exchanges occur (her "entrepôt").

[4] Nor need models be tyrannical and unyielding templates; as von Reden (1995: preface) points out, models can be improved and refined in the light of ancient as well as anthropological evidence. Also Möller 2000: 3-6.

The inclusion of a range of material evidence in the identification of type-sites and the sorts of residence implied has been explored by Bronze Age archaeologists, who have generally been more open to model use (e.g. Sherratt and Sherratt 1991: 351). Of particular relevance here are studies into the character of the "Minoan thalassocracy": did it entail Minoan settlement in the various Cycladic islands, and if so, of what sort? Following Warren's list of material criteria by which to judge settlement of Minoans, Branigan developed a typology of Minoan colonies detectable in the material record which could be applied as predictive models to suspected cases of Minoan colonisation (Warren 1971: 101; Branigan 1981; 1984).

The steps he used to derive the models are adapted in the next section to devise an acceptable classification of the "port of trade", one that includes the entire "gamut" of type sites (Arnold 1957a: 155), and that can be used on the ground. For, while Dalton regarded the wide applicability of the term as a positive reflection of the institution's flexibility (1978: 102), most archaeologists have ultimately found that its applicability to such a bewilderingly wide variety of sites weakened its use as a neutral tool of analysis (e.g. Rathje and Sabloff 1973: 221; Hodges 1978a: 97-100; 1982: 24; Bresson 1983: 163-164; Figueira 1984; Zaccagnini 1993: 130). It is clear that there are many different types of port which conform to Polanyi's important conception of the port of trade as a repeatedly-used locus of cross-cultural exchange; inventing new terms only demands new definitions which are no more likely to be universally accepted.[5]

A typology of ports of trade

Step 1. Case studies. Identify different types of 'ports of trade' from historical case studies.
Step 2. Behavioural characteristics. Distil the behavioural characteristics of each type.
Step 3. Material characteristics. Extrapolate the material characteristics of each type.

Step 1: Case studies

Using a variety of case studies (listed in the "documented examples" column of Table 1), ports of trade can be divided into three main groups on the basis of who exercised political control over the port. While other variables also influence port characteristics, such as number of migrants, permanence, social complement of colonies etc (Curtin 1975: 62-66 discusses some in relation to trading diasporas), it is the political factor which seems most to dictate the behavioural characteristics of the sites, and often explains the other factors - a port controlled by a trading community is, for example, more likely to be inhabited by traders' families than a port in potentially hostile host territory.

The first group, type A, includes sites controlled by the hinterland power in whose territory the port lies and which the port primarily serves.

Type B sites are politically and administratively autonomous, independent from all other polities.[6]

Type C sites are under the control of the trading community.[7]

Table 1: Port of trade type-sites

	Political control	Documented examples	Excavated examples
A	hinterland	Sri Lankan and Indian ports of the Portuguese period; Middle Saxon Hamwic; Medieval Icelandic ports; Medieval Kaupang and Birka; Dahomean Whydah; 18th century Canton.	Kaupang; Jewish London
B	autonomous	Aztec-Mayan ports, eg Cozumel, c.1000 CE-1500 CE; pre-Dahomean Whydah; Medieval Dorestad and Hedeby; LBA Ugarit;[8] 16th century Banten.	Cozumel; Dorestad and Hedeby; Ugarit; 3rd-2nd century BCE Delos.
C	traders	Second millennium BCE Assyrians in Anatolia;[9] Naukratis; Europeans in East and Africa, 17th-19th century CE; European treaty ports in China, 19th-20th centuries CE; contemporary Chinese in Bangkok; Aztec Tochtepec in Oaxaca, Central Mexico; Phoenician trading colonies.	Assyrians in Anatolia; Naukratis; EMII/LMIB Kastri on Kythera; Phoenician trading colonies.

---

[5] For example, Freidel and Sabloff (1972: 2) distinguish "ports of trade" (where all trade is non-local) from "trading ports" (where local and non-local exchange meet). But both ports require the exchange of goods across cultural boundaries, with all the problems entailed.

[6] Despite Polanyi's emphasis on political neutrality, it was this type of site that most interested him ("our port of trade" is one inhabited by natives (1963: 36)). He interpreted the invariably separate administration of the port as a result of the hosts' desire to avoid contamination from traders who often hailed from the market economies so repugnant to Polanyi himself.

[7] The three types accord with the most important types of loci of cross-cultural exchange previously stressed by commentators. Polanyi (1963: 34-35) himself recognised two types of "emporia": Lehmann-Hartleben's archaeological vestiges of "silent trade" and the trading quarter of a Classical town, both of which he distinguished from Pirenne's *Portus*, which was a settlement of traders. These accord here with types B, A, and C respectively. Humphreys, in her critique of Polanyi's work,

extrapolates the same three types of port on the basis of political control (1969: 191). In archaeological trade studies, type A is the locational equivalent of Renfrew's Mode 8, "emissary trading", being the physical locus of the transportation of goods, type B equates with his Mode 10, "Port-of-Trade", and type C with his Mode 9 "colonial enclave" (Renfrew 1975: 42-43). Likewise Hodges distinguishes his Class 1 port of trade, the "Dorestad-Hedeby" type, from Class 2, the "Kaupang-Hamwih" type (1978a: 97-101). These are equivalent to types B and A respectively.

[8] Documentary evidence shows that merchants from many origins both traded and resided in Ugarit. Like many type B ports, Ugarit sometimes found itself under the protection of larger states, but was, for most of its history, an independent kingdom (e.g. van Wijngaarden 1999: 9-10; Cherry and Knapp 1994: 136).

[9] The Assyrians had a diaspora of trade settlements in Anatolia, with its apex at Karum Kanis, whence much of the documentary evidence comes. Some goods were sold to the palaces, some in the Assyrian part of town (e.g. Curtin 1984: 67-70).

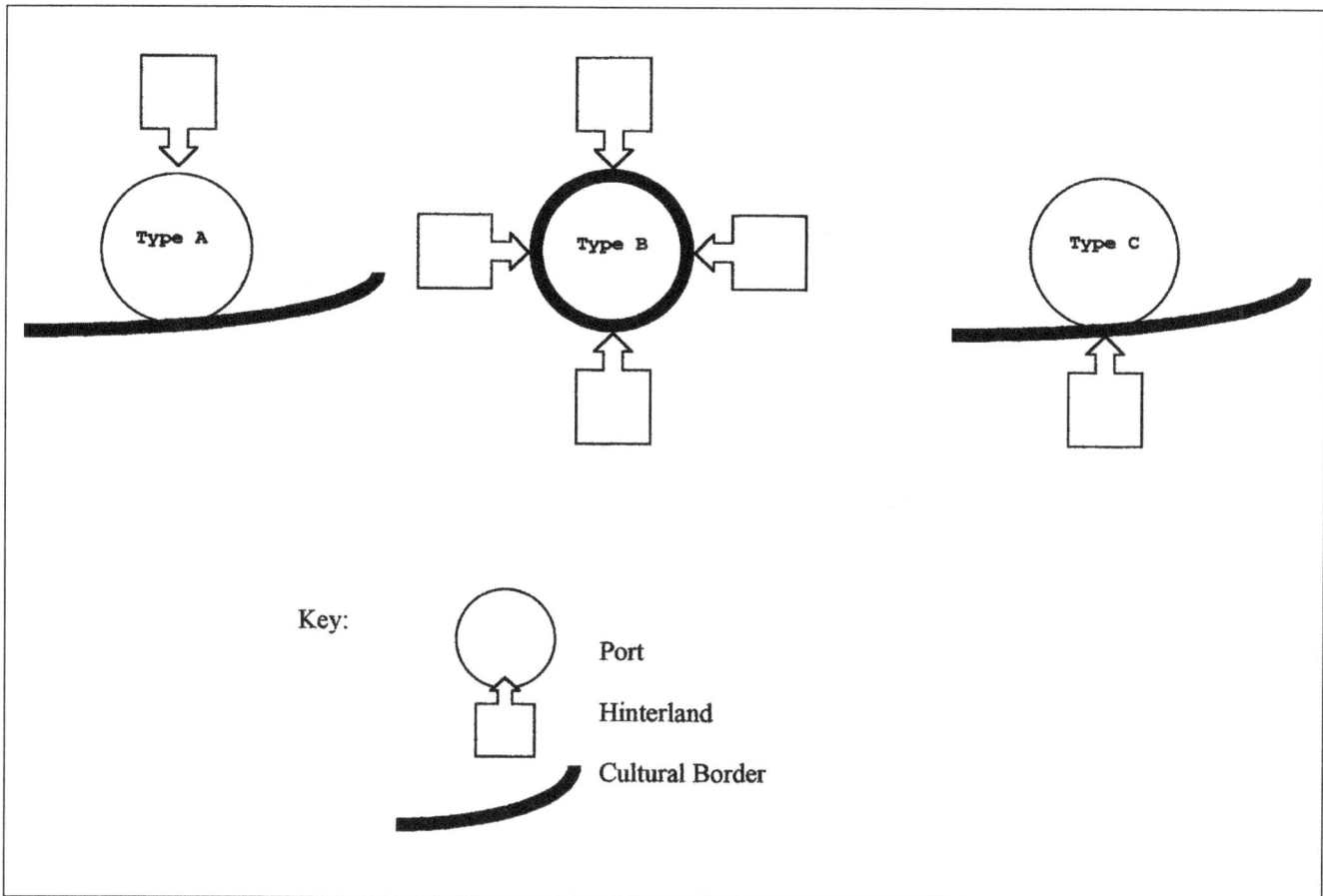

Figure 1. The relationship of each port of trade to its hinterland

For the purposes of this study, hinterland is defined as the "area served by the port". So, in the case of type A ports, the host community is the principal area served by the port and is therefore the technical hinterland, even though other areas may also benefit. In the case of type B ports, the hinterlands are multiple and correspond to all of the individual areas that the traders serve. In the case of type C ports, the hinterland is the homeland of the traders who originally found the ports for their own benefit, not the host community of the ports. These differences are represented diagrammatically in figure 1.

Step 2: Behavioural characteristics

A few general points may be outlined:

1. There is often a period of sporadic contacts prior to institutionalisation as a port (to Hodges' type B emporium (1982: 51-2)). The material correlates of this pre-institutionalisation period may result in theories of 'pre-colonial trade'.

2. Many ports evolve into another type, through political intervention by the hinterland, or by one of the trading partners. The autonomous type B port is the most vulnerable of all, its visible prosperity and ease of access acting as particular attractions for those wishing to monopolise trade.

3. Many ports evolve into central places, by attracting to themselves additional non-economic functions as a result of

their success. Such ports become indistinguishable from settlement colonies.[10]

Behavioural characteristics of Type A Ports

Institutionalisation. The institutionalisation of the port by the hinterland may mark the recognition that the supply of imports must be regulated in order to prevent a crisis of leadership consequent upon the loss of imports. It is for this reason that Leeds calls the port of trade "an organ operated for ends of state" (1971). Icelandic chieftains were governed by "status motives" in their requirement of luxury goods obtainable only through her ports (Porláksson 1978: 112).

Control of imports. Hinterland leaders have exclusive access to imports. Control enhances their status, through the redistribution of necessities, and the display, deposition and choice distribution of imported luxuries to dependent élites, in the withdrawal system of wealth (Hodges 1988: 36; Leeds 1961: 28). For example, the king of Narsynga in Sri Lanka redistributed imported horses to his faithful lords, which they passed on to their own knights (Leeds 1961: 36). The same mechanism prevailed in Persia, wherein Cyrus redistributed luxury gifts to his friends and "no-one there is ever allowed to have such things (*sc.* bracelets, necklaces, horses) except those to whom the king has given them" (Xenophon,

---

[10] This is Hodges' type C emporium (1982: 52), and evolution marks the '*apoikia* stage' in Minns' colonial process, and the third stage in the development of Burghardt's 'Gateway Cities' (Minns 1913: 348; Burghardt 1971: 284).

Cyropaedia 8.2.7). In Whydah's redistributive economy, imports were consumed only by dignitaries (Arnold 1957a: 173-74). The imports thereby regarded as attributes of status in Whydah (shoes and umbrellas) were not ones upon which the European providers laid any value. Even to the Dahomean élite, these goods were not the *raison d'être* of the port's institutionalisation (arms were), but, as imports, they came to be associated with high status: they became luxuries, to be rationed and displayed.

This type of port is often found in a redistributive economy, which facilitates the most efficient collection of exports as well as the redistribution of imports. In Whydah, slaves were brought to the king prior to transport to the port and were the property only of the king and of those to whom the king granted the right of ownership (Arnold 1957a: 171). The mechanism is colourfully illustrated by Barbosa's account of a Sri Lankan kingdom where

> "All the good cinnamon...the king of the country sells...himself to the merchants...because no-one can gather it except the king. There are likewise...many wild elephants which...all have to be brought and presented to the king. There are many jewels in this island...all these stones are gathered in by the king and sold by himself"

> (Leeds 1961: 37).

Because of the involvement of the élite, this type of port lends itself to the practice of administered trade between leaders, usually through their representatives. Administered trade may take the form of gift exchange. In a request highly reminiscent of those posed of each other by Near Eastern monarchs in the second millennium BCE, the king of Calicut (paraphrased by Da Gama) unabashedly conveyed to the king of Portugal that:

> "my country is rich in cinnamon, cloves, ginger, pepper, and precious stones. That which I ask of you in exchange is gold, silver, corals and scarlet cloth"

> (Leeds 1961: 36-37).

Terms of trade. All exchanges inside the port are conducted on the hosts' terms. In Dahomean Whydah all equivalencies were fixed in Dahomean law (Arnold 1957a: 168). In Medieval Iceland, inspectors and sheriffs were legally obliged to settle prices of foreign goods on arrival (Þorláksson 1978: 113).

Port location. The port is usually situated on the boundary of the host territory, such as Whydah, Goa, Hamwic etc. Part of the reason lies in the desire to keep foreigners away from the core of the host community. More pragmatically, such a location is most efficient for the bulking of goods. This type of port therefore acts as a gateway community: all goods enter and leave the territory through the port (Burghardt 1971: 269).

Freedom of traders in port.[11] Foreign representatives are discouraged from penetrating beyond the port, as at Hamwic,

---

[11] Although merchants are the most obvious representatives of a foreign community likely to be present in a port of trade, an inscription giving the title of the Sidonian *koinon* on Delos indicates other personnel likely to be present: "the *koinon* of the Berytian Poseidoniasts of merchants and shippers and warehousemen" (cited Carter 1997: 99).

Whydah and in India/Sri Lanka. Containing foreign traders in the port area prevents foreign traders exchanging their wares with anyone outside the élite stratum; it keeps local and long-distance exchange separate; it also limits the social, economic, and cultural contamination of the native population. Inhabitants of the peripheral port areas may be tainted by association: Whydasians were regarded as being of 'metic' status in Dahomey (Arnold 1957a: 163 and n. 26). In many societies, traders from other cultures are (for good reason) suspected of being spies (*ibid.*: 169). The Aztecs formalised this with a class of trader-spies, the *naualoztomeca*, who sat in foreign markets disguised as traders (Chapman 1957: 124). Xenophon (*Cyropaedia* 6.2.2) reports that Indian traders were persuaded to act as spies by the Persian king.

Within the port, traders are carefully supervised. Da Gama and his crew were provided with food and lodgings and were supervised to a stifling extent during their sojourn at Goa (Leeds 1961: 30, 31). At Whydah, traders were provided with servants, carriers and other attendants (Arnold 1957a: 165). Such intense supervision discourages the permanent residence of foreign traders at the port: as a result, traders are unlikely to bring families or recreate their full domestic lifestyle to any degree.

For ease of supervision, resident traders are often billeted in enclaves; at Whydah, the Brazilians, British, Portuguese and French had permanent factories, each of which constituted a distinct quarter of the town (Arnold 1957a: 166). In the Indian ports, natives and Europeans were strictly separated (Leeds 1961: 27). In Canton, foreign merchants were assigned quarters outside the city walls, and were regularly ordered to leave (Curtin 1984: 242).

Behavioural characteristics of Type B Ports

Institutionalisation. No specific act of institutionalisation is necessary, and these ports emerge naturally on important nodes in cross-cultural exchange networks. They need never be institutionalised on a formal basis; a periodic meeting place or fair, fitting readily into the existing matrix of local fairs and markets, could satisfy the import needs of all parties. For example, Mansangaar, a Senegambian village, was transformed twice a year into a port of trade by the Afro-Portuguese (Curtin 1975: 99), and fairs were an important part of Central American long-distance trade when the Spaniards arrived (Freidel and Sabloff 1984: 186-187).

Control of imports. There need be no separation of local from long-distance exchange. Exchanges can occur between traders, and between traders and port inhabitants (who may also exact tolls, as at Dorestad (Hodges 1982: 57, 60, 90)). Freidel and Sabloff note the importance in Central Mexico of local production of goods for export, and the markets of Tlateloco and other settlements in the Mexica valley were filled with exotic luxuries (Freidel and Sabloff 1984: 186, 188). At Banten, Chinese traders brokered both local and overseas trade (Curtin 1984: 170).

If there is no separation of local and long-distance trade, a wide range of people may have access to imports. Sub-élite involvement means that utilitarian wares are also traded in these ports. For instance, Sahagún, a Spanish commentator on Aztec society, noted that a trader had brought stone knives, bells and needles to trade (Chapman 1957: 125), and Freidel and Sabloff point out that even the *pochteca*, administered traders par excellence, carried utilitarian goods such as flint knives and combs for ordinary purchasers (1984: 188).

The port may prosper, from local goods entering the markets, toll income, and the presence of so many visitors to provision. The presence of large amounts of gold in, and only in, the Aztec-Mayan ports was the cause of much delight to the Spanish Conquistadors (Chapman 1957: 133). The Rheneians regarded Delos as a source of wealth (Duchêne 1993: 123, 116).

The ports are politically neutral. This neutrality is expressed in the fluidity and flexibility of their behavioural and material culture, denoting a cosmopolitan attitude to foreigners and their influences (Rathje and Sabloff 1975: 9-13). For example, of all the Aztec-Mayan ports only Cozumel offered the Spaniards safe haven on their journeys, an ironic gesture of neutrality given the region's, and indeed the site's, ultimate fate. Delos was Apollo's personal island, belonging to none and offering sanctuary to all. Intermarriage and cultural interaction created a mixed culture in Banten (Curtin 1984: 170).

Terms of trade. Exchanges may take place either under the aegis of a neutral authority or independently. Measures and currencies will be of diverse forms, and there may be evidence of the use of several different languages. At Delos, docking and storage facilities were attached to the shrine complexes belonging to the various trading groups present (Duchêne 1993: 83).

Port location. Such ports are located on central transition points of an ecological, transportational or economic nature. Dorestad was located at the confluence of the Lek and the Rhine, and at the junction of a multiplicity of transport routes (Hodges 1982: 74), and islands are obviously advantageous in this respect, as the success of Cozumel and Delos demonstrates.

Freedom of traders in port. Foreigners of different origins reside freely at these ports, recreating as much of their domestic lifestyles as they wish. To minimize conflict, foreigners may inhabit separate enclaves, such as the Aztec barrios (Chapman 1957: 121), and on Delos (Rathje and Sabloff 1972: 8-9). At Hedeby, King Godfred seems to have planned a part of the settlement especially for the foreign traders (Hodges 1982: 56). The cosmopolitan and safe nature of the port can encourage traders to bring their families. This factor in particular encourages the appearance of:

· Foreign styles of interior decoration and furniture.
· Foreign rituals. Tyrians and Sidonians transported their *marzeah* to Delos (Carter 1997: 99-100).
· Foreign personal belongings.
· Foreign production of goods.
· Foreign kitchenwares.

Behavioural characteristics of Type C Ports

Institutionalisation. Since a permanent migration is implied, a specific act of institutionalisation is required in each case. This may result in the port being planned according to its specific function; the European ports in Africa, for example, were all stone-built and heavily fortified (Curtin 1975: 101, 121).

Control of imports. The port is founded and controlled by a trading community, typically to tap the resources of a less economically developed area. As Branigan (1981: 25-27) showed with regard to colonies, three types of ports can be distinguished, any of which can belong to a *diaspora*: settlement ports, enclaves, and governed ports, with an element of political control.

Terms of trade. Measures, currencies and the business language are foreign. For example, the size and weight of the iron bars used in the Dutch trade with Africa were based on Dutch measures (Curtin 1975: 241), and the Chinese community in Bangkok continue to conduct their business in Chinese (Branigan 1984: 50).

Port location. Except for enclaves, ports tend to be situated at the edge of the host region, that being the most efficient location for the funnelling of goods and the safest one for a foreign community. European ports at the heads of their respective African *diasporas* all had coastal locations (Curtin 1975: 108, map 3.3). Naukratis was at the Canopic mouth of the Nile.

Freedom of traders in port. The permanent nature of the traders' presence means that many bring families. African traders in the *juula* towns were accompanied by their families, who tended the surrounding fields. By contrast, the contemporary all-male European trading ports relied for their sustenance on the nearby African towns (Curtin 1975: 119). The Assyrians who first settled Karum Kanis were all male (Aubet 2001: 109)

The initial presence of unaccompanied male foreigners often gives rise to relationships with native women, and the emergence of a generation of cross-cultural brokers. The best documented example of this is the case of the Afro-Portuguese, offspring of Portuguese traders and native wives, who created their own independent and successful trade *diaspora* in Senegambia (Curtin 1975: 95-100). The Kültepe texts attest the marriage of Assyrian merchants into Anatolian families with whom they wished to do business (Coldstream 1993: 94), and evidence from Pithekoussai suggests that native wives were common (*ibid.*).

Such permanence encourages the recreation of a lifestyle based on that familiar in the traders' homeland, although the restricted availability of materials and the presence of local inhabitants, such as spouses, may encourage modifications. In the course of recreating a home-from-home, any or all of the following can appear:

· Foreign styles of architecture (except in enclaves, where the architecture is local, as in the Chinese quarter of

Bangkok). In contrast to Chinese cities, foreign treaty ports in China had race courses, upmarket clubs and tidy public parks. This was despite having overwhelmingly Chinese populations (Abbey 2000).

- Foreign styles of interior decoration. The Bangkok Chinese used their own styles of furniture (Branigan 1984: 50-1).

- Foreign rituals. Herodotus records the use of temples and altars by the Greeks who frequented Naukratis (2.178). The temple of Melqart in Cadiz and the Phoenician rites practised therein were famous in antiquity (Aubet 2001: 275-7).

- Foreign personal belongings. Even after several centuries of existence, and some inter-marriage, the Chinese community in Bangkok imports some pottery and jewellery from China (Branigan 1984: 50).

- Foreign production of foreign goods. The Bangkok Chinese also produce pottery and jewellery in Chinese styles (*ibid.*)

- Foreign kitchenwares.

Step 3: Archaeological correlates of ports of trade

A few points pertain to the archaeological features of all ports:

1. The features outlined reflect 'perfect' type-sites.[12] Quite apart from the major differences in excavated information available from different sites, it would be unrealistic to expect every characteristic to be observable at each site. For this reason the notion of a *Kriterienbundel* is proposed, providing a 'checklist' against which sites can be compared.

2. Only institutionalised ports are detectable. Prior to institutionalisation, contacts are sporadic, and traders only temporarily present. This stage may be indicated by the presence of imports in the hinterland and on the future site of the port. In the case of type B ports, institutionalisation may never occur, with fairs taking place periodically (as at Senegambian Mansangaar). For the other ports, traders initially unsure of their welcome may reside in temporary accommodation, such as boats, from which trade can take place (Hodges 1982: 62; Smith 1987: 148). Trade can also be silent (Herodotus 4.196).

3. In cases where traders are in control of their part of the port, signs of foreign residence are likely. Ports are, by definition, "multi-ethnic situations" (Hall 1997: 131) so ethnic identity and its material expression may, where it is permitted, be marked. However, several recent studies (such as Hall's), have demonstrated that the relationship between the material record and ethnic identity need not be obvious or direct, or even exist at all. Regrettably migrants, particularly those who depend for their lives and livelihood on the welcome of foreigners, do not carry suitcases full of the material correlates of their ethnic identity, to be unpacked at their final destination, and found by archaeologists millennia later. Consideration of a wide range of material factors is crucial.

---
[12] Möller 2000: 3-5 has a lucid discussion of ideal types.

The behavioural characteristics summarized above can be used to extrapolate a *Kriterienbundel* of the expected material characteristics of each port type. The number of each point in the following typology corresponds to the behavioural one of which it is a material correlate.

Material correlates of type A ports of trade

Institutionalisation. The pre-institutionalisation stage may be represented not by finds at the port site itself but by imports to the hinterland earlier than the date of institutionalisation.

Control of imports. In the hinterland, imports are concentrated in central places. The central place at the apex of the politico-economic hierarchy attracts the greatest quantity of imports, which may be displayed or deposited. Imports may be redistributed to subordinates in hierarchically-ordered lesser central places, who may in turn ostentatiously display or deposit them. The prestige goods that are often the focus of administered trade may be present at the port. There is no deposition of traded goods at the port itself, which is not materially wealthy.

Terms of trade. Measures, currencies and the language of trade are of native types.

Port location. At political border.

Freedom of traders. Close supervision of traders, and provision for their needs, can involve:

- Native architectural styles.

- Native furniture types.

- Absence of families. This factor may account for the imbalance between adult and sub-adult graves in the main cemetery at Hamwic, where only five of the seventy-six burials were those of children (Hodges 1982: 63).

- No foreign rituals.

- No foreign kitchenwares.

- Morphological range of imported wares low, not representing full functionality of domestic assemblage.

- No foreign production of foreign artefacts.

- Restriction of visible aspects of foreign culture (such as personal belongings) to enclaves. At Hamwic, this was the area nearest the waterfront (Hodges 1982: 57-8; Morton 1992: 67).

- No imitation of foreign goods; certainly none of the "dissemination of style" encouraged by the presence of foreign producers (Papadopoulos 1997: 450-1). Foreigners are culturally suspect. At Hamwic, very few imports were imitated on the site (Morton 1992: 67).

- No scattering of imports along the border except in the area of the port itself: foreign goods outside the port are items of trade

Material correlates of Type B ports of trade

Institutionalisation. Although it may be possible to infer the existence of periodic ports from the presence of imports in the hinterlands, only permanently instituted ports are visible. Naturally emerging, there will be no evidence of planning, as at Dorestad (Hodges 1982: 60-61).

Control of imports. Since there need be no physical separation of local and imported goods in the port, imports may be distributed over the whole site, as seems to have happened at Cozumel (Sabloff and Rathje 1975b: 27), and at Dorestad and Hedeby (Hodges 1978a: 98). At Ugarit, royal and private merchants traded goods alongside each other and imported Mycenaean wares had a wide spatial distribution (Cherry and Knapp 1994: 137; van Wijngaarden 1999: 11), with Mycenaean stirrup jars being found in most tombs (*ibid.*: 14).

The port's prosperity encourages the withdrawal and deposition of imports, including luxuries, at the ports. Dorestad for example displays "an exceptional range of metalwork" (Hodges 1982: 75).

Terms of trade. Different systems of measures, currencies and languages co-exist at these sites. No one language of trade need be dominant, and multi-lingual documents may occur, as on Delos (Rathje and Sabloff 1972: 15, n. 5).

Port location. Such ports are located at good transportation nodes, with islands (such as Cozumel and Delos) being particularly common. Ugarit stood at the intersection of a myriad of trade routes, both maritime and overland (Cherry and Knapp 1994: 136). Goods from different ecological systems may be evident.

Freedom of traders. The pre-existing nature of the site means that most architectural styles are likely to be native. Otherwise, the permanence of traders enjoying a high degree of personal freedom, can involve:

- Foreign furniture styles.

- Presence of families. The cemetery at Hedeby indicates the presence of women and families (Hodges 1982: 63).

- Foreign rituals. At Delos, about forty small shrines were clustered into separate Greek, Phoenician and Jewish sectors (Rathje and Sabloff 1972: 8).

- Foreign kitchenwares.

- Some mirroring of the morphological range of domestic goods.

- Local production of various foreign goods.

- Imitation of imports consequent on the port's cosmopolitan nature. Imported vessels were imitated at Cozumel (Connor 1975: 129).

All of these foreign factors may be found in discrete clusters, corresponding to different enclaves. At Hedeby for example, imports abound in the area of king Godfred's settlement, whilst being very rare in the south settlement (Hodges 1982: 56).

Material correlates of Type C ports of trade

Institutionalisation. Since the ports are deliberately instituted, there is likely to be evidence of careful planning (although this may not be possible in enclaves).

Control of imports. Hinterland control of imports means that imports are passed back to the hinterland, or to the hinterland's customers. The port itself does not accrue wealth in its early life.

Terms of trade. Measures, currencies and the prevalent business language will be of homeland varieties. For example, the Assyrians in Anatolia recorded all their business transactions in Assyrian (Branigan 1984: 51), and brought cuneiform to Karum Kanis (Özgüc 1964: 48). A clay weight inscribed with a Linear A sign has been found at Kastri (Branigan 1981: 32).

Port location. The port will usually be at the edge of a foreign polity.

Freedom of traders. The permanence and freedom to recreate a domestic lifestyle can involve:

- Architecture in foreign styles (except in enclaves, where the traders will inhabit native structures, as in Kültepe (Branigan 1984: 51)). At Kastri, a street drain is reminiscent of Minoan building practices (*idem* 1981: 32).

- Furniture in foreign styles.

- Families, either foreign or mixed. At the Assyrian port of Kültepe, the excavators suggest that there was a "good deal of intermarriage" between the Assyrian traders and Anatolian women (Branigan 1984: 50).

- Foreign rituals. At Kültepe, burials beneath the floors of Anatolian buildings recall a native Assyrian practice (Özgüc 1964). Sanctuaries belonging to some of the Greek states with interests at Naukratis have been excavated (Boardman 1999a: 119). At 30 Gresham Street, a thirteenth century *mikveh* (ritual cleansing bath) attests the presence of London's Medieval Jewish community (Kingsley 2002: 7).

- Foreign kitchenwares. In the Chinese quarter of Bangkok, preparatory kitchenwares are distinctively Chinese (Branigan 1984: 50).

- A wide morphological range of foreign products to service a permanent community. At Karum Kanis, for example, a very wide range of pottery appeared during the Assyrian colonial period (Emre 1963: 87-8).

- Local production of foreign goods by foreign artisans. At Naukratis, for example, vases in a Chian style may have been produced locally (Boardman 1999a: 123). There are many locally-produced foreign wares at Kastri (Branigan 1981: 32).

- Dissemination of foreign styles to native population.

The predicted material characteristics of the port types are summarised in Table 2.

Table 2: Predicted material characteristics of ports of trade

Material Characteristics	Type A	Type B	Type C[13]
Institutionalisation	Pre-colonial trade	Organic growth	Ex novo
Prosperity	Little	Much	Little
Terms of trade	Native	Some foreign, varied origins	Foreign
Location	Border	Central	Border
Architecture	Native	Native	Foreign
Furniture	Native	Some foreign, varied origins	Foreign
Families	No	Yes, varied origins	Yes
Rituals	Native	Some foreign, varied origins	Foreign
Kitchenwares	Native	Foreign, varied styles	Foreign
Morphological range of foreign goods	Low	Medium, varied styles	High
Foreign production	No	Some, varied styles	Yes
Imitations	No	Yes, varied styles	N/A
Distribution of imports in hinterland(s)	Central places; deposited; élite contexts	Whole site; in local markets	Varies

---

[13] Different types of Type C ports have almost the same predictable material correlates, although an enclave will probably not show signs of foreign architecture and will not be founded *ex novo*.

Chapter 2
Al Mina as a port of trade

Reshisuri, Mount Sapuna, Ahta,

the emporium on the sea-shore—the royal 'store-house'—the boxwood mountain

I annexed to Assyria.

I am Tiglath Pileser, king of Assyria, who from east

to west personally conquered all the lands

Stele II B, Iran (Tadmor 1994: 104).

The characterisations of Al Mina discussed in the previous chapter have ranged through virtually all of the port types. Initially a port founded and controlled by Greeks (type Ca), on reconsideration she became a Levantine site with a Greek *enoikismos* (type Cb), or a free port (type B). Orientalists have stressed her native hinterland (type A).

Most of these characterisations have been derived from differing interpretations of the same body of Greek finewares at the site. The argument for Greek presence is wholly predicated on the presence of these finewares. The port of trade model, which employs a wide range of material characteristics, places these finewares in the context of the wider material assemblage known from the site.

The political status of Al Mina

Al Mina lay on the Orontes, the only outlet to the sea for the Amuq plain (see map 2). The polity based on the plain was, by the ninth century BCE a neo-Aramaean kingdom, Unqi,

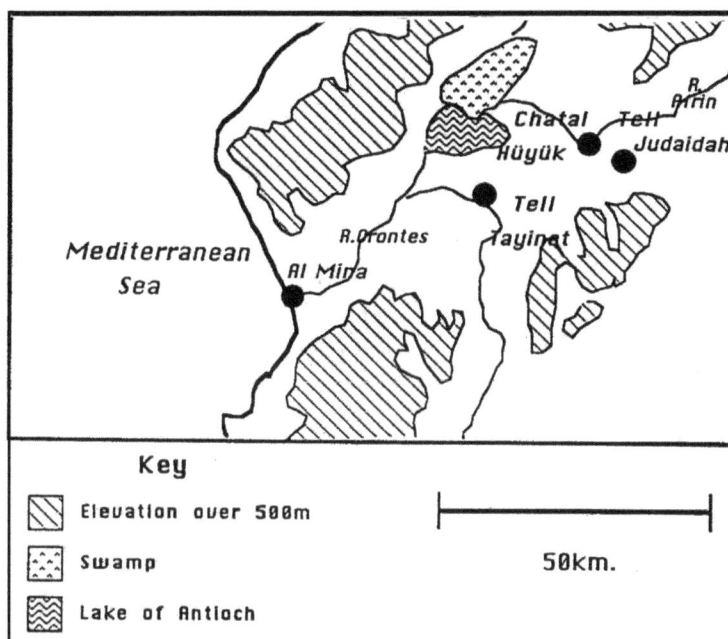

Map 2. The Amuq Plain: excavated sites with Greek Geometric pottery

with a capital at Kinulua (Harrison 2001; Hawkins 1974: 81-3), and, despite periodic interference of the Assyrians in her affairs, she enjoyed at least partial autonomy in the centuries prior to 738 BCE when Tiglath-pileser III provincialised her.

> "In anger ? ...of Tutammû, together with his nobles...The city of Kinalia, his royal city, I captured...in the midst of the palace of Tutamû, I set up my throne...Kinalia, I rebuilt. Unki to its furthest border I subjugated...my official I set over them as governor."
>
> (Luckenbill 1926: 273-274 (§769))

So Unqi was a petty, largely autonomous, kingdom, whose leader occupied a palace in the capital Kinulua, and who controlled other settlements in the province: an Assyrian document reports Assurnasirpal's capture of Aribua, a border town (like Al Mina), "?belonging to the king of Unqi" (*ibid.*: 266 (§478)). From all of this we may surely infer that Al Mina, the only port town at the "furthest border" of Unqi, was controlled from Kinulua, and by whoever held sway there—first the various kings, and then the Assyrian governor. It has recently been suggested that Al Mina was the "Ahta, the emporion (karum) at the sea-shore", mentioned on a stele of Tiglath-pileser III (Zadok 1996; Tadmor 1994: 104-5). In neo-Assyrian times "karu" was applied to special areas in which commercial activities were carried out by royal representatives in places whose economies could not be exploited through regular administrative means; in Arvad's harbour, for example, the Assyrian kings maintained a karu where the king and his merchants enjoyed special trading privileges (Elat 1978: 20, 27)

The political status of Al Mina indicates that it a type A port of trade, with the Amuq plain as its hinterland. It is time to examine the site's material culture, to see if the use of a wide range of material evidence can cast any light on its function.

Material characteristics of Al Mina

The criteria listed in Table 2 are examined in turn, in relation to the Geometric levels at the site.

Levels 10-7 at Al Mina fall within the Greek Geometric period. Their dating has been highly controversial, particularly between scholars using the Near Eastern pottery and those using the Greek imports. The nugatory state of Levels 10-9 means that they will probably never be dated with any confidence.

Among others, the following dates for the early levels have been suggested:

Levels 10-8   *c.* 825—*c.* 720 (du Plat Taylor 1959)
             c. 770—?*c.* 720 (Boardman 1999b)
             —*c.* 720 (Coldstream 1968: 313)
Level 7   *c.* 720—696 (Boardman 1999a: 46)

Lehmann's seriation analysis of Near Eastern pottery into 8 assemblages now enables dates for Level 8 onwards to be derived from the Levantine wares (1996; 1998: 12-15; n.d.

31-32). Assemblage 1, to which Al Mina Level 8 belongs, is dated *c.* 740-*c.* 720; Assemblage 2 (Al Mina Level 7), dates to *c.* 720-*c.* 700/680 BCE.

Institutionalisation. Level 10 lies on virgin soil (Woolley 1938: 16) suggesting, from the conventional dating of the Greek pottery, that a new settlement was institutionalised here *c.* 770 BCE. However, Woolley postulated that a catastrophic flood had washed away the earliest levels. Although most have been sceptical of this claim, much earlier imports have been found in the Amuq plain (p.20), for which Al Mina remains the only practicable point of access; a period of irregular, pre-institutionalised trade, is therefore likely. There are a few scraps of SPG imports at the site that may date to this pre-institutionalisation period (e.g. Popham and Lemos 1992: 155; Kearsley 1999: 115; Boardman 2002b: 18, n.25).[14]

Prosperity. Woolley noted the insalubrity of the tell (1938: 13). The dismal picture he paints is little alleviated by the material assemblage at the site. There are very few luxury finds from the earliest levels, such as a few pieces of bronze and gold in Levels 6-8 (Woolley 1938: 155, 169-170),[15] a poor haul when compared to the wealth of tribute which was passing from Unqi to the Assyrians. For example, Ashurnasirpal II (883-859 BCE) received from the king of Unqi 20 talents of silver, one talent of gold, 100 talents of tin, 100 talents of iron, 1,000 oxen, 10,000 sheep, 1,000 linen garments with multi-coloured trim and so on (Grayson 1976: 142). Even after tributes such as this, the conquering Tiglath-pileser III was able to carry off 300 talents of silver, 100 talents of unknown, weapons and multi-coloured garments etc. (Tadmor 1994: 57).

So Unqi was a wealthy polity in its own right. Much of the material that came by sea must have come via Al Mina. Yet Al Mina withdrew very little wealth for its own benefit, as we might expect for a site in control of its own fortunes, either as an independent type B port, or as a type C migrant-controlled port.

Terms of trade. The graffiti and weights at Al Mina come largely from the upper levels, wherein Greek, Aramaean and Phoenician inscriptions have all been identified (Graham 1986: 55). Only one graffito is notably early, coming from Levels 7/6, on a possible Late Geometric Attic sherd (Boardman 1982a: 366) (plate 1).

The inscription consists of an unusual string of Greek letters in an unknown dialect, apparently reading "ναβεο". By analogy with most contemporary Greek (and, indeed, Near Eastern) inscriptions on pots (Johnston 1983: 67), it is likely that it is a proprietorial and not a trade inscription. Moreover, applied post-firing, it is impossible to say where the graffito was added.

---

[14] The circles skyphos in Cambridge (AG26) believed to be from the site (Popham and Lemos 1992: 155) is from the Athenian Agora. AL26 ("AL" standing for Al Mina) is a L/SG krater sherd. Thanks are due to Mr John MacDonald of the Museum of Classical Archaeology in Cambridge for his help regarding the Cambridge Al Mina sherds, and to Professor Snodgrass for his advice.

[15] The "ivory" from Level 9 is from domesticated buffalo horns (Francis and Vickers 1983).

Plate 1. The Greek inscription at Al Mina. Photo courtesy of Professor John Boardman

In fact, the absence of Euboean writing at LG Al Mina is striking: Euboean sites are a prolific source of early Greek graffiti (*ibid:* 63). At Pithekoussai, over 35 pre-675 BCE inscriptions (mainly proprietorial) have been found, many from settlement contexts and most in the Chalcidian alphabet of the settlers. Pithekoussai also has several examples of Aramaic and Phoenician inscriptions (Ridgway 1992: 111-118), and a lead weight that coincides with the Euboean weight standards known from later times (Ridgway 2000a: 185).

Location. Al Mina's only physical advantage was her strategic position at the Mediterranean end of the Orontes, at the "furthest border" of Unqi.

Architecture. The plans are reproduced in Figures 2-5.

1. *The floors.* The floors are usually of beaten clay or mud; floors in Levels 10-8 sometimes had pebble foundations and, in Levels 5 and 6, there were also pebble and gravel floors

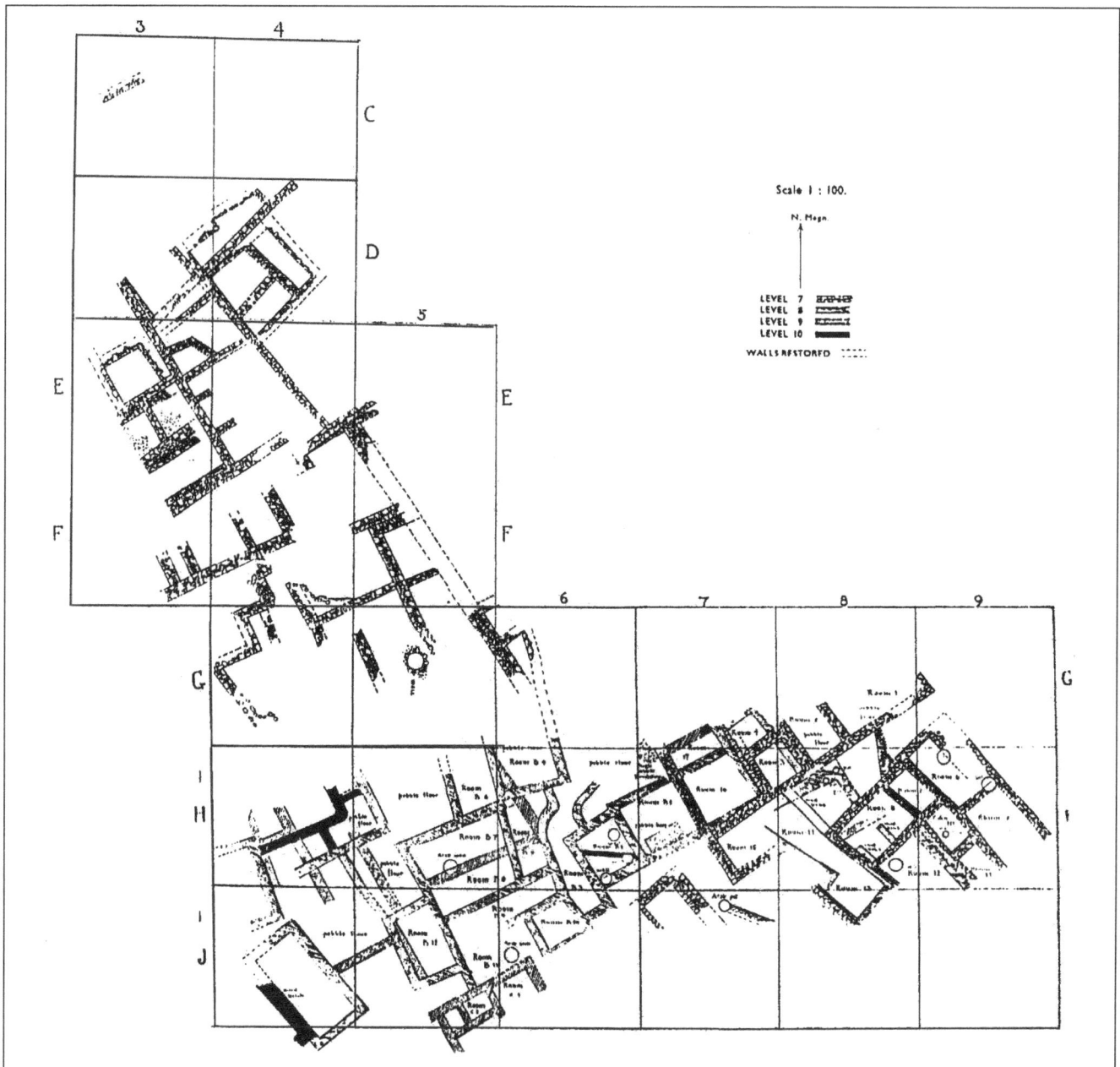

Figure 2. Levels 7-10 at Al Mina. Woolley 1938.

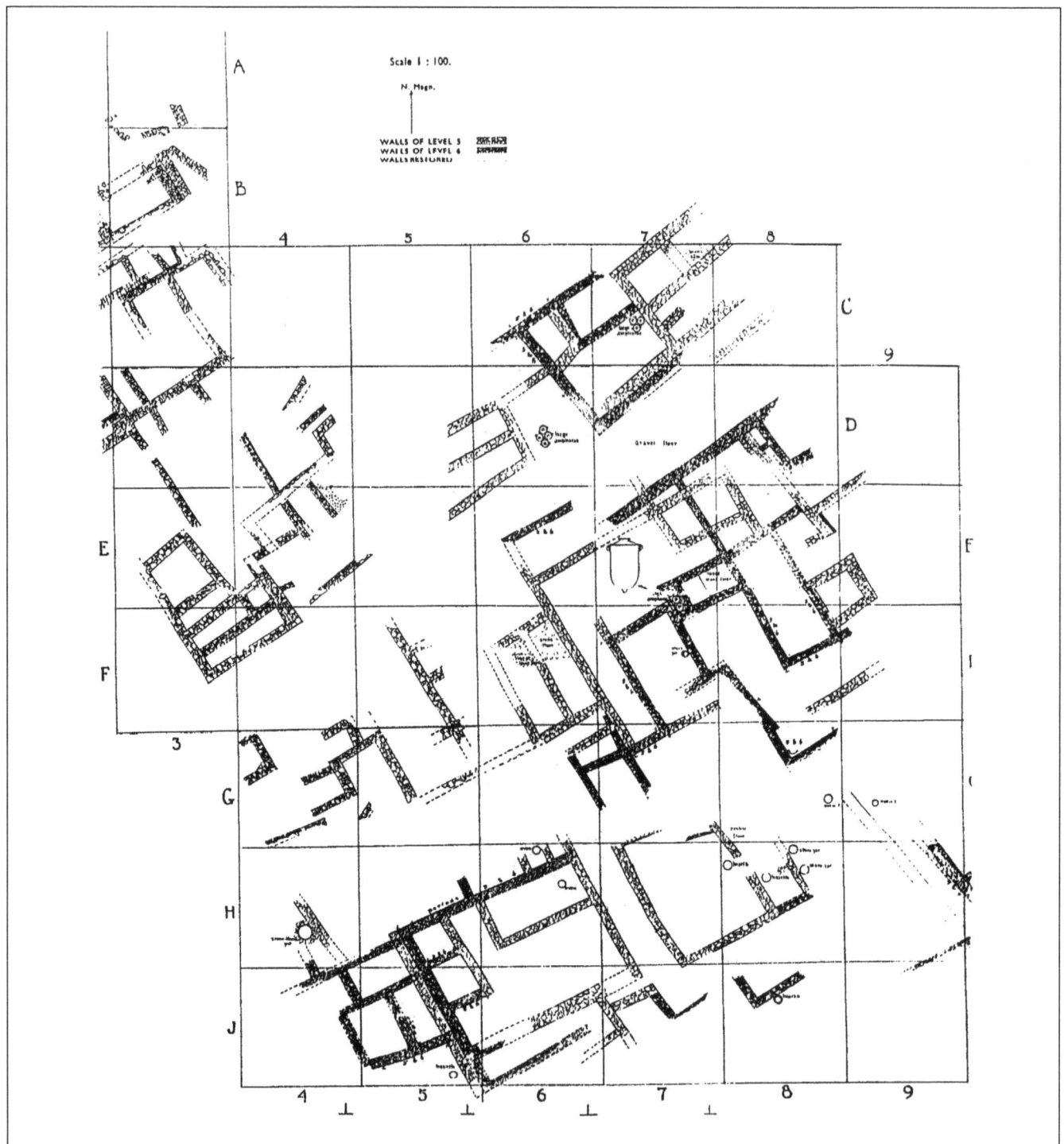

Figure 3. Levels 5-6 at Al Mina. Woolley 1938.

(e.g. Woolley 1938: 11, 152 and Level 5/6 plan). These are all contemporary Levantine characteristics, the three usual types of flooring being beaten earth (often with a pebble foundation), gravel and pebble (Braemer 1982: 138).

2. *The walls*. Beneath exterior walls, foundations are of stone. Some interior foundations are omitted. Initially they are very shallow, consisting of one course of pebbles laid on the ground. In Level 7 and above, several courses of foundation placed in trenches are usual, and the boulders that replace the early pebbles are mixed with rubble. The plans show the boulders facing an inner core of rubble. Later walls often utilise the remains of lower levels as foundations (Woolley

1938: 10, 154). Once again, these features are in sympathy with what is known of Levantine architecture. Foundations are conspicuously shallow, are generally composed of stone, and are often omitted in the case of interior walls (Riis 1970: 18 (Tell Sukas); Braemer 1982: 112-114). This technique is common at nearby Chatal Hüyük (Haines 1971: 6). Levantine courses often face a rubble interior, and the re-use of older walls as foundations is commonplace (Riis 1970: 18; Braemer 1982: 112, 114).

Al Minan walls are usually constructed of dried mud-brick, with a thickness of *c*. 70cm. Extant bricks are of the following dimensions: 40cm x 30cm(?) x 14cm; 40cm x 20cm x 12cm;

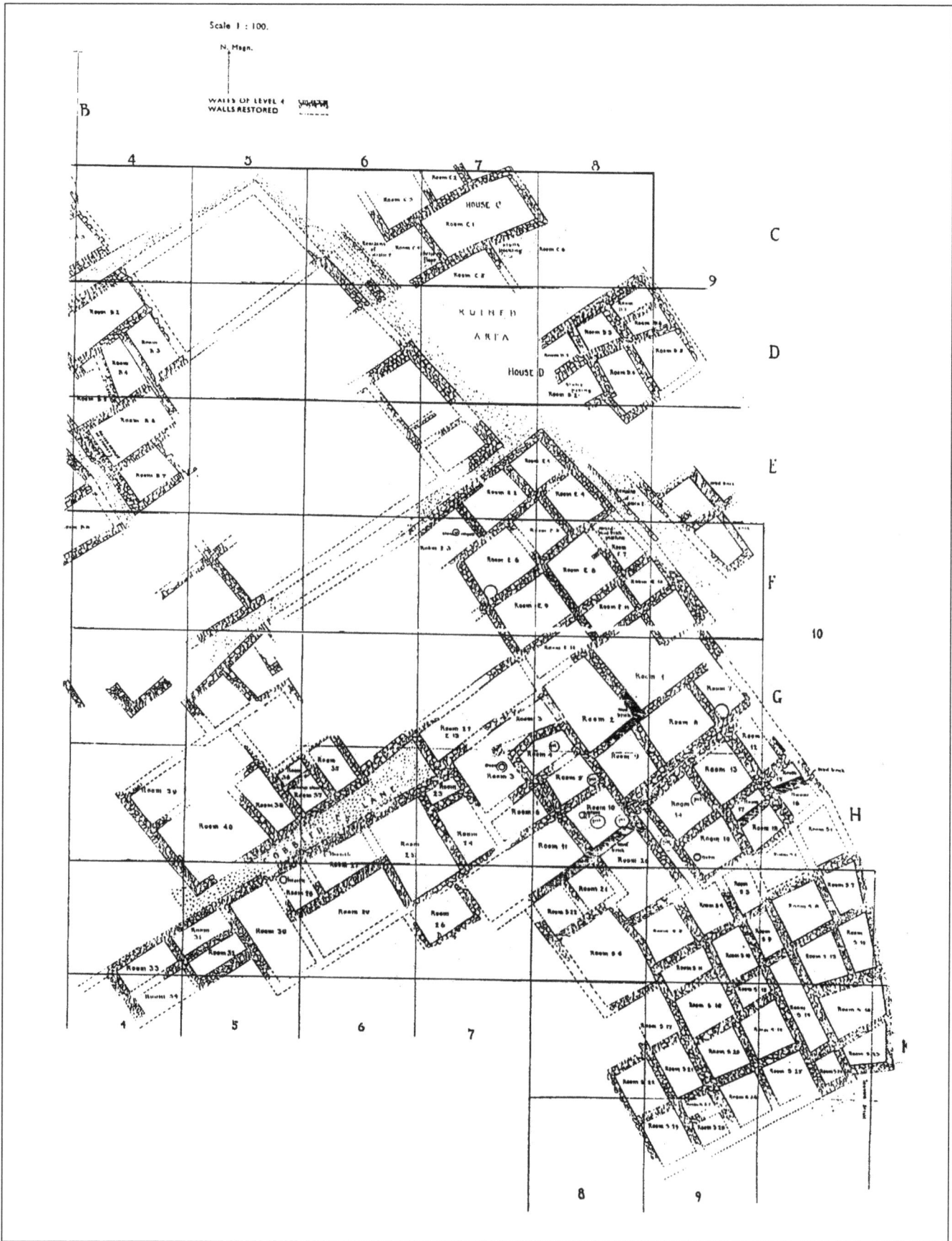

Figure 4. Level 4 at Al Mina. Woolley 1938.

40cm x 27cm x 12cm; 40cm x 22cm x 11cm (Woolley 1938: 10-11, 137, 154), which fall within normal Levantine bounds (Braemer 1982: 123). Mud-brick is a common construction material in the Iron Age Levant, particularly in the north where the pillar walls of Palestine and Phoenicia are rare (Braemer 1982: 122, 124). As for wall thickness, pre-700 BCE walls in the Levant average a thickness of 60-80cm, again in perfect accord with Al Mina.

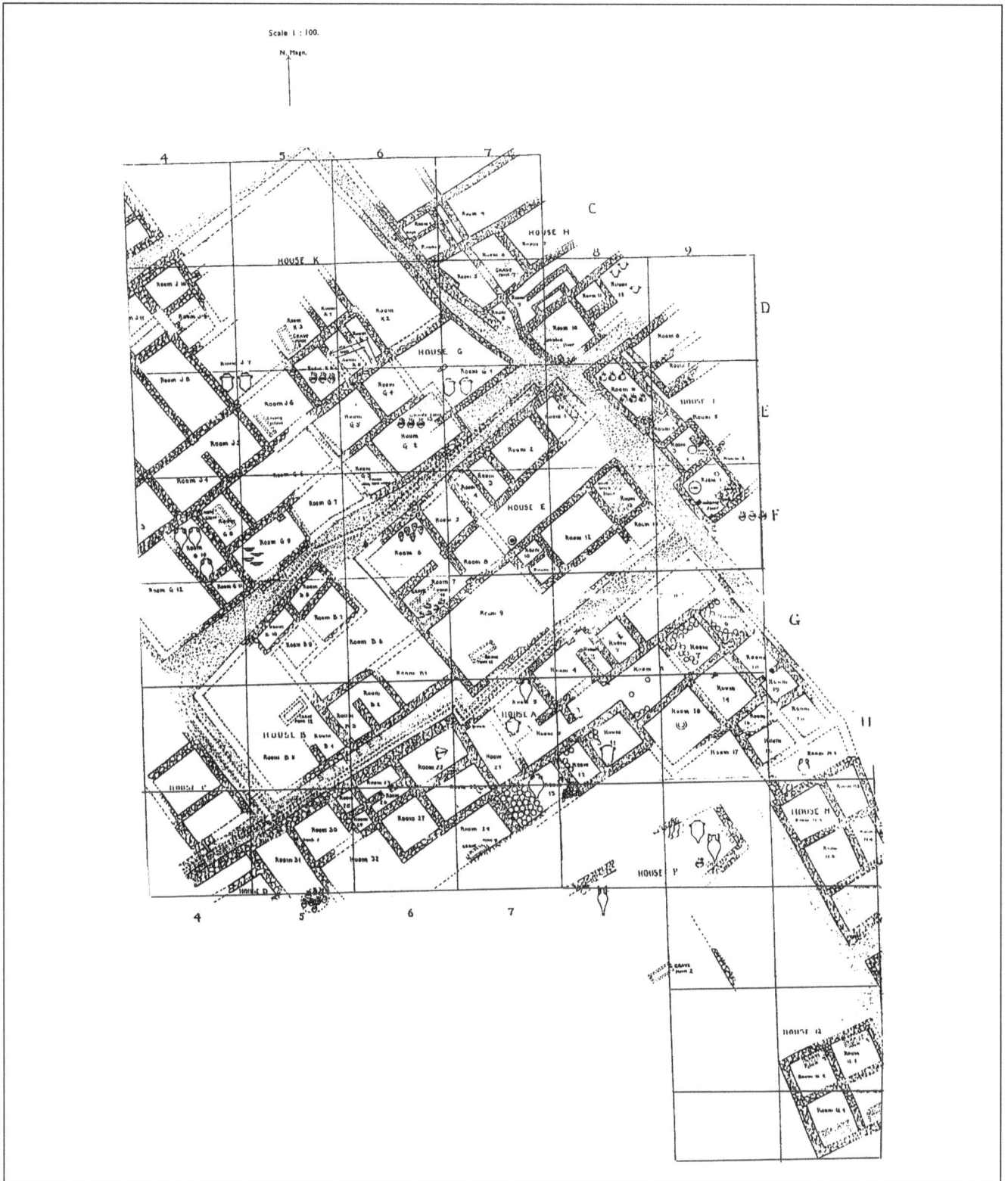

Figure 5. Level 3 at Al Mina. Woolley 1938.

3. *The doors*. Foundations at Al Mina were usually carried over the doorways, although a sill was found in Level 4 (House A, rooms 4-5) and apparent door fittings in Level 3 (House A, room 15) (Woolley 1938: 139, 144). Levantine doorsills, where they exist separately from the foundations, are often of a single large stone such as that found by Woolley, and continuous foundations are a convention of Levantine architecture (Braemer 1982: 113, 132), for example being used at Chatal Hüyük (Haines 1971: 6).

Hinge stones, an example of which was discovered at Al Mina (Woolley 1938: 144), are a specifically North Syrian characteristic, virtually unknown further south (Braemer 1982: 133).

4. *The roof*. No roof tiles were noted (Woolley 1938: 11). Tiling was not commonly employed in the Iron Age Levant, roofs being constructed of wooden branches beneath a layer of earth (Braemer 1982: 137).

5. *Settlement layout and house form.* The principal characteristic of the early strata at Al Mina is their muddled appearance. That this is an ancient North Syrian tradition is demonstrated by the plan of Bronze Age Ugarit (Ras Shamra) (Riis 1982: 245; Yon 1992: 27) and at Chatal Hüyük where the circulation of the relevant levels is tortuous (Haines 1971: 6 and pl. 24).

Overall, the architecture of the buildings is consonant with north Syrian styles.

Furniture. Lamps constitute the sole extant class of evidence at Al Mina. Lamps belonging to three main types were found (Woolley 1938: 138, fig. 15). The earliest is type I, the "pinched saucer type", which appears in Level 8 (*ibid.*: 154) (figure 6), and is a Near Eastern type (e.g. Lehmann 1998: 14 fig. 3.20); they are very common at Tell Sukas, for example (Buhl 1983: 62, fig. xviii) (figure 7).

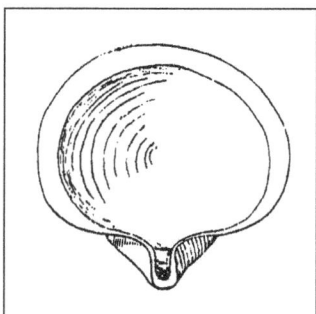

Figure 6. The pinched saucer lamp at Al Mina. Woolley 1938: 138, fig. 15 no. 1

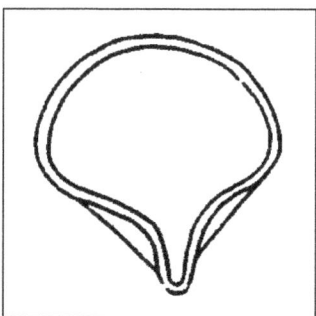

Figure 7. The pinched saucer lamp at Tell Sukas. Buhl 1983: 62, fig. xvii, no. 333. Courtesy of the Royal Danish Academy of Sciences and Letters

Families. No evidence for the Geometric period.

Rituals. No evidence for the Geometric period.

Kitchenwares. Minoan archaeologists have demonstrated that kitchenwares can be useful evidence for foreign settlement (e.g. Branigan 1984: 50-1; Schofield 1983: 298-9).

For analytical purposes, kitchenwares may be divided into the three stages of food use: storage, preparation and consumption. Unselfconsciously functional products, suited to a particular culture's dietary habits, usually serve the first

two stages.[16] They are likely to be plain or coarse wares, and unlikely to cross cultural borders unless accompanied by migrants. In the Chinese quarter of Bangkok, for example, the preparatory kitchenwares are distinctively Chinese (Branigan 1984: 50). The final stage, consumption, may be served by finewares.

Although Woolley did not make explicit his strategy for keeping and recording finds, there are some hints that "redundant" material—such as undiagnostic plain wares— were not kept (e.g. Woolley 1938: 133). Nonetheless, there are some potentially diagnostic data from Geometric Al Mina:

1. *Storage wares.* Woolley noted "type 2" amphorae (Level 8 and possibly Level 9) and "type 11" amphorae (Level 8) (1938: 154 and figs. 26.2, 27.11). A number of SOS amphorae were also found (Robertson 1940: 19, fig. 8e; Johnston and Jones 1978: 106-107). "Type 2" amphorae (figure 8) are of Phoenician type, Sagoma's type 2 amphorae (1982: 73-78; cf. Bikai 1978: pl. xiv, no. 10). Such amphorae are distributed prolifically over Cyprus and the Levant (e.g. Courbin 1993a: 56-57, pl. 32, nos. 1-3, 7). Although the Euboeans did produce a class of the widely-distributed SOS transport amphorae, scientific analysis of some SOS samples at Al Mina indicates that they are of Attic origin (Johnston and Jones 1978: 126-7, figs. 5 and 6, nos. 60 and 61). The wide distribution (and rounded bottoms) of these foreign amphorae suggests that they were containers for traded goods rather than storage vessels.

In bare outline the flat-bottomed "type 11" neck amphora (figure 9) is familiar from the Greek ceramic repertoire, and has usually been identified as Greek (e.g. Boardman 1999b: 146, n.17). However, it is also a very common shape in the Levant, particularly on the excavated Amuq plain sites (e.g. Haines 1971: pl.4C) (plate 2), and is likely to be a North

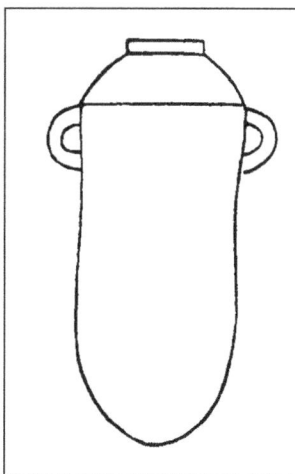

Figure 8. Type 2 amphora at Al Mina. Buhl 1983:149, fig. 26, no. 2

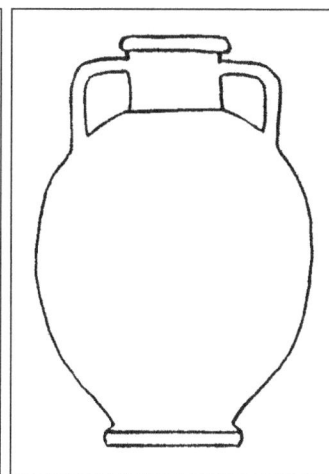

Figure 9. Type 11 amphora at Al Mina. Buhl 1983: 151, fig. 27, no. 11

---

[16] That is not to say that kitchenwares never cross cultural boundaries. For example, the thermal tolerance of some clays recommends them for export, which may explain the presence of Aiginetan cooking pots in the Athenian Agora. Waldbaum cites the modern American trend for using French, Scandiniavian and Mexican kitchen equipment against always equating imported kitchenwares with imported people (1997: 8 and n.16).

Plate 2. Syrian storage jar at Chatal Hüyük (corner of room V-13/3). Haines 1971 plate 4C.
Courtesy of the Oriental Institute of the University of Chicago

Syrian storage amphora, for water or other liquids (Lehmann forthcoming: 12 and *pers. comm.*).[17]

2. *Preparatory wares*. The retained cooking wares from Levels 8-6 are mainly holemouth north Syrian types, with very close Amuq parallels. Cooking vessels, whereabouts now unknown, whose descriptions match north Syrian types were also registered in the pottery catalogue of the 1936 season as coming from Levels 8-9 (Lehmann 1998: 13; n.d. 13, 17).

There is also an unstratified example of a Phoenician (or coastal) cooking pot (*ibid.*: 13).

3. *Wares for consumption*. Under this heading might fall the flat coarse dishes, probably of Levels 8-7, which are a very frequent, highly localised north Syrian type (Lehmann forthcoming: 7). This category should also include the finewares, often believed to be the chattels of resident Greeks, Phoenicians and Cypriots. They are discussed in the following chapter.

Morphological range of foreign goods. This factor is discussed in the following chapter, together with the other evidence for Greek and Phoenician residence.

Foreign production. Ceramics, the most well preserved and exhaustively studied of materials—particularly at Al Mina—

are the usual focus for diagnosis of foreign production in the ancient world. In Blakeway's classic and transferable typology of Greek pottery in Italy the relevant class of vases is "class ii", comprising in that case vases made in Italy by Greeks (1932-1933: 184).

Locally produced foreign wares are made (a) in local clay[18] (b) in a foreign style (c) by a foreign hand.

The second criterion is detectable in the adoption of new shapes or decoration. The first criterion is more difficult; visual fabric analysis can be problematic and scientific analysis is not foolproof, as researchers of the suspected Euboean pottery at both Al Mina and Pithekoussai have discovered (e.g. Ridgway 1978; Popham, Hatcher and Pollard 1980). The third criterion is the most crucial but also the most subjective of all, being entirely dependent on visual diagnosis,[19] and which may (albeit subconsciously) be informed by our expectations: would we expect to see members of this foreign group at this site or not? If so, we might see foreign production; if not, imitations.

---

[17] Amphora 575-1 at Pithekoussai, of uncertain fabric, but similar shape and carrying Aramaic inscriptions relating to volume could therefore be another candidate for north Syrian production (illustrated in Buchner 1978; 133, fig. 1; Ridgway 1992: 112).

[18] Although ethnological research points to reluctance on the part of potters to travel any great distance for their clays (e.g. Jones 1988: 872), it has been suggested that clay was transported in the ancient world, possibly as ballast (e.g. Gill 1987).

[19] Mössbauer analysis permits the distinction of different firing temperatures, indicating different production techniques and so, perhaps, different producers. In the case of the Pithekoussai material, Deriu *et al.* (1986: 113) were able to identify two consistently different temperatures used in the firing of 'Corinthian' wares, one of which corresponded to Euboean and Corinthianising pottery, the other to Corinthian imports.

It has been suggested that Greek, Cypriot and Levantine/Phoenician wares were produced by potters from their respective traditions at Geometric Al Mina, although, given the small size and specialised nature of the site, it may be that no pottery was produced *in situ* (Liddy 1996: 486; Lehmann forthcoming: 33).

1. *Greek.* The shape of Boardman's (1959) eponymic Al Mina ware vessels (all skyphoi) fulfilled criterion (b). As for criterion (a), the fabric appeared to be local. Through a delicate weighing of the various decorative traits, which indicated Eastern/Cypriot influences, Boardman concluded that the ware was Greek-made at Al Mina. However chemical analysis has demonstrated the fabric's compatibility with Eastern Cypriot clays as well as its incompatibility with north Syrian Bronze Age clays (Jones 1986: 694-5; cf. Liddy 1996: 486). Recently once more, Greek production in the Levant, perhaps even at Al Mina, of a few examples of this ware (rechristened "Euboeo-Levantine) has been championed (Kearsley 1989: 143-4; *eadem* 1995: 77-8; Boardman 1999b: 148).[20] Further analysis is obviously required, but there is currently no reliable evidence for Greek production of Greek wares at Geometric Al Mina.

2. *Cypriot.* The Cypriot material, mainly from Level 8 onwards, constitutes about 32% of diagnostic Geometric pottery (Boardman 1999b: 143). Woolley recognised that the vessels were both local and imported (1938: 16), and du Plat Taylor (1959) isolated the relevant classes as White Painted, Bichrome and Black-on-Red.

Distinguishing local production from imports has proven difficult (e.g. Bonatz 1993: 136). Recent scientific studies have shown that the Black-on-Red material at Al Mina was imported from Cyprus, probably Kition (Matthers *et al.* 1983; cf. Brodie and Steel 1996: 271), and that the White-Painted and Bichrome wares may have been Cypriot imports (Liddy 1996: 486; cf. Boardman 1999b: 149). By contrast, using stylistic analysis, Gjerstad argued that the better-quality Cypriot wares were manufactured by Cypriots at Al Mina, due to the "structure of the clay" (i.e. criterion (a)) and the "uncanonic and peculiar" decoration of the pieces (i.e. criterion (c)) (1948: 255 and n. 2; 1974: 115). Given the lack of certainty even within the scientific studies (e.g. Liddy 1996: 486-7), the possibility of local production in a Cypriot style remains.

However, local production of "Cypriot" wares need not entail the presence of Cypriot potters introducing a foreign style (criterion b), but rather the existence of a Cypro-Levantine ceramic *koine* in north Syria, expressing itself through the production of "Cypro-Levantine" wares (Boardman 1999b: 149). Saltz noted "the locally manufactured Cypriote-like pottery of Al Mina and the Amuq, as in the case of Tarsus, appears to have belonged to an indigenous, though related, tradition and development" (1978: 53-4). The Amuq plain has its own tradition of Black-on-Red and Bichrome, which may be derived from the Cypriot tradition (Swift 1958: 125,

138, 151; Saltz 1978: 31-2; 53-4). Locally produced wares in a "Cypriot" style are present at many north Syrian littoral sites (e.g. Bounni *et al.* 1976: 243; Courbin 1978a: 54-5; Buhl 1983: 124).

In other words, whether imported or locally produced, wares in a Cypriot style are not foreign to Al Mina.

3. *Levantine/Phoenician.* Phoenician pottery is usually associated with the Red Slip wares, which constitute *c.* 21% of the diagnostic Geometric pottery at Al Mina (Boardman 1999b: 151). The obvious difficulty in evaluating both the place of production and the origin of the producers of Red Slip wares (i.e. criteria (a) and particularly (c)) is the lack of decorative features. In addition, Red Slip pottery was produced in many areas, including Cyprus, the Amuq and north Syria (e.g. Swift 1958: 125-128, 141; Taylor 1959: 79; Birmingham 1963; Culican 1982), and a *koine* is emerging (e.g. Bikai 1987: 70; Boardman 1999b: 150). As a result, there has been total divergence of opinion, some identifying the Red Slip at Al Mina as Phoenician (e.g. Culican 1982: 79), some as Syrian (e.g. Boardman 1999b: 150).

The most recent scientific study suggested several (unidentified) sources for Al Mina Red Slip (Liddy 1996: 485). Lehmann notes the similarity of Al Mina Red Slip to Tyrian Red Slip, and its dissimilarity to north Syrian types (1996; 1998: 13; n.d: 33). Differences are detectable in the quality of the slip and the fabric and in the shapes of the vessels; these are presumably imports.

As for the Cypriot pottery, Red Slip is not an intrusive, foreign, tradition. Syrian Red Slip is certainly present at the site (Lehmann 1997). The British Museum's catalogue lists 126 Syrian Red Slip bowls of the 7th and 8th-7th centuries BCE.[21] Cluster analyses of Lehmann's assemblages 1-2 show two different "fields of interaction", one continental, the other spread over the whole littoral area, reflecting close maritime links all along the coast (*idem* 1998: 28). Both the "Cypriot" and the "Phoenician" wares fall within the littoral field of interaction. This field meets the continental one in the Al Mina area, reflecting its central position in intra-Levantine communications.

In sum, there is no evidence for the production of foreign wares by foreign potters at the site.

Imitations. Imitative production (Blakeway's "class iii") is distinguishable from "foreign production" by substituting "foreign hand" by "native hand" in criterion (c) of the previous section. Of the three main ceramic styles at Al Mina only the Greek is in a style foreign to the region, and with the re-assignment of Al Mina ware to Cyprus, there is no evidence for any local production of Greek wares at the site by either Greeks or 'natives'.

Distribution of imports in the hinterland. The dissertations that provide most of the available information on the Amuq

[20] Kearsley has also suggested that the few LG PSC (her 'type 6') skyphoi were manufactured in the East Mediterranean (1989: 143-4). Others doubt its survival into the LG period at all (Popham and Lemos 1993: 154).

[21] Thanks are due to Alexandra Villing for providing information on the database, and access to both it and the collections.

imports do not discuss the distribution or context of either the Phoenician or the Cypriot pottery, so Greek Geometric pottery must form the focus of the discussion.[22]

Greek Geometric pottery is known from only three tells in the Amuq plain—Tell Tayinat, Chatal Hüyük, and Tell Judaidah (see map 2), although the plain was densely settled in the Iron Age, and all the tells were surveyed (Braidwood 1937: 6, 20-37; Swift 1958: 147). Some have been excavated, including seven with Iron Age remains (Hood 1951; Swift 1958: 6, n. 2). Most Greek Geometric pottery was unearthed at Tell Tayinat. Fewer sherds were found at Chatal Hüyük and fewer still at Tell Judaidah (where, however, the area of exposure was more limited) (Saltz 1978: 81). Overall, "several hundred" Greek sherds and a small number of whole vases belonging to Phase O (950-550 BCE) were excavated (Swift 1958: 153, 198-199). Saltz saw well over two hundred Geometric Greek sherds from Tell Tayinat and Chatal Hüyük at the Oriental Institute Museum in Chicago (1978: 81).

Are these three findspots random and undifferentiated, "various sites in the Amuq plain"? (Boardman 1999a: 45). It is instructive to compare the imports' distribution with Unqi's political topography discussed at the beginning of the chapter. Kinulua, the capital of the kingdom of Unqi, has been identified with Tell Tayinat in both pre and post-Assyrian periods (Gelb 1939: 39; Liverani 1992: 74-75; Harrison 2001).[23] Chatal Hüyük stands on the river Afrin, an important transportational route through the plain. She was the second largest city on the plain, and was protected during the Iron Age by a fortification wall (Haines 1971: 3-25; Harrison 2001: 123). Evidently, then, the site was less important than Tell Tayinat, but nevertheless enjoyed sufficient central control and organisation to construct a fortification wall. Tell Judaidah is a similar, but slightly smaller, site (Swift 1958: 7).

So the Greek Geometric imports in the hinterland of Al Mina are found in major locations in the polity, including the principal central place, wherein most imports were found. This limited distribution suggests that access to them was restricted in ways related to the political structure of the polity: Tell Tayinat, its capital, enjoyed the greatest access to imports. Chatal Hüyük, the second largest city, enjoyed some access to the imports, and Tell Judaidah, the smallest site of the three, had least of all. The Assyrian reference to "Tutammû, together with his nobles" suggests the existence of a political hierarchy, with monarch and aristocrats closely linked (Luckenbill 1926: 273 (§769)).

While there is no specific evidence that the vessels were deliberately deposited at these inland sites (no graves were excavated, for example), the fact that some were whole suggests that they were. Although most of the material comes from unreliable loci, some evidence points to high-status consumption of these imports: at Tell Tayinat, PSC skyphoi were found in Building XIII of the First Building Period, Building I (or XIV) of the Second (or First) Building Period, and Buildings IV and VI of the Second Building Period (Haines 1971: 64-66 for Building Periods; Saltz 1978: 106, n. 382, 83). Of these, at least three were *bit-hilani*, north Syrian palace buildings: Buildings XIII, IV and I (Haines 1971: 38, 41-42, 44).

Cypriot pottery was also found in the area of the Assyrian governor's house at Tell Tayinat (Gjerstad 1948: 257). So Greek and Cypriot finewares reached the important sites of the polity for which Al Mina served as port, wherein some were deposited and some penetrated élite areas of the site.

Most of the imports date to the period ca. 900-725 BCE, although there may be several earlier pieces at Chatal Hüyük. For example, an amphora, dated stratigraphically to the tenth century BCE, was identified by Saltz as Attic (1978: 81-3). Its motifs, though unparalleled in this exact combination, have Euboean analogies, and the vessel, once properly accessible, may well be added to the growing catalogue of Atticising Euboean material in the Levant. Its very fine mica and matt paint is characteristic of early Euboean pottery (Catling 1990: 9). The amphora is belly-handled, a rare shape in the early Euboean ceramic assemblage (but which may be the form of several of the Lefkandi parallels cited below) and one that "may reflect a specialized and prestigious function, perhaps as an item of feasting equipment" (Catling and Lemos 1990a: 35). It has black paint and a beige-white slip. The shoulder zone is decorated by a series of registers. From the top down these are: a band of paint with reserved cross-hatched lozenges, some of which are joined; a series of broad-based isosceles triangles; a series of compass-drawn concentric semicircles with eight half-rings per semicircle (non-pendent, inferred from the parallels Saltz cites) which are partly reserved in a broad band of paint; a narrow band; a broad band; a narrow band. On the handle are obvious brush marks, and on the belly fragment are two wavy lines. Concentric semicircles and wavy lines are the norm on Euboean belly-handled amphorae (Lemos 1990: 213-8), as well as being common in Attic PG. Reserved versions are rare in both classes. Saltz was able to cite two Attic parallels, but more vessels with reserved non-pendent semicircles have since been unearthed from Lefkandi (e.g. Popham *et al.* 1979: pl. 133, no. 17; Catling and Lemos 1990c: 120 and pl. 33, nos. 556 and 557 (a likely belly-handled amphora and an amphora/hydria); *ibid*.: 121 and pl. 34, no. 582 (a likely belly-handled amphora)).[24] A micaceous (and so probably not Euboean) hydria was also found in tenth century levels at Chatal Hüyük (Saltz 1978: 284).

Currently, many more imports are known from the port than from the proposed hinterland (*c.* 1500 against *c.* 200, plus a

---

[22] The Amuq Valley Regional Project team is currently re-examining Braidwood's material (including the Greek and Cypriot imports) and has been undertaking a new survey of the region since 1995. The project is headed by K. Aslihan Yener, the survey by Tony Wilkinson (both of the Oriental Institute, Chicago).

[23] Tell Tayinat is the findspot of a bronze horse frontlet dated to the eighth/seventh centuries BCE and iconographically related to the horse-blinkers found in an eighth-century context in the temple of Apollo Daphnephoros at Eretria. This latter piece shares an inscription with a horse's forehead ornament found in the Samian Heraion. The inscription could be dated to the ninth century BCE and reads "That which Hadad gave our lord Hazael from 'Umqi in the year that our lord crossed the river" (Kantor 1962; Eph'al and Naveh 1989).

[24] Three of the Euboean parallels are MPG (Catling and Lemos 1990b: 94).

lesser number of whole vases). When considering this imbalance, it should be recalled that the Iron Age levels at the inland sites were at or near the surface, and were badly disturbed, a problem exacerbated by the slope of the mounds (Saltz 1978: 77-8, 107, n. 383). Moreover, only a small portion of any of the inland sites has been excavated (e.g. *c.* 5% of Tell Tayinat (Haines 1971: pls. 18, 53 and 93)). Lastly, no scholar of Greek Geometric pottery has examined the excavated material, so there may be more sherds lurking unrecognised. By contrast, Woolley believed that he had excavated the entirety of Iron Age Al Mina, which was the bottom stratum (Saltz 1978: 107, n. 383). And, whilst a full publication of the Al Mina sherds is wanting, there has been no shortage of scholars searching through the various collections, and publishing their opinions.

Kriterienbundeln: conclusions

The following table summarises the material characteristics of Al Mina, the port, and should be compared to Table 2.

If we compare the results of these criteria to those set out in Table 2, we can see that, despite a number of 'unknowns', one type of port is consistently indicated: type A i.e. a port founded and controlled by the hinterland power, first the Aramaean kings of Unqi and then the Assyrian governor. Apart from the mere presence of imported Greek Geometric finewares, there is nothing about Al Mina that is reminiscent of the earliest Euboean colonies in the West; and even there, settlements like Pithekoussai were soon producing rather than importing Euboean pottery.

Such a conclusion does not preclude the presence of Greek residents in the restricted way common to foreigners in type A ports, for example; positive material evidence for Greek presence is examined in the next chapter.

The institutionalisation of Al Mina as a port of trade

The institutionalisation of Al Mina cannot, on the basis of current evidence, be accurately dated. If Al Mina is Ahta, the port's activities were already of note by 738 BCE. A sustained Greek interest at the site is not indicated until the LG period of most of the Greek imports.

For the port's controllers, either Aramaean princes, or after 738 BCE, an Assyrian Governor, Al Mina's institutionalisation would have regularised the supply of certain imports. Metals are the obvious candidates; the aggressively expansionist neo-Assyrian economy of the 9th century often required metal tribute from Levantine vassals, including the iron in which Euboea is so well-endowed, and Unqi's tribute often included it. Besides these prime value goods, the dignity of the Assyrian monarchs required a constant supply of the latest luxuries from the West (including Unqi) to be displayed in capitals, temples and palaces (Postgate 1979: 199).[25]

The institutionalisation of Al Mina may also have been intended to regulate in one place the pre-institutional trade indicated, for example, by the earlier imports in the Amuq plain. Such pre-institutional trade may have involved less formal modes, such as piracy and raiding—the Assyrian governor of Tyre and Sidon reported an apparent slave raid by 'Ionians' on a city under his control (cited Braun 1982: 15). A regulation of pre-existing trade would explain the appearance of imported Greek, and, in much smaller quantities, Cypriot and Phoenician, pottery at the very earliest levels of the site, without recourse to the idea of *ex novo* settlement by Greeks bringing their finewares as chattels (cf. e.g. Kearsley 1995: 72; *eadem* 1999: 117).

After 738 BCE Al Mina provided for the Assyrian conquerors of Unqi a gateway for goods arriving by sea. This gateway

Table 3: Material characteristics of Al Mina, port of trade

Material characteristics	Results for Al Mina
Institutionalisation	Pre-colonial trade
Prosperity	Little
Terms of trade	?
Location	Border
Architecture	Native north Syrian
Furniture	Native north Syrian
Families	?
Rituals	?
Kitchenwares	Storage and preparation: north Syrian
Morphological range of foreign goods	Low (Greek): see next chapter
Foreign production	No (Cypriot/Phoenician *koine*)
Imitations	No
Distribution of imports in hinterland(s)	Central places; some deposited; some élite contexts

[25] See p.47 for social definition of "luxury imports".

was convenient for direct access to the Assyrian hinterland and was not dependent on Phoenicia, where ports such as Tyre had been attracting Aegean goods for several hundred years. This is the period during which Assyrian customs officials were posted at Tyre and when Assyria seems to have been most anxious to preserve access to goods entering Tyre and Sidon (Aubet 2001: 57). Assyrian interest at Al Mina is reflected in the appearance of Assyrian-style "Grey ware" pottery in Levels 5 and 6 (Saltz 1978: 32; Lehmann forthcoming: 18). The later LG period also sees the importation of Greek pottery from a wider range of producers than before, particularly East Greek.

Chapter 3
Evidence for Greek residence at Al Mina

From there Nausithous, the godlike, had removed them,
and led and settled when in Scheria...
about the city he had drawn a wall, he had built houses
and made temples for the gods and divided the ploughlands"
Homer Odyssey VI. 7-10.

In terms of her material assemblage, Al Mina is a typical north Syrian settlement, and has been characterised as a port of trade under the control of her hinterland, initially Aramaean Unqi and then the Assyrians. Such a characterisation does not preclude the presence of Greeks or residents from other parts of the Mediterranean at the site, for example in the restricted fashion common to type A ports (p.6).

It is time to review the evidence for foreign, particularly Greek, settlement at the site in the Geometric period.[26]

The architecture

Many Al Minan architectural features (summarised on p.13ff.) are not uniquely Levantine. For example, mud floors are in use at Lefkandi (Popham *et al.* 1980b: 24). Euboean Geometric walls had rubble-faced interiors and shallow foundations (Popham *et al.* 1980b: 15, 24). Shallow foundations and wall-facing are also features of the Pithekoussan structures (Klein 1972: 36) (figure 10). Mud bricks are also commonly employed in contemporary Greek structures, including those at Lefkandi (Coulton 1993: 37) and at Eretria (Mazarakis 1987: 8).

However, Greek walls tend to be considerably thinner than those at Al Mina (70cm); the width of most Geometric Eretrian walls is 40-45cm (Mazarakis 1987: 17), while the walls of the house at Lefkandi are 40cm wide (Popham *et al.* 1980b: 24). The Euboeans transported this relative thinness to Pithekoussai, where the plans show that wall thicknesses vary between *c.* 45-75cm, with the earliest walls on the apsidal

---

[26] Some problems inherent in mapping archaeological data onto ethnicity have been discussed (p.8). In addition, early Al Mina has none of the graves or ritual monuments that can be the clearest indicator of foreign presence.

buildings being the thinnest. Increased awareness of the dangers of this location may have encouraged the construction of wider walls. In fact, 70cm is the absolute upper limit for the majority of Greek Iron Age walls: mud brick walls on the mainland tend to be 40-50cm thick (Fagerström 1988: 119).

Further, in Euboea, walls were commonly strengthened by the use of wooden posts (e.g. Eretria: Schmid in Blackman 2001: 63, Mazarakis 1987: 12, n. 41, 17; Lefkandi: Popham *et al.* 1980b: 24, Coulton 1993: 31; Kyme: Sapouna-Sakellaraki 1998). This style of construction was transported to Pithekoussai, where postholes surround the walls of Structure III (Klein 1972: 36). These were not reported at Al Mina.

The continuous foundations employed at Al Mina were not a feature of Euboean architecture. Gaps for doorways appear at Lefkandi and Eretria (Popham *et al.* 1980b: 14; Mazarakis 1987; Coulton 1993: 43), which convention seems to have been transported to Pithekoussai.

No tiles were found at Al Mina. At Geometric Lefkandi tiling may have been used: although the mass of tiles found at the site was of Archaic date, one inscribed tile was found associated with purely SPG/LG material, and the Heroon at Kyme contains some tiles (Popham *et al.* 1980d: 85; Sapouna-Sakellaraki 1998: 63).

A more certain feature of contemporary Euboean roofing absent from Al Mina is the use of posts as additional support, indicated by post supports in the centre of the rooms at Eretria and Lefkandi, and by burnt remains at Kyme (*ibid;* Popham *et al.* 1980b: 14; Mazarakis 1987: 10, 13; Coulton 1993: 41). Such posts were used at Pithekoussai (Klein 1972: 36).

Finally, while Al Mina had a rather jumbled layout, contemporary Euboean settlements were usually composed of isolated apsidal or oval units (Popham *et al.* 1980b: 14-15; Mazarakis 1987: 17; Sapouna-Sakellaraki 1998: 61ff.) (figure 11). That early Al Minan structures were neither oval nor isolated, is clear even from the meagre remains of Level 10, where the walling in Squares H4 and J4 is angular, not curved, and where the conjoining walls of H4 betray a multi-

Figure 10. The Mazzola site at Pithekoussai. Buchner 1970: 65. Courtesy of Giorgio Buchner

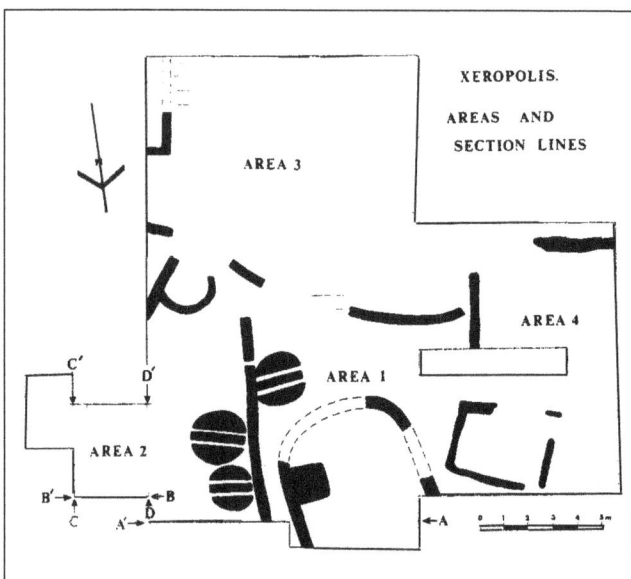

Figure 11. The house at Lefkandi. Popham et al. 1979, pl. 9.
Reproduced with permission of the British School at Athens

roomed structure. Indeed, there is no sign of any apsidal, oval or isolated buildings in the early levels. The Euboean builders at Pithekoussai retained their familiar apsidal shapes (Structures I and IV), which are then superseded by rectilinear structures, reflecting a mainland development (Mazarakis 1987: 17).

Overall, it seems unlikely that the earliest extant buildings at Al Mina were constructed by architects from a Euboean

tradition.[27] What then is the evidence for Greeks living within north Syrian buildings?

Writing

The Greek inscription (p.12) constitutes the best evidence for Greek presence at the site (Graham 1986: 56), although it could have been made before reaching Al Mina. Even if inscribed at Al Mina, the rarity of the 'string' (ibid.: 55), and the incompetence of the style (Jeffery, in Boardman 1982a: 366), suggest that the writer was inscribing a non-Greek name/ phrase in unfamiliar letters, perhaps to "display alphabetic prowess" (Johnston 1983: 67).

Pottery

The only possible evidence for Greek settlers at Al Mina is the pottery.

Kitchenwares. While the imported Greek amphorae at Al Mina are likely to have been containers for traded goods (p.17), at Pithekoussai the interred pot of Structure I in the Mazzola compound recalls the Lefkandian and Kymeian habit of interring storage vessels (Buchner 1971: 65; Popham et al. 1980b: 19, 20; Sapouna-Sakellaraki 1998: 81), and there are other storage jars (of both Greek and Eastern derivation) at the site (Buchner 1982b: 286-287).

---

[27] Boardman 2002b: 9 argues that constraints of local building materials could account for architectural differences.

Euboean coarse wares (which constituted a high proportion of the total ceramic assemblage at Geometric Lefkandi and Kyme) are often decorated with quite elaborate incisions and impressions, and some burnishing (Boardman 1980: 72-73; Popham *et al.* 1979: pls. 58, 59) (figure 12). Hence it could be conjectured that if Euboean coarse wares had been present at Al Mina, they would have been recovered and kept. There were also plenty of coarse kitchenwares at Pithekoussai, mainly chytrai (Ridgway 1992: 89).

Figure 12. A coarse ware from Lefkandi. Popham et al. 1979, pl. 58, no. 333. Reproduced with permission of the British School at Athens

Finewares and the pots=people equation. Much has been written on the positivist fallacy of equating the modern visibility of an ancient object with its ancient importance (Snodgrass 1980: 126). Ceramic material is all but indestructible and, for reasons related to ease of diagnosis, and to the historical interests of archaeologists, fund-giving bodies, collectors and museums etc, finewares are often the major published class of evidence. This is particularly true in Classical Archaeology and is exemplified in the case of Al Mina.

Indeed, the identification of Al Mina as Posideum—a Greek colony—had an unanticipated theoretical fall-out in shoring up both the positivist fallacy and the so-called "pots=people" equation (Sherratt 1992: 337). Sidney Smith first explicitly formulated the equation between Greek pottery and Greek settlers at the site (1942: 96), and, at least in Classical Archaeology, he has been largely followed in this interpretation ever since (e.g. Kearsley 1999; Boardman (1999a: 44) "all (*sc.* the Greek imports) must have been for daily use, since there was no organised trade in Greek pottery at that time"). The equation has been extended to all the imported finewares at the site. For example, Culican (1982: 79), noting that the Red Slip pottery shares the slip of "metropolitan Phoenicia", concludes that Al Mina is "exactly...Phoenician" and Coldstream notes that "a similar claim could be made there for resident Cypriot traders, on the basis of a considerably larger body of Bichrome and White Painted pottery made in the Cypriot manner" (1989: 94).

Ironically, the equation between pottery and residence is not what Woolley himself had visualised. For him, only the sudden deluge of Cypriot finewares in Level 8 and the Greek style of the local pottery in Level 3 could be extrapolated to indicate actual residence of foreigners. All of the other imports were items of a luxury trade, perhaps carried by traders of each origin, but not for their personal use at the site (Woolley 1937: 9; 1938: 16).

In the case of the Greek pottery, two other beliefs supported the pots=people equation. First, Greeks always carried their skyphoi with them (e.g. Riis 1970: 129; Coldstream 1979: 255); Greek travellers would always have Greek pots as chattels. Secondly, Early Iron Age Orientals (unlike Italians) had no interest in Greek wares, so they could not be items of trade (e.g. Cook 1972: 276; Boardman 1999a: 45).

Moreover, wares such as Attic and Corinthian have long been known to have a ubiquity that could not entirely correspond to Attic or Corinthian presence. Euboean pottery only became well-recognised after Boardman's groundbreaking 1952 study, and its wide distribution—from the North Aegean to North Africa, the Levant to the Far West—has only recently emerged. Such a wide distribution suggests that a non-Greek taste for Euboean pottery and its transportation by non-Euboeans is perfectly possible. Specifically, the presence of quantities of Euboean material in the Amuq plain (p.20) suggests that north Syrians in the ninth and eighth centuries BCE had such a taste.

So there is no *a priori* reason why the presence of finewares, alone, can demonstrate the presence or even trading involvement of those from the producer state. Essentially, the mere presence of imported finewares indicates nothing more than cross-cultural contact at some level and invites further research regarding the involvement of the producers of the ware at that specific time and place.

However, some features of a fineware assemblage in a settlement context may be more likely to indicate residence than not (see Appendix for an example of the impact of context on pottery complexion).

1. *Range of shapes at port.* When the range of foreign fineware shapes (imported or locally-produced) mirrors that of a domestic comparandum, in proportions reflecting that comparandum, it is more likely that members of the foreign community are in free residence, for example at Type C ports of trade and settlement colonies.

At Karum Kanis, for example, a very wide range of pottery appeared during the Assyrian colonial period (Emre 1963: 87-8). Conversely, when just a portion of the domestic ceramic range is evident or important functional forms are significantly over- or under-represented, unrestricted residence is more unlikely (for example at Type A ports of trade).

Because the overwhelming majority of Greek Geometric imports to Al Mina are Euboean,[28] it is Euboean imports that

---

[28] Initially suggested to be Euboean on stylistic grounds by Boardman (1959: 64), scientific tests on the PSC skyphoi have confirmed their likely Euboean origin (Popham, Hatcher and Pollard 1983; Jones 1986: 691-694), and excavation in Euboea, particularly at Lefkandi, have revealed parallels for all the posited Euboean forms at Al Mina. The Greek Geometric pottery in the large unpublished collection in the British Museum is also predominately Euboean. Precisely which Euboean site

Table 4: Morphological distribution of LG Euboean imports at Al Mina

	skyphoi	cups	kotylai	kraters	amphorae	plates	hapax legomena	total
Qu.	175	7	18	27	2	2	3	234
%	75	3	8	11	1	1	1	

Table 5: Morphological distribution of LG local finewares at Lefkandi

	skyphoi	cups	kotylai	kantharoi	tankards	kraters	amphorae	oinochoai	bowls	pyxides	hapax legomena	total
Qu.	95	10	15	2	7	48	9	29	2	5	2	224
%	42	5	7	1	3	21	4	13	1	2	1	

Table 6: Morphological distribution of LG Euboean imports to Pithekoussai

	skyphoi	kotylai	kraters	amphorae	oinochoai	plate	aryballoi	jug	mug	other	total
Qu.	68	17	33	5	165	1	4	2	1	20	316
%	22	5	11	2	52	0	1	1	0	6	

offer the best chance of detecting settlement. Here, the selected domestic comparandum is Lefkandi (Boardman 1980).

At Al Mina, most Euboean imports date to the LG period. Besides skyphoi, the following LG Euboean forms have been noted: kotylai, kantharoi, kraters, a few dinoi, a few plates, a lekanis and a pyxis (e.g. Robertson 1940; Coldstream 1968: 310-6; Descœudres 1978: 17-8; Popham, Pollard & Hatcher 1983: 283 table 1; Popham and Lemos 1992: 155; Kearsley 1995; Boardman 1999a: 40-1; *idem* 1999: 145).[29] While it is impossible to extract reliable percentages for the entire assemblage, owing to the dispersal of the material, it is possible to gain an impression. Kearsley presented 274 Geometric pieces scattered around many museums (1995). The majority of the wares are Euboean, and are shown in Table 4.[30]

An overwhelming 75% of all catalogued Euboean imports in Kearsley's study are skyphoi, and 86% are vessels for drinking. This figure corresponds well with that derived from the British Museum's recently catalogued collection of 907 Euboean Geometric sherds, which are divided into the following shapes: 713 skyphoi, 194 kotylai i.e. 79% skyphoi, 21% kotylai. Even allowing for some other shapes, undiagnosed, the Euboean sherds at Al Mina clearly relate mainly to drinking.

Before any comparison with a domestic comparandum is made, it seems that such a restricted morphological corpus is a poor basis on which to postulate presence, particularly when no other evidence for such presence exists.

The domestic comparandum. Certainly, the skyphos is a very common Geometric form, being the most common fineware shape at Late Geometric Lefkandi. However, the proportions differ considerably, and the overall range of forms is wider, reflecting fuller functionality. Most notably, oinochoai, completely absent from Al Mina, constitute *c.* 13%. Table 5 is based on Boardman 1980: 62-72.

The colonial comparandum. There are about three hundred Euboean fineware imports from the settlement at Pithekoussai (Coldstream 1995a).[31] Their morphological distribution is summarized in Table 6.

---

produced most of the material is impossible to say: Lefkandi, Chalcis and Eretria seem to have used the same clay beds, confounding attempts at scientific anaylsis (Boardman 1996: 156). Stylistically it seems that pottery from all three sites is present at Al Mina (e.g. Boardman 1980: 77; *idem* 1996: 156; Kearsley 1989: 144-145).

[29] Of the other published imported Greek shapes at Al Mina, the amphorae and tankards are likely to be Attic or East Greek (e.g. Robertson 1940: 7, 3b; Coldstream 1968: 312-13; Descœudres 1978: 8 nos. 5 and 6; Kearsley 1995: 23, 55, 62-3); the oinochoai and jugs East Greek (e.g. Kearsley 1995: 53, 55; Descœudres 1978: 7 no. 1); and the aryballoi and the pyxides Corinthian (Coldstream 1968: 315; Riis 1970: 156; Neeft 1987: 48).

[30] I have assumed all pieces are Euboean unless stated otherwise, a total of some 234 pieces. Al Mina wares excluded (Kearsley 1995: 48).

[31] Euboean imports constitute only 3% of the total painted assemblage in this period (Ridgway 1992: 89).

Once again skyphoi form a sizeable portion of the assemblage and as at Lefkandi the range of forms is broader than that found at Al Mina. However, the large proportion of Euboean oinochoai imported for use at the settlement at Pithekoussai, totalling some 52% of the published assemblage, is striking.[32] This preponderance is mirrored in the necropolis, where most oinochoi were locally-produced (Ridgway 1992: 89). Coldstream has linked this huge provision in pouring shapes to the volcanic soil of Ischia, which encouraged the cultivation of the vine (1998: 304).

If the Euboean pottery at Al Mina represents Euboean settlement, we have to assume either that oinochoai, in common use at Lefkandi and prolific at Pithekoussai, were supplied by other producers, in quantities which have left virtually no trace (there are a few East Greek oinochoai, see n.29), or that pouring with ceramic objects was not undertaken at Al Mina. Yet the absence of imported oinochoai is not unique to Al Mina: in the Geometric period, there are just 3 Greek oinochoai in the whole Levant, all at Ras el Basit. Oinochoai continue to be a very rare import to Al Mina and to the East in general (e.g. de Vries 1977; Boardman 1979: 38).

Indeed, leaving aside the plates (which are virtually all pre-LG and found only in Phoenicia), the morphological distribution of the Euboean ceramic assemblage at Al Mina is atypical of a Euboean settlement assemblage but very typical of what is found elsewhere in the Levant (p.41), being virtually restricted to various types of cups, with some kraters and fewer amphorae.

2. *Comparison of imports in port and hinterland.* In cases where a port-hinterland structure appears to obtain, where the hinterland receives pottery (a) from the same provenances as the port and (b) in the same forms as the port, then, unless foreign settlement in the hinterland as well as in the port is likely, the pottery in the port represents trade of some description, not residence.

Information on relevant imports to Al Mina's hinterland, the Amuq plain, is available only in general form and is largely restricted to the Greek material (which, as at Al Mina, is exclusively ceramic).

The Greek Geometric imports are overwhelmingly open shapes (Saltz 1978: 81); one very early amphora (p.20) also testifies to the presence of that shape. As at Al Mina, PSC skyphoi are common, with at least 90 known examples (Swift 1958: 153). Attica is a suggested provenance of Early Iron Age imports to the Amuq, although the decorative motifs of the vessels (maeanders and chevrons (*ibid.*: 154)) are now known from the Atticising repertoire at Lefkandi, so may be Euboean. The Rhodian and Samian material at Al Mina could be subsumed under Swift's "East Greek" category of Greek imports in the Amuq, which includes some eighth century examples. Even the one Corinthian sherd at Al Mina finds an Amuq counterpart (1958: 154). Only the SOS amphorae

fragments from Al Mina do not find reported parallels in the Amuq. The similarities led both Saltz and Swift to stress the parallel nature of the ceramic assemblages from Al Mina and the Amuq plain (Swift 1958: 153; Saltz 1978: 41, 81).

Cypriot imports are also reported from the Iron Age Amuq plain. It has been estimated that 10% of all Amuq pottery, and 35% of Amuq painted pottery, is Cypriot (Gjerstad 1948: 257), and, although some vessels were locally produced, others were imports (p.19). Unfortunately, no information is available regarding the forms of this material, other than that the majority of vessels were one-handled jugs, a form also present at Al Mina. In general, the wares are those present at Al Mina: White Painted, Bichrome and Black-on-Red, as well as some Black Slip (Gjerstad 1948: 257; Swift 1958: 151).

The data concerning Phoenician material in the Amuq are even less serviceable, for neither Swift nor Saltz distinguish between Red Slip imports and locally-produced wares. Certainly though, Swift's catalogue of Amuq Red Slip forms (1958: 131-7) shows that they have a very wide range, within which Red Slip imports from Al Mina could be located.

All the major provenances of ceramic imports at Al Mina—Phoenician, Cypriot, and, in her various wares, Greek—did reach the Amuq plain behind her. Individual forms of vessels are only known in the case of the Greek material, which seems to be similarly represented in both port and hinterland.

We can conclude that Al Mina did not receive imports that were not also received in the Amuq plain; in other words, on the basis of the range of ceramic material, there is no more evidence for the settlement of Greeks at Al Mina than at Tell Tayinat, Chatal Hüyük or Tell Judaidah.

Features of Greek Geometric finewares at Al Mina

Since the Greek finewares are the sole evidence for Greek settlement at the site, and the only evidence for Greek Geometric contact elsewhere in the Levant, in may be helpful to draw together the features of the pottery that bear upon the question of Greek residence and the role of pottery in Al Mina's early levels:

1. *Greek production.* There are no agreed examples of pottery produced by Greeks, suggesting that there was no Greek settlement that was sufficiently permanent, populous, or free to require local production of familiar pottery. By contrast, 81% of the LG finewares at Pithekoussai were locally produced, with only 3% of the assemblage being imports from the Euboean homeland (Ridgway 1992: 89). Local production seems to have started very early in the colony's life (Coldstream 1995a: 266). These figures suggest that, for Euboeans overseas at least, the continued importation of pottery, such as we see at Al Mina, indicates non-residence, while local production of Euboean pottery is a better guide to settlement.

2. *Imitations.* There are no imitations of Greek material, indicating that there was none of the "dissemination of a

---

32 Coldstream's 67% is from a total assemblage which excludes amphorae and kraters (1995b: 267, n. 93).

ceramic style" (Papadopoulos 1997a: 458) we might expect from the presence of Greek producers at the site.

3. *Kitchenwares*. No Greek kitchenwares are known from early Al Mina, although seventh century examples have been found elsewhere in the Levant (p.41).

4. *Range of shapes*. Euboean forms are essentially limited to fine drinking wares, a morphological restriction not mirrored in the domestic or colonial comparandum.

5. *Comparison of imports in port and hinterland*. The forms and provenances of the Greek imports at Al Mina recur in the immediate hinterland of the site.

6. *Distribution of imports in hinterland*. In the hinterland, sometimes whole vessels were found in impressive areas of important sites, suggesting that they were admired, appreciated and sometimes deposited by those who frequented such places.

In sum, the Greek Geometric pottery found at Al Mina and its hinterland is not evidence for Greek settlers at Al Mina. Nor is there any non-ceramic evidence for any Greek residents, in terms of architecture, measures or, indeed, personal belongings. The fibulae are Levantine (Woolley 1938: 138, fig. 17; Stronach 1959: 195-201), the seals and faience alabastra (As)syrian (Boardman 1999b: 158-9).[33]

In theory, the cosmopolitan ports of the Levant may all have had mixed populations (Waldbaum 1997: 12), and Al Mina need be no exception. The presence of Greeks living in north Syrian buildings, eating food cooked and stored in north Syrian pots is certainly possible, but the pottery does not provide reliable evidence for it or for any other type of presence.

Indeed, the identical nature of the imported material in port and hinterland suggests that the pottery (presumably with now-perished imports) was an item of trade, being passed through the port to the central places in the hinterland.[34] The very restricted distribution (and, in some cases, palatial contexts) of the imports suggests that the élite of Unqi were, at the least, not unaware of Greek pottery imports and may even have appreciated them in their own right. This possibility is explored in more detail in Chapter 5.

Phoenicians at Al Mina?

As Kestemont (1985) has shown, epigraphical data and the Assyrian annals attest a strong Phoenician interest in parts of north Syria and Cilicia in the early first millennium BCE. This interest had a physical dimension—a Phoenician harbour installation at Myriandros is recorded in the Assyrian annals, Xen. *Anabasis* 1.4.6 and Ps-Scylax *Periplus* 102, and

Phoenicians were present at Carcemish in the reign of Tiglath-pileser III; official Phoenician inscriptions and the invocation of the Tyrian god by the King of Aram testify to political and religious influence (Aubet 2001: 50). Influence seems to have been particularly strong in Cilicia, where five Phoenician inscriptions dating from the 9th to 8th centuries BCE have been discovered (Röllig 1992). Presumably, access to the rich Anatolian metal deposits was the main focus of interest, although other goods are possible: Aubet notes that Solomon acquired horses and carriages from Cappadocia around this time (2001: 48-50).

In recent years, the Phoenicians (principally the Tyrians) have been rehabilitated from the academic doldrums in which they languished for much of the nineteenth and twentieth centuries CE, and have been appreciated as pan-Mediterranean traders and explorers. This, coupled with their certain presence in the North Syrian/Cilician region, and their documented role as suppliers for the Assyrian Empire, does mean that Phoenician activity at this gateway site is possible.

However, by the second half of the ninth century, the Aramaean kingdoms were increasingly powerful. In 800 BCE an alliance between the north Syrian kingdoms and Urartu allowed those regions to dominate the main routes from the Mediterranean to the metalliferous areas of Cilicia and Anatolia, and excluded Tyre. The beginning of the Assyrian shortage of silver, normally supplied by Tyre, dates to this period (Aubet 2001: 90). By 800 BCE Phoenician presence in north Syria and Cilicia was curtailed and Tyre looked westwards, to Kition and beyond, for new sources of the materials—particularly metals—craved by its main market, Assyria (*ibid.*: 51, 83-4, 87).

As for the material evidence at the site, indicators of Phoenician presence are, as for the Greek, entirely ceramic. The peculiar wall construction often employed by Phoenician (and Israelite) builders, the pillar and rubble ('*a telaio*') construction technique, is absent (Isserlin and Taylor 1974: 91; Braemer 1982: 119). This technique is known both in the Phoenician homeland, at Sarepta and Tyre (Pritchard 1978: 93-4; Bikai 1978: pl. LXXXIX 5 and 6), and later at the overseas Phoenician settlements, such as Motya, Nora, and Carthage (Isserlin and Taylor 1974: 90; Pritchard 1972: 19; *idem* 1983: 522). The tripartite pillared warehouse structure familiar from Western Phoenician settlements such as Motya and Toscanos is also absent (p.30).

Nor is there any sign of the Phoenician two-spouted lamp (Szentléleky 1969: 24-5 and n. 13), which is found at Western Phoenician settlements (there is even an example at Pithekoussai) (Pritchard 1972: 18-19; Buchner 1982b: 285). Wall brackets, ubiquitous on Phoenician sites for the suspension of lamps (e.g. Pritchard 1978: 95), were also not reported at the site.

There is a Phoenician-style cooking pot, but it is unstratified (Lehmann forthcoming: 13).

The Red Slip evidence is harder to interpret than the clearly intrusive Greek. Most of the Levantine pottery types at Al

---

[33] Pithekoussai, with its Campanian fibulae, warns us that fibulae are not reliable indicators of Euboeans overseas (Coldstream 1993).

[34] Like the apparently unused mortaria of levels 6-5, destined for onward transmission (Lehmann forthcoming: 22).

Mina fall into the same coastal class as the metropolitan Phoenician wares (although there is a possibility that, being more elaborately decorated than the native Syrian wares, they were more likely to be retained (Lehmann forthcoming: 28)).

The material evidence shows only that some Phoenician pottery was reaching the port. There is no other evidence that suggests that it was being used at the port by metropolitan Phoenicians, rather then being an item of trade. As for the Greek material, this does not preclude the presence of Phoenicians at Al Mina, cooking, or being cooked for, in Syrian cooking pots and living in Syrian-lit and built residences in an archaeologically undetectable way. It does, however, seem to preclude the possibility that this was a wholly Phoenician settlement (cf. Culican 1982b; Graham 1986: 58).[35]

Warehouses at Al Mina?

There is an added architectural issue at Al Mina: Woolley, reacting against the perceived barbarity of the structures (understandably, given his usual palatial perspective), and in line with his overall objective of finding a trading settlement, identified the buildings at the site as warehouses.[36] Woolley's interpretation has been generally accepted. Thus both Elayi (1987: 257) and Graham (1986: 53-54), although both highly sceptical of the general Greekness of the site, accepted the notion that the structures were warehouses.

Despite this general acceptance, the logical corollary of the interpretation—that the imports (including the pottery) are traded goods—is often rejected. While Woolley's interpretation of his site was at least internally consistent, with traded goods being stored in warehouses, under the current orthodoxy we are left pondering the presence of chattels in warehouse buildings. It would therefore seem to be worth re-examining the architectural layout of the site for this reason too.

Woolley based his proposal that the site was composed of warehouses whose merchant owners were Greeks on the following analysis:

"Had this been a residential town, we should have judged it, on the evidence of its buildings, to have been poor, if not barbarous; mere huts of *mud brick*, of *one storey*, with *mud-plastered walls* and with no pretence to architectural style or decoration would seem to call for no more flattering description. But the *lay-out* of the buildings, at least in the later times of Levels II, III and

IV, and their *contents* throughout the entire period, are not consistent with such a judgment. The fact is that it was not a residential town, and its buildings, which would have been *poor as private houses*, were perfectly adequate to their purpose; what we have here are the *stores and business premises* of merchants" (my italics)

(Woolley 1938: 11, 15).

As we have seen, mud-brick walls were consonant with contemporary Levantine practice. The layout of the buildings in the early levels is typically Levantine. Moreover, the layout of the buildings in the later levels, which best supports Woolley's case, also conform to Levantine architectural practices: the units of the refounded town of Level 5 onwards are detached and larger, inspiring Woolley to see in them "early examples of the type of office and magazine building which was to become the standard for future times" (Woolley 1938: 18). Although no unit is sufficiently well preserved to class with any certainty, the best-preserved unit on Level 5, in Squares H/J-5/6, accords with Braemer's class II.b.4 (1982: 69, fig. 23d) (Megiddo III is roughly contemporary with Al Mina Levels 6-5). Tell Sukas, Period G3 (which is also contemporary with Al Mina Levels 6-5), also has class II units, this time of subtypes A3 or B1 (Lund 1986: 190).

A number of features suggest that some buildings had upper storeys. First, Woolley noted that the walls were probably thick enough to sustain a further storey (1938: 11). Second, Level 2 (House F, room 12) contains a flight of stone steps (*ibid.*: 11, 136). Similar stone steps occur at Beer Sheba, buildings 25, 75 and 76, above which the excavators postulate the use of wooden staircases or ladders (Biet Arieh 1973: 32, 34). The use of alternative methods of elevation, such as wooden staircases and ladders were probably commonplace in the Levant: there are many examples of activities taking place either on the roof or in a second storey (e.g. Wright 1978: 151), when no evidence of staircases has been found. At Bronze Age Ugarit, where staircases have been found, the excavators have suggested that the living quarters were actually situated on the upper floors, with the ground floors (and the roofs, as today) being used for many everyday activities (Yon 1992: 29). Lastly, the difference in level between contiguous houses was probably exploited. Woolley remarked that "buildings of the same date, even though adjacent, are not necessarily on the same horizontal plain" (Woolley 1938: 7): artificial means of access may not have been required.

Levels 4-2 at Al Mina apparently constituted a new town, composed of regular blocks of 'insulae' facing into regular streets (figures 4-5). This regularity also reflects the pan-Mediterranean influence of Hippodamian ideals, as evidenced by their appearance at the Phoenician outposts of Solunto and Carthage (Isserlin 1973: 87), rendering futile all attempts to characterise ethnicity (and function) on the basis of town plans at this period. As regards the actual house types, Braemer classifies them as Class III.4 (1982: 82).[37]

---

[35] The payment by Phoenicians to various Assyrian kings harrying north Syria may have been a purely precautionary measure, designed to stave off attacks from the next region—metropolitan Phoenicia itself (cf. Kestemont 1985). This strategy seems to have paid off in the short-term: Tiglath-pileser III was the first Assyrian monarch to attack Phoenicia and, although he provincialised north Phoenicia, including Arvad and Byblos, Tyre was left independent, albeit suffering from a swingeing tribute and customs officials in her port. But the writing was on the wall and, after gradually losing territory and independence, she became an Assyrian province *c.* 640 BCE.

[36] The modern Al Mina known to Woolley was represented by a few houses, a Customs Officer's house and a warehouse (1938: 4).

[37] Though Braemer refers to Level 4, the page references he gives in his n. 76 are to Woolley's account of Level 3, and the type of structure he is describing is so much more clear in that level that I presume he means Level 3.

Generally then, the layout of Al Mina and of its buildings is typical of the contemporary Levantine, and, more specifically, north Syrian milieu. Consequently, from an architectural point of view, these buildings are no more or less likely to have been warehouses than those at any of the other sites in the region.

In fact, a number of Levantine structures have been positively identified as warehouses. Shiloh defined the typical Israelite storehouse as being composed of three parallel rooms of equal width, which tend to dominate their surroundings (e.g. Shiloh 1970: 182; Kochavi 1998: 471). No Al Minan unit qualifies for such a description. Neither do they conform to the typically Phoenician warehouse, the form of which was evidently transported overseas in these years, for example to Toscanos in southern Spain (Niemeyer 1982b: 192-9; *idem* 1990: 480, 482 fig. 13; Aubet 2001: 319).

Nonetheless, it remains possible that structures, although not built in recognised warehouse styles, could function as warehouses. Only an examination of the contents of the structures can indicate their actual usage.

Woolley claimed that the contents of the buildings "throughout the entire period" indicated that they were "stores and business premises". The most compelling feature of the contents in demonstrating this claim is the sorting of imports (Woolley 1938: 11-12). The first indication of such sorting appears in Levels 6/5, and is only fully expressed in Level 3 (*ibid.*: 16, 24). The earlier levels (and most of Levels 6/5) are interpreted along the same lines purely on the basis of analogy (e.g. *ibid.*: 12, 18), and there is no independent indication of the original distribution of the goods in these levels (presumably because they were not found *in situ*, being both scattered and shattered (*ibid.*: 19)). So no judgment as to the function of the buildings can be made on the basis of the contents in the early levels; and even Woolley himself seems diffident about invoking the warehouse hypothesis for Levels 5/6 (*ibid.*: 12, n. 14). This being the case, it would seem to be worthwhile to examine just how the goods in the supposedly paradigmatic later levels are spatially distributed. Elayi (1987: 257) noted that in Level 3, of the 16 units excavated, only one (H) contained exclusively Greek goods, three contained only local goods, seven mainly local goods, and five she (reasonably) suggests were devoid of Greek goods, since their contents were not described by the excavator. From this information, she concludes that only the owner of the H 'warehouse' was a Greek merchant. However, examination of the spatial distribution of these finds within the structures reveals that only a minority of rooms in any one unit contains such goods. Indeed, Unit H contains Greek goods in only three of its twelve extant rooms (Woolley 1938: 142, and plan of Level 3). But this spatial distribution of imports would be an irrational non-maximisation of space for a structure functioning entirely as a warehouse.

This is not to suggest that imports were not stored at Al Mina throughout the lifetime of the site, any less than at all of the other ports for which warehouse hypotheses have not been invoked (such as Ras el Basit and Tell Sukas). Indeed, the bulk storage of *in situ* goods in the later levels, and the evident functioning of these sites as ports, demonstrates that goods were stored and break-of-bulk operations took place there. But the distribution of the contents in the later levels when they can be properly analysed (and when they are generally considered to most support the warehouse hypothesis) corroborates the evidence of the architectural style and layout of the buildings throughout the lifetime of the settlement: these structures were not 'warehouses' in any modern (or, if the identification of the Phoenician and Levantine 'warehouses' is correct, ancient) sense of the term, as structures devoted to the wholesale storage of traded goods.

Perreault goes further, and suggests that the site's early levels are virtually all domestic in character (1993, 65-6, and n. 28). Kearsley too casts Al Mina as an "occupation site" for mercenaries (1999: 128). But as Woolley himself pointed out (1938: 13), the low-lying Al Mina had no natural advantages as a residential settlement. By contrast, its position at the mouth of the Orontes, giving it access to the Amuq plain and the Assyrian heartlands, gave it tremendous advantages as a site dedicated to trade. In sum, the architectural style of the buildings, the layout of the site and of its structures, and the contents of the buildings in the later levels point to their use as mixed residential and storage facilities. As Riis (1982: 246) points out, such a combination of mixed residential and storage units is not unusual in the Levant.

Release from the tyranny of the warehouse hypothesis permits the otherwise inexplicable presence of intra-mural burials, ovens, hearths and loomweights and the domestic assemblage of Room 8 Level 8 (Woolley 1938: 13,142,146,169), which had compelled Woolley to postulate a modicum of settlement by the poor residents.

Conclusions

The available evidence for the early years does not show that Greeks resided at Al Mina, either as traders or mercenaries. The only evidence of Greek interest in the port is the finewares, and that is an item of trade, being passed through the port to the hinterland beyond.

The available material evidence suggests that Al Mina was a place where traded goods were stored and where people (presumably those controlling the physical aspects of the trade) lived: a working port, and, as Woolley saw, a gateway to the East.

Chapter 4
Greek Geometric pottery in the Levant

You ask me whether the Orient is up to what I imagined it to be.

Yes, it is; and more than that, it extends far beyond the narrow idea I had of it

Flaubert in Egypt (Steegmuller 1973: 173)

Greek Geometric imports have now been found at many other coastal and inland sites in the Levant (map 1). As at Al Mina, finewares constitute the sole type of import.

This wide distribution allows us to discern whether the character and function of Al Mina—at least as regards Greek Geometric pottery—was unique. If Al Mina was not unique in these characteristics, instead being part of a Levantine-wide pattern, then that pattern will be all the more amenable to interpretation through the utilisation of a larger, and, in many cases, more reliable, database.

There follows a catalogue of Greek Geometric pottery in the Levant.[38] After the catalogue comes a short description of the find-sites, considered within their geo-political context: before 720 BCE, when the Assyrians had provincialised most of the Levant, the region was divided into separate polities, whose leaders made constantly-shifting alliances in an effort to contain Assyrian power. Territory changed hands frequently. After 720 BCE, political borders between states were fewer, and cultural differentiation between states less marked: for example, measurements were unified and intra-Levantine transport expanded (Lehmann 1998: 30).

A catalogue of Greek Geometric pottery in the Levant

For the sake of consistency, and since much of the material has proven to be Euboean, the chronological scheme adopted is that devised by the excavators of Lefkandi. The synchronisms between this and the orthodox Attic chronology are noted in Table 7.

Table 7: Euboean and Attic synchronisms in the Geometric period

Lefkandi Chronology[39]	Attic Chronology[40]	'Absolute' Dates BCE[41]
E/MPG	EPG	1050/1025-980
MPG	MPG	980-960/950
LPG	LPG	960/950-900
SPGI	EGI	900-875
SPGII	EGII	875-850
SPGIII	MGI	850-800
SPGIII	MGII	800-760/750
LG	LGI	760/750-735
LG	LGII	735-700

[38] Following Waldbaum (1994: 62, n. 5), I exclude sites noted by Wenning (1981: 33-34; 1991: 209) as findspots of Greek pottery unless elsewhere documented. I also exclude the kantharos sherd reported by Austin "near Koropi" (1968: 183, n. 29). This sherd was published in "Sumer" (Clairmont 1952). The choice of publication seems to reflect the sherd's final resting place—Baghdad Museum—not its findspot: there is no ancient or modern Koropi in the area. But Attic Koropi flourished in the LG Attic period (Coldstream 1977: 133-134) (significantly perhaps, the Koropi kantharos is reported as coming from near Koropi—like the Stathatou amphora and gold necklace (Cook 1951: 45)). This proposed re-attribution is supported by the findspot of the only other positively provenanced sherd in Clairmont's article—Phaleron, another Attic site.

[39] Popham et al 1980a: "abbreviations"; Popham 1993b: 101; Catling and Lemos 1990b: 95.

[40] Desborough 1952: 294 (PG); Coldstream 1968: 330 (Geometric).

[41] Absolute dates from Coldstream 1968; both the upper and lower ends of the Geometric chronology have come under recent scrutiny (e.g. James et al. 1991; Morris 1998; Kopcke 2002: 114-7), as has the relative sequence (Papadopoulos 1998).

Table 8 lists by period Greek Geometric sherds in the Levant (excluding Al Mina and sites in the Amuq plain).

Table 8: Greek Geometric Pottery in the Levant

Where	Qu.	What	Provenance	Context
E/MPG (1050/1025-960/950)				
Luhuti (later Hamath)				
Tell Afis	1	deep skyphos	Argive? (figure 13)	settlement[42]
Israel				
Tell Hadar	1	lebes	Chalcidian? (figure 14)	public storeroom[43]
Total	2			
LPG (960/950-900)				
Hamath				
Ras el Basit	4	amphorae	Lefkandi	settlement[44]
Phoenicia				
Tyre	3	amphorae	Euboean	settlement[45]
	1	krater	Euboean	settlement[46]
	1	cauldron	Euboean	settlement[47]
	3	CC skyphoi	Euboean	settlement[48]
Israel				
Tell Abu Hawam	1	PSC skyphos	Euboean	settlement[49]
Total	13			
SPGI-II (900-850)				
Hamath				
Ras el Basit	1	oinochoe	Lefkandi	settlement[50]
Phoenicia				
Tyre	1	amphora	Euboean	settlement[51]
	1	PSC skyphos	Euboean	settlement[52]
Assyria				
Nineveh	1	PSC skyphos	Euboean?	temple of Nabu[53]
Total	4			
SPGIII (850-760/750)				
Hamath				
Ras el Basit	1	PSC plate	Cyclades	settlement[54]
	1+	PSC skyphoi	Cyclades	settlement[55]
Tell Sukas	2	PSC skyphoi	Cycladic/Euboean	settlement[56]
	1	skyphos	Euboean	settlement[57]
Tabbat al Hamman	Few	PSC skyphoi	?	settlement[58]

[42] TA.89.E.214/2. Bonatz 1998: 214-5. A deep bell-shaped tall-bodied bowl without handles, decorated with scribbled zigzags bordered by 4 diagonal encircling lines. *per* Bonatz, its nearest parallels are with EPG Argolid. Two similar vessels have been identified as Argive imports at Lefkandi (Popham *et al*. 1979: 23, pl 49: 166-7). Elsewhere in the Levant, Argive pottery has only been identified at Tambourit. Early Cypriot imports were also present at Tell Afis.

[43] Coldstream 1998a: 357-359; Kochavi 1998.

[44] Courbin 1993b: 95 (no. 1), 97 (nos. 2 and 3), 98 (no. 4) (inv. C.1895, C.5235, C.4006, C.6519a-c).

[45] Bikai 1978: pl. XXX: 1 (A 30), which is Coldstream 1988: 40, no. 69, and not no. 68 (cf. *ibid*.: 37, n. 16). Also *ibid*. nos. 70 and 71.

[46] Coldstream 1988: 40, no. 24.

[47] *Ibid*.: 40, nos. 72-5.

[48] 42 PSC/CC skyphoi in Coldstream 1988: 39-40, of which 3 CC skyphoi (nos. 45, 68, possibly 26) dated to LPG. Remaining 39 dated *c.*850-*c.*750 i.e. SPGIII. Bikai 1978: 53 "Import 3" has 24 examples, stratified as follows (strata from *ibid*.: 54, Tab 13A; dates *ibid*.: 68): 1 SPGI-II; 19 SPGIII; 4 LG.

[49] Hamilton 1935: 24, no. 96 and pl. 12; Heurtley 1935: 181 and pl. 88; Lemos (in Waldbaum 1994: 62, n. 6). Cf. Kearsley who classes it as Type 6 (1989: 104), that is, of late eighth century date.

[50] Courbin 1990a: 505 (inv. C.6638); 1993b: 105, n. 52.

[51] *Ibid*.: no. 76.

[52] See n.48.

[53] Campbell Thompson and Hutchinson 1929: 138; Hamilton 1932: 130; Clairmont 1955: 98, no. 1; Riis 1970: 144; Boardman 1987: 375, for early SPG date and provenance.

[54] *Idem* 1976: 64; 1978a: 55; 1982: 193, n. 1 (inv. C.2098); 1986: 190. Courbin's dating of 850-800 BCE (1982: 202) replaces 1976 one of 775-750 BCE.

[55] *Idem* 1975: 60; 1978a: 55.

[56] TS 2018 (37) and TS 1012 (38). Ploug 1973: 11-14, pl. II, nos. 37-38. Coldstream 1989: 92 for SPGIII date of all Levantine PSC skyphoi.

[57] TS 3520 (39). Ploug 1973: 13, 14; pl. II, no. 39. Atticising.

[58] Braidwood 1940: 191 (fig. 4, no. 9), 193. Coldstream 1968: 311, 345. Here dated SPGIII by analogy with majority of PSC skyphoi (see ns.48,58).

Table 8: Continued

Where	Qu.	What	Provenance	Context
Ras Ibn Hani	2	PSC skyphoi	?	settlement[59]
Hama	1	krater	Attic	between palace and temple[60]
	1	cup	Euboean	near little palace[61]
	4	PSC skyphoi	Euboean/Cycladic	royal sanctuary[62]
			Euboean/Cycladic	palace/patrician house
			Euboean/Cycladic	cemetery
			Euboean/Cycladic	cemetery
Phoenicia				
Khaldeh	1	PSC skyphos	Cycladic/Euboean	burial[63]
Tambourit	1	pyxis	Argive?	burial[64]
Tell Rachidieh	1	PSC plate	Euboean/local	élite burial[65]
Sarepta	2	PSC skyphoi?	?	settlement[66]
Tyre	3	kraters	Attic	settlement[67]
	2	pyxides	Attic	settlement[68]
	1	skyphos	Attic	settlement[69]
	1	?	Attic?	Settlement[70]
	1	krater	Euboean	Settlement[71]
	1	skyphos?	Euboean?	Settlement[72]
	2	skyphoi	Euboean	Settlement[73]
	59	PSC skyphoi	Euboean	Settlement[74]
	28	PSC plates	Euboean	Settlement[75]
Israel				
Tell Abu Hawam	1	1-handled cup	Euboean?	settlement[76]
	1	skyphos	Cycladic/Euboean?	settlement[77]
Megiddo	2	skyphoi	Attic/(ising) Euboean	temple/governor's house[78]

[59] Bounni *et al.* 1978: 282-284, fig. 29, nos. 1 and 6; Stratum dated to eighth-sixth centuries BCE. Dated SPGIII by analogy with majority of PSC skyphoi (see above).

[60] 2D 724. Riis and Buhl 1990: 184 no. 668.

[61] 2A6 77. Riis 1970: 154, 160 (fig. 55d). Riis compared this black-glaze cup with that from Tell abu Hawam and a Siphnian example. All find parallels in the SPGII-III area at Lefkandi (Desbourough and Dickinson 1980: 49, 52), whence this piece dated.

[62] Riis 1970: 152, 153 fig. 51a-d. 7B 23, L 941, 6A 290, 8A 181; Coldstream 1968: 310-11; *idem* 1977: 93. Riis and Buhl 1990: 184, nos. 666, 665). Niemeier suggests it was offered as a votive in the shrine (2001: 13).

[63] Saidah 1971: 194. Dated SPGIII by analogy with majority of PSC skyphoi (see above).

[64] Courbin 1993b: 105, n. 53; Coldstream 1988: 41, n. 79

[65] Doumet 1982: 90. Thanks are due to Dr Doumet for providing offprints of her articles on the Tell Rachidieh excavations.

[66] Herscher 1975: 96; Kearsley 1989: 194 (who (p.6) suggests that Herscher's piece may be a plate); Doumet 1982: 125; Koehl 1985: 136. Dated SPGIII by analogy with majority of PSC skyphoi (see ns.48,58).

[67] *Ibid.*: 40-41 (nos. 77, 85, 86).

[68] Coldstream 1988: 41, nos. 87, 90-96.

[69] Bikai 1978: pl. XXIIA, no. 3 (A 34); Coldstream 1988: 40, no. 78.

[70] Bikai 1978: pl. XIA, no. 24 (A877). Coldstream in *ibid.*: pl. XIB, n. 24 for frequency of such decoration in MGI Attic.

[71] Coldstream 1988: 41, nos. 97-98.

[72] Sherd found in strata IX-VIII (850-800 BCE) (Bikai 1978: 68). Bikai 1978: pl. XXIIA, no. 2 (A 35). Cf. Coldstream 1988: 41, no. 103, and pl. XIII, where provenanced as Euboean, and Popham *et al.* 1979: pl. 47, nos 131-147.

[73] *Ibid.*: 40, nos. 79, 80.

[74] See n. 48.

[75] 16 in Coldstream 1988: 39 (nos. 9-18, 20-22, 54, 57, 67), dated SPGIII by Lefkandi parallels; seven in Bikai 1978: 53 ("Import 4"), of which one comes from strata 2-3, dated to LG period (*ibid.*: 34 Tab. 13A, 68, pl XI.B A559); six in Courbin 1982: 198 and n.19 (dated here to SPGII by analogy, see ns.48,58)

[76] Hamilton 1935: 23-24, no. 95 and pl. 8; Heurtley 1935: 181 and pl. 88; Coldstream 1968: 303. Euboean attribution supported by the finds from Lefkandi, especially Popham *et al.* 1979: pl. 28, no. 70/P7. All three pieces hail from stratum III, the dating of which has been the subject of endless controversy. Dates ranging from the tenth to the seventh century BCE (Balensi 1985: 73, n. 26) have been used to date the Greek pottery by *termini ante quos*.

[77] Balensi 1985: 69 and fig. 3; Herrera and Balensi 1986: 170, fig. 1c. Herrera and Balensi suggest either a Corinthian or a Cycladic fabric. Possibly LG: the influence of Attic pottery on Euboean LG is worth noting (e.g. Coldstream 1968: 192-193; Popham *et al.* 1980c: 368). There is a parallel for the star motif on a LG krater sherd at Lefkandi (Boardman 1980: 61; Popham *et al.* 1979: pl. 44, no. 66) on which the star is irregular like the Tell Abu Hawam example, in contrast to the neater Dipylon exemplars of Attica (e.g. Coldstream 1968: pl. 7a).

[78] Clairmont 1955: 99, nos. 4 and 5 and pl. 21:1a-b, 2a-b. Coldstream 1968: 303 (where Clairmont's "nos. 1-2" refers to figs. 1a-b and 2a-b, actually nos. 4 and 5 in Clairmont's text). Avi-Yonah and Stern 1977: 853. Good parallels in Attic MGI (Coldstream 1968: 303-304). SPG III is the date of most of the Lefkandi Levelling Material containing Atticising sherds, and of comparable imports to Tyre. cf. similar Euboean and Attic imports to Tyre (Coldstream 1988: 40-41 and pls. XII-XIII). Desborough and Dickinson 1980: 41-42, nos. 407-412, illustrated in Popham *et al.* 1979: pl. 21 for similar SPGIII Atticising multiple zigzags at Lefkandi. Both sherds may be from one skyphos.

Table 8: Continued

Where	Qu.	What	Provenance	Context
Samaria	1	mug	Attic/(ising)/Euboean	settlement[79]
	1?	krater	Attic	Settlement[80]
	1	plate	Attic/(ising) Euboean	settlement[81]
	2	?	Attic/(ising) Euboean	settlement[82]
	1	?	Cycladic	settlement[83]
	1	?	Attic/(ising) Euboean	settlement[84]
Philistia				
Askalon	1	PSC skyphos	Euboean	?[85]
Ekron	1	cup	Attic?	élite zone[86]
Assyria				
Tell Halaf	1	PSC skyphos	Euboean	settlement[87]
Total	132+			
LG (760/750-700)				
Hamath				
Tell Afis	1	PSC skyphos	Euboea? (figure 15)	storerooms[88]
Ras el Basit	Many	cups	Euboea	settlement[89]
	1	krater	East Greece?	Settlement[90]
	1	oinochoe	Attic?	settlement[91]
	1	oinochoe	Cyclades	settlement[92]
	5+	skyphoi	East Greece	settlement[93]
	1	skyphos	Euboea	settlement[94]
Tell Sukas	1	aryballos	Euboean	settlement[95]
	1	amphoriskos	Euboean	settlement[96]
	2	kraters	Cycladic/Euboean	settlement[97]
	1	pyxis?	Parian?	settlement[98]
	1	cup	East Greek	settlement[99]
	1	kotyle	Euboean	Settlement[100]

[79] Reisner *et al.* 1924: 282, no. 9a and fig. 157, no. 9a (0467); Coldstream 1968: 304. *Ibid.* ascribes all Greek Samaritan sherds an Attic/ising origin; later notes that they could be Cycladic imitations (1977: 94).

[80] Crowfoot *et al.* 1957: 210, nos. 1-6 (Q4710, Q4589, Qy84, Q4576 *et al.*); fig. 34, nos. 1-3, and fig. 34a; pl. XVIII, nos. 1-2 (Argive krater). The excavators believed that all fragments were from one krater, which opinion Coldstream (1968: 304) supports, although Saltz (1978: 186) suggests the presence of at least two kraters. Waldbaum (1994: 57, n. 10) notes the existence of two similar sherds in the study collection of the Institute of Archaeology, Hebrew University of Jerusalem (nos. 3769 and 8533/2) which may hail from Samaria.

[81] Reisner *et al.* 1924: 281, no. 1a (2604), and 282, fig. 157, no. 1 and "Rim"; Coldstream 1968: 304. Since a maeander decoration is unknown for Lefkandian plates, which are all of the PSC variety, an Attic origin may be more likely.

[82] Reisner 1924: 282, no. 10a and fig. 157, no. 10a (0496); Crowfoot *et al.* 1957: 213 and pl. XVIII, no. 18; Coldstream 1968: 304.

[83] Reisner 1924: 288, no. 12m and 289, fig. 164m (0400). Classified with "White-ground lekythi," but redeemed by Riis (1970: 146, 149 (fig. 49b)).

[84] Reisner *et al.* 1924: 281, no. 6b and 282, fig. 157, no. 6b (4359); Riis 1970: 149 (fig. 49c).

[85] Hamilton 1935: 24; Riis 1991: 208; Waldbaum 1994: 57 and n.8.

[86] Waldbaum 1994: 58 and fig. 6. According to Seymour Gitin (the Director of the Tel Miqne-Ekron Excavation and Publication Project), in a letter dated May 19th, 1993 the sherd (no. M2/88 IVNW.23.30) may have been part of a fill, and was not associated with any architectural construction, although it was found in the "élite zone". Thanks are due to Professor Gitin for this information.

[87] Hrouda 1962: 84 and 101 (no. 188), pl. 69; Courbin for *terminus post quem* of 850 BCE (1990b: 55, n. 34); Coldstream 1968: 311, 345.

[88] TA.86.D.280/1. Bonatz 1998: 220; Mazzoni 1987: 27. Sherd found in a mid-eighth century context, so an SPGIII date possible. Thanks are due to Dr Bonatz for this information.

[89] Courbin 1975: 60 (although described as "fragments", the succeeding "une de ces coupes" indicates that they were mainly cups); *idem* 1978a: 56; 1983a: 292; 1986: 193 (inv. C.2558 and C.5768 etc.); 1990a: 506. Boardman's total of 25 Greek Geometric sherds at Ras el Basit (1990b: 173), includes Al Minan (i.e. Cypriot) wares (Courbin 1993b: 107, n. 65).

[90] *Idem* 1975: 60. Courbin does not provenance the krater, besides noting that is not Cycladic. Metopal birds are a regular motif of East Greek potters of the LG and later periods (Coldstream 1968: 278, 285). Metopal birds on kraters are also known from LG Euboea (e.g. Boardman 1980: 68; Popham *et al.* 1979: pls. 52, no. 234 and 55, no. 264).

[91] *Idem* 1990a: 506 (inv. C.6515).

[92] Courbin 1983a: 291-292.

[93] Courbin 1977-1978: 30; 1978a: 56; 1978b: 41 and pl. XV, fig. 1; 1986: 193 (inv. C.2515); 1990a: 506 (inv. C.2077 and C.7054); 1983a: 292.

[94] *Idem* 1986: 194; 1990a: 506 (inv. C.7517); Courbin describes the sherd as imitation EPC. Though the sigma kotyle is a Corinthian EPC invention (Coldstream 1968: 105), Corinth is a rare source of Greek Geometric material in the Levant and EPC kotylai were faithfully copied in Euboea (*ibid.*: 191).

[95] TS 4416 (64). Ploug 1973: 17, 21; pl. III, no. 64 and fig. a, no. 64. Riis 1982: 243 notes of all four PC types (the aryballos, amphoriskos, pyxis and kotyle) that they are probably Euboean.

[96] TS 5551 (70). Ploug 1973: 17-18, 22; pl. III, no. 70.

[97] TS 1394 (40); TS 969 (41). *Ibid.*: 13-14; pl. II, nos. 40-41; Riis 1982: 243.

[98] TS 520 (62). *Ibid.*: 17, 20; pl. III, no. 62.

[99] TS 4577 (100). Ploug 1973: 28-29, 33; pl.V, no. 100; fig. a, no. 100.

[100] TS 517 (49). *Ibid.*: 17, 20; pl. II, no. 49.

Table 8: Continued

Where	Qu.	What	Provenance	Context
Hama	1	krateriskos	Parian?	near little palace[101]
	1	amphora/jug	Euboean/Cycladic	near royal palace[102]
	2	kraters	Naxian/Parian	west of little palace[103]
Phoenicia				
Tyre	8	skyphoi	Euboean	settlement[104]
	1	PSC plate	Euboean	settlement[105]
	2	kraters	Atticising Euboean	settlement[106]
	5	kotylai	Euboean	settlement[107]
Tell Kabri	1	skyphos	?	?[108]
Israel				
Tell Qiri	1	dinos	Euboean	public building[109]
Babylonia				
Babylon	2?	lekythoi	East Greek?	settlement[110]
Total	41+			

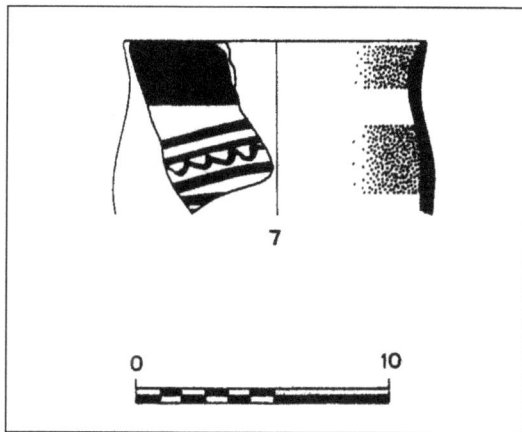

Figure 13. E/MPG Argive (?) deep skyphos
from Tell Afis. Bonatz 1998: 225,
fig. 3.7 (TA.89.E.214/2).
Courtesy Edizioni ETS, Pisa

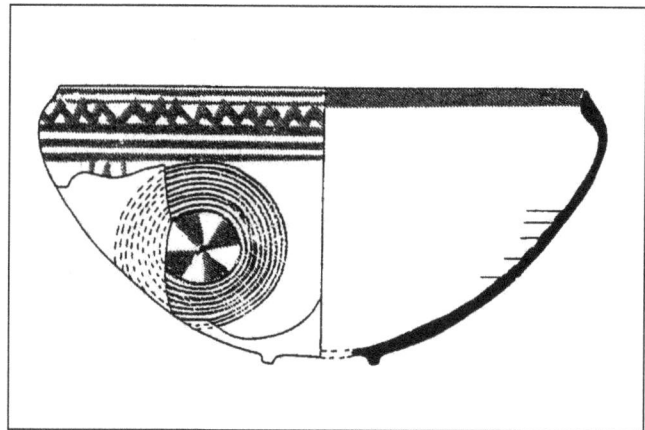

Figure 14. E/MPG Chalcidian(?) lebes
from Tell Hadar. Coldstream 1998: 358, fig. 1.
Scale 2:5.
Courtesy Israel Exploration Society, Jerusalem

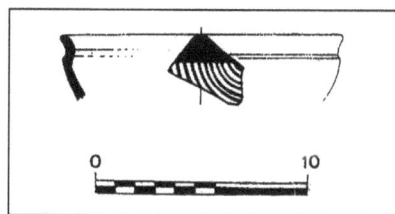

Figure 15. LG PSC skyphos from Tell Afis.
Bonatz 1998: 229, fig. 5.3 (TA.86.D.280/1).
Courtesy Edizioni ETS, Pisa

[101] 2 E 76. Riis 1970: 154 and n. 628, 160 (fig. 55e); Riis and Buhl 1990: 184 no. 667. Coldstream 1968: 310. For Lefkandi parallels of metopal crosses on LG kraters, see Popham *et al.* 1979: pl. 54, nos. 248 and 252. A few earlier examples are known, such as *ibid.*: pl. 18, no. 328, but the motif is atypical (Desborough and Dickinson 1980: 38).

[102] 7 A 47. Riis 1970: 154, 160 (fig. 55f). Coldstream 1968: 311. Apart from the PSC skyphoi and the Attic krater, none of the sherds were found in their original contexts. Nonetheless, the excavator believes it significant that they were all found around the important structures of the ninth to the eighth centuries BCE

[103] 4 C 321, 7 A 47. Riis 1970: 154 and n. 629, 160 (fig. 55b). Coldstream 1968: 310. Riis and Buhl 1990: 184 nos. 669-670. For linked blobs on LG Lefkandi kraters, see Popham *et al.* 1979: pl. 53, nos. 243-244. Also 2 D 724. Riis 1970: 154 and n. 631, 160 (fig. 55c).

[104] *Ibid*: 41, nos. 99, 102, 103, 105, 106, 108, 109, 111.

[105] See n.75.

[106] Coldstream 1988: 41, nos. 81-82, 84, 88-89; 83 (although *ibid.* has no. 82 as a separate piece, that sherd has already been noted as part of a krater (nos. 81-82), while no. 83 has not).

[107] Coldstream 1988: 41, nos. 100, 101, 107, 112, 113, of which 107 possibly Corinthian.

[108] Waldbaum 1994: 59. Possibly SG.

[109] Ben-Tor and Portugali 1987: 110; Waldbaum 1994: 59. Possibly SG.

[110] Deubner 1957: 52, nos. 2 and 3 (Bab. 43 597 and 29 663). Possibly SPGIII.

Findspots of Greek Geometric pottery

Hamath

Tell Afis. Tell Afis has been identified with Assyrian Khatarikka (Aramaean Hazrak/Assyrian Apsu), the capital of Lu'ash, which by the eighth century had become Hamath's northern province: Tiglath-pileser III calls the city one of the 19 districts of Hamath (Mazzoni 1991: 279; *eadem* 1995: 181). According to the Zakur stele found at the site, Zakur, king of Hamath and Lu'ash, was rescued from a siege of northern kings by divine (and probable Assyrian) intervention at Khatarikka in *c.* 796 BCE (Hawkins 1982: 389, 403).

Like nearby Ebla in the Bronze Age, Iron Age Tell Afis occupied a crossroads position overlooking routes between the coast, particularly between the Amuq and the Aleppo area. It was a large settlement, comparable in layout and size to Tell Tayinat (Mazzoni 1987: 25), and has yielded evidence of overseas contacts earlier than the rest of Syria (Bonatz 1998: 216). The sector from which the LG sherd comes was dedicated mainly to storage (*ibid.*: 220; Mazzoni 1987: 27).

Ras el Basit. Ras el Basit lies on the coast *c.*25 km south of Al Mina.[111] Although its nearest central place is Tell Tayinat, capital of Unqi, it seems to have been part of Hamath.

In 738 BCE, Unqi, 19 districts of Hamath (including Luhuti) and the coastal plain revolted against the Assyrians (Hawkins 1982: 411). The coastal plain is likely to be the region of the twelve kings of the sea-coast, which was independent in the time of Shalmaneser III in 853 BCE, but which by 738 had been swallowed up by Hama. Its territory stretched from the Nahr el-Kebir to modern Gebel el-Aqra, which lies between Ras el Basit and Al Mina (Kessler 1975-1976: 59-63). It is therefore likely that, for much of the period under consideration, Basit lay within the coastal territory of Hamath, after having served one of the twelve coastal kingdoms, and that, in 738 BCE, she became incorporated into an Assyrian province. In support of this contention is the fact that a rare form of burial practice is common to Basit and Hama (Courbin 1986: 190). There is an overland route from Basit through the hills to the Orontes valley (1982: 11).

The Geometric material from Ras el Basit has four notable characteristics:

1. The early date of the amphorae.

2. Its quantity: over 16 individually catalogued and published vessels, "many" cups and unknown numbers of PSC skyphoi. Whilst this pales beside the Al Mina material, it compares very favourably with the finds from Tell Sukas, although Sukas is the most frequently discussed site after Al Mina, as a glance at the index of any book on Greek colonisation will attest. But the comparative catalogue of the material suggests that Ras el Basit was the most important port serving Hama in the Geometric period, with Sukas only becoming significant in the later seventh century BCE.

3. Its similarity to the Al Minan material, both in the Geometric period (with Euboean, Cycladic, East Greek and Attic provenances) and afterwards (both sites continued to receive Greek material after the end of the eighth century BCE (Courbin 1983b: 120), unlike most Levantine ports). This may reflect the similarity in the political histories of the two sites, both lying in areas close to the Assyrian heartlands and both being provincialised in 738 BCE.

4. Its contexts. Unlike Al Mina, Geometric graves have been excavated at Basit, but the early cemetery has yielded no Greek material (Courbin 1990a: 507). One grave contains one of just two imitations of Greek pottery in the Levant, a globular shoulder-handed amphora which combines a familiar Greek form with Levantine decoration (*idem* 1993a: 52-3, pl. 5).

Ras Ibn Hani. Ras Ibn Hani was part of the same coastal territory as Ras el Basit, incorporated into Hamath before 738 BCE and the Assyrian provincialisation. Like Basit, access must have been overland, across to the Orontes, and thence down to Hama.

Despite quite extensive excavation of the tell, the Geometric Greek material is very sparse, although the site did continue to attract Eastern Greek vases in greater quantities in the seventh and sixth centuries BCE (Bounni *et al.* 1978: 282).

Tell Sukas. Tell Sukas is a coastal site roughly equidistant between Ras el Basit and Tabbat al Hammam. The Danish Expedition that excavated both Sukas and Hama also undertook a survey of the other sites in the plain: no Geometric Greek pottery has been reported from any of the other fifty-odd known sites (Riis 1958-1959: 110-4; *idem* 1970: 9, fig. 2).

Situated in the area discussed under Ras el Basit, its pre-738 BCE (that is, pre-Assyrian conquest) central place is likely to have been Hama. Indeed, the range of imported Greek pottery at Sukas and Hama is similar (Saltz 1978: 112). The PSC skyphoi from the two sites which have been analysed by Kearsley belong to the same type (5b), a group to which none of the Al Mina skyphoi belong (1989: 99-100).[112] An overland route within Hamath to the upper Orontes and thence directly to Hama is plausible, and there is some supporting evidence for this: a direct route leading from Tell Sukas directly to Hama was used even in recent times, and the Eastern gate of modern Gabla (*c.* 5km north of Tell Sukas) was until recently known as the Hama Gate (Riis 1970: 156, 161, fig. 56).

---

[111] The modern Arabic name of Ras el Basit contains a clue as to its ancient toponym: Posideum, a connection made by the seventeenth century (Courbin 1993b: 65, n. 6). Its very name therefore indicates that it was, at one time, Hellenised. Why should a modern Levantine site embody a Greek name? If this site was founded by Greeks in the Bronze Age, any Greek presence had entirely dissipated by the inception of the Iron Age. More likely, the name was given later, and retrospectively applied to the Bronze Age site by Herodotus. Certainly, a later Archaic Greek presence at the site has been postulated (Courbin 1990a: 509).

[112] Despite queries over some of the dating conclusions (particularly the continuation of the PSC into LG: critique in Popham and Lemos 1992), Kearsley's system is very useful in enabling geographically disparate sherds to be grouped.

Sukas is often distinguished from other Levantine findspots of Greek pottery in being regarded, along with Al Mina, as a site harbouring a Geometric Greek *enoikismos* (Hanfmann 1956: 166; Riis 1970: 129; Frederikson 1979: 282; Wenning 1981: 34; Braun 1982: 9-11). Its elevated status regarding Greek residents lies in the identification of a "Greek sanctuary" established at the site *c.* 675 BCE (Riis 1970: 126; *idem* 1982: 146-9), a period when the Greek ceramic imports to Tell Sukas actually dry up (Ploug 1973: 93). Whatever the credentials of this identification (and, in general, building forms at Sukas are related to contemporary north Syrian types (Lund 1986: 187-9)), there is no justification for the consequent appellation "Greek Settlement Period" of the immediately preceding period (cf. Riis 1970: 127-28). Indeed, it is only after 625 BCE, and especially in the sixth century BCE, that Sukas attracts quantities of Greek material (Ploug 1973: 95).

Tell Sukas is the most southerly site where Geometric East Greek pottery has been found.

Tabbat al Hammam. Another coastal site, located just to the North of the Nahr el-Kebir (Eleutheros) river, she would have lain within the territory of the "twelve kings of the sea coast", and then of Hama. This is therefore the most southerly of the four ports serving Hama and then the Assyrian governor of the territory. It enjoyed easy access to its hinterland (Riis 1970: 158).

Hama. Hama was the capital of Hamath, an independent and powerful Syro-Hittite state in possession of a large territory. Prior to 738 BCE she is likely to been served by Tabbat al Hammam, Tell Sukas, Ras Ibn Hani and Ras el Basit, for reasons given *supra*. Tiglath-pileser III provincialised the coastal and an inland portion of her territory in 738 BCE, and in 720 BCE Hama herself was destroyed by Sargon II (Hawkins 1982: 415). Fugmann (1958: 264, 277) claimed that she became the seat of the Assyrian governor, although she may have been abandoned.[113] All Greek imports would therefore predate 720 BCE (Coldstream 1968: 311), if not 738 BCE when Hama's access to the sea would have been blocked by the provincialisation of the coast.

Thus, prior to 738 BCE, Hama apparently had access to at least four ports, partly perhaps to compensate for the difficulty of coastal access through the mountains. Originally

landlocked, it seems reasonable to presume that the coastal strip was seized in an attempt to reach the littoral. Nonetheless, it is probable that all four of her ports did not serve this function simultaneously. Indeed, in terms of volume of Greek imports, Basit seems to have been the most important port in the early first millennium BCE.

Although there are some individual sherds at Hamath ports which are not duplicated at Hama, PSC skyphoi and other Euboean wares form the majority of imports to Hama as to all of her port sites. The one marked difference between port and hinterland is the presence of four LPG amphorae (a rare form combined with an early date) at Ras el Basit. None of the other Hamath sites have correspondingly early imports. This may be due to the fact that, at this early period, Ras el Basit would have served not Hama, but one of the twelve coastal kingdoms, whose capital is now unknown.

Hama is the only Hamath site where imports were deposited. Moreover, the contexts of some vessels are élite, encompassing palace and temple.

Hamath's leaders had pan-Levantine contacts, with Aram-Damascus, Egypt and Israel (Grayson 1982: 261; Hawkins 1982: 393). For example, King Toi of Hamath presented metal vessels (among other treasures) to King David of Israel, who deposited them in his temple (Prausnitz 1966: 178).

Conclusions. Ras el Basit, Ras Ibn Hani, Tell Sukas and Tabbat al Hammam all passed Greek Geometric material to Hama, the major central place in the region, where some was deposited and penetrated élite parts of the settlement. Most of these imports are Euboean, and date to the SPGIII-LG period. The Assyrian domination of the region seems to have had a detrimental effect on the functioning of Sukas and perhaps Tabbat al Hammam, at least as regards the reception of Greek pottery. Such a noticeable northerly orientation of the ports continuing to receive Greek material may have been the result of a rationalisation of trade: both Ras el Basit and Ras Ibn Hani were close to Cyprus (which after 709 BCE was also under Assyrian control) and to Assyrian-controlled Unqi, as well as nearer to the Assyrian heartland itself.

Phoenicia

Khaldeh: Berytus? Khaldeh lies approximately 12 km south of modern Beirut (Saidah 1966: 53), and its identification by Rouvier (1896) as Berytus (or a close suburb thereof) seems plausible. Berytus was a major Phoenician city. Certainly, the site is massive, the excavated 422 tombs constituting a mere fraction of the "vaste nécropole phénicienne" (Saidah 1971: 193).

Tambourit/Sidon. Tambourit is the findspot of five Phoenician cremation graves, *c.* 6 km south-east of Sidon (Saidah 1977: 135, and fig. 1). Nothing more is known of the Iron Age site, although its close proximity to Sidon suggests that it was a suburb of that major Phoenician city; it is for that reason marked on Map 1 as Sidon. This is one of only two possible Geometric Argive imports to the Levant, the EPG bowl from Tell Afis being the other. The shape, a pyxis, is also very rare.

---

[113] As Hawkins 1982: 425, n. 428. cf. Francis and Vickers 1985: 133. There is little support for an Assyrian construction of Square I 10, aside from the "position particulière" of the stratum. The literary evidence is unconvincing: the relevant Assyrian document merely attests that Sargon set a governor over the "land of Hamath" (Luckenbill 1927: 102 (§183)), not that he was based in the settlement known as Hama. *Ibid.*: 28 (§56) "I deported and settled in the land of Hamath" is a reference to Sargon's enthusiastic policies of enforced migration with reference to the Hamath region, not to a garrison on site. The cited references to Hama in the neo-Babylonian cuneiform texts demonstrate that the town existed in the mid-sixth century BCE, not that it had existed continuously, or that the governor there resided. The claim that "sous Assurbanipal (669-626 av. J.-Chr.) la ville est mentionnée comme la capitale de la province", seems to be an extrapolation from the fact that the city is mentioned in a geographical list, which does not in itself confirm provincial status (Hawkins 1972-1975: 69). Finally there are no post-Assyrian references to a governor of Hama, most unusual for the seat of a governor (*ibid.*). This seat was probably elsewhere (Khatarikka?), and Hama virtually unoccupied until Hellenistic times.

Sarepta. Sarepta was a major Phoenician port city, under the overall hegemony of Tyre in the early first millennium BCE (Aubet 2001: 66).

Tell Rachidieh. Situated just 4 km south of Tyre, Tell Rachidieh was probably a suburban cemetery of that major settlement, and is therefore subsumed on Map 1 under that site (Doumet 1982: 90; Coldstream 1988: 38). The grave containing this piece has been described as "the nearest available thing to a Phoenician élite assemblage in the homeland" (Coldstream, *pers. comm.*). Certainly, along with plentiful pottery the grave contained a bronze ring, pearls set in gold and cornelian beads, and many other metal objects (Doumet 1982: 99-100, 130-131). The sherd's original Euboean attribution was revised to admit the possibility of local production (Doumet 1982: 124; Doumet and Kawkabani 1991: 7). This re-attribution would make it only the second known Levantine imitation of a Geometric Greek vessel outside Cyprus. As in the case of the Basit imitation, the flattery was not wholly sincere, since the vessel may have had bichrome banding on its interior (cf. Courbin 1993b: 104, n. 48 for doubts over presence of bichrome).

Tell Kabri. Tell Kabri lies about 25 km south of Tyre (Kochavi 1992: 10). Although its Iron Age credentials are not clear (other than it must have lain within the overall hegemony of Tyre), in the Late Bronze Age it was a very important mercantile city boasting its own palace with the sort of painted plaster floors better known to Classicists as "Minoan" (Niemeier 1993: 332).

Tyre. Prior to Tyre's fall to Sennacherib in 701 BCE, Tyre exercised political hegemony over much of Phoenicia, from the Nahr el-Kelb to Acco (Bikai 1978: 74), although settlements within this territory retained a measure of independence. Tiglath-pileser III's reign saw a more aggressive Assyrian policy towards Phoenicia. Although Tyre escaped provincialisation, Assyrian inspectors and customs officials were present at the port and the burden of tribute increased, particularly of precious metals (*ibid.*: 57). Assyria allowed Tyre enough autonomy to procure the goods it wanted, while asserting enough control to skim off tolls and tribute, and to stop Tyre trading with that other mighty Empire, Egypt.

After Al Mina, Tyre is the findspot of the greatest number of Greek Geometric imports in the Levant. There are three notable characteristics:

1. Their early date. The material from Tyre balances the early Phoenician material in Greece, especially Euboea. Coldstream has drawn out a plausible early trade route operating between Euboea and Tyre via south Cyprus, particularly Eteo-Cypriot Amathus, whose early Greek imports mirror those of Tyre (Coldstream 1982: 264-5; *idem* 1988: 43) and where the similarities between Cypriot and mainland Phoenician and Palestinian pottery types are closest (Culican 1982a).

2. The quantity of PSC plates is unparalleled at any other Levantine (or Greek) site.

3. Genuine Attic imports are in greater abundance here than at any other Levantine site.

Tyre's great wealth and power was dependent upon her trading contacts, which, in the early first millennium BCE seem to have had both state and private dimensions (e.g. Aubet 2001: 92). Her prophesised downfall in Ezekiel 27 is expressed by reference to the cessation of imports from far and wide (p.46). Isaiah 23, probably composed after Tyre's fall to Sennacherib, states that her "merchants were princes and her traders the most honoured men on earth". In Biblical times, merchants who traded overseas (as opposed to traders, who were more locally based) did enjoy a high status (Katzenstein 1973: 249-50, n. 157), and, given Tyre's trading might, Isaiah's choice of phraseology may have been very apposite. The reference to merchants as princes finds an Homeric analogue in Mentes, who actively seeks out imports (*Od.* 1.179-318), and of course there are plenty of ethno-historical parallels for external trade being the prerogative of those in control of other aspects of life. Although relevant literary evidence is sparse, the description of sixth century BCE Tyre by Ezekiel portrays her as a classic type B port of trade, with a huge variety of goods and traders coming from all over the Mediterranean. Typical of such ports, she also fed her own products into the trade system, such as textiles and worked ivory.

Tyre promoted diplomatic relations with neighbouring areas such as Israel (Jezebal of Tyre married Ahab), Aram-Damascus, and Egypt (Mitchell 1982b: 547). As well as matrimony, gift exchange is a documented part of her diplomatic offensive with potential trading partners. For example, Tyrian envoys are depicted bringing gifts, including monkeys and linen, on the occasion of the opening of Assurnasirpal II's palace, probably for the right to gain access to raw materials (Aubet 2001: 55, 90).

Conclusions. While all the Phoenician sites with Greek imports were either important political and trading sites themselves, or were very closely associated with them, Tyre was the most powerful of these and exercised some form of hegemony over them all. This hegemony is reflected in the huge disparity of imports between Tyre and her underlings. On present evidence, Greek contacts with Phoenicia were stronger in the pre-LG period. As in Hamath and Unqi, Euboean imports predominate. East Greek wares do not seem to have reached this far south. There were several cases of the deposition of imports at Phoenician sites, in one case (Tell Rachidieh) at least in an élite context.

Israel

Tell abu Hawam. This harbour town is situated on the River Qishon, on the last section of the main trunk road between Mesopotamia and the Mediterranean habours (Kochavi 1998: 476). Some believe that its ancient name lurks behind Section 33 of Shishak's 926 BCE campaign, giving that date for the *terminus ante quem* of the stratum in which the Greek sherds were found (e.g. Yeivin 1962).

Uncertainty surrounds the political affiliations of the site after Solomon, who ceded 20 cities in this area to the king of Tyre

(1 Kings 9.10-13). It seems likely that the Assyrian provincialisation of the coastal region of Israel into Dor in 734 BCE included this site (Otzen 1979: 255 and 252, map), although there may have been Tyrian settlers at the site and Phoenician influence was certainly strong (Aubet 2001: 69). Certainly, Tell abu Hawam is better connected to Israel's transportational routes than to the Phoenician littoral, being on the route to the settlements of the western Jezreel Valley including Taanach and Megiddo, which was certainly served from here.

Tell Qiri. Tell Qiri was a satellite town of Yoqne'am, a major centre and one of the most important sites in the strategically crucial Jezreel valley (Ben-Tor and Portugali 1987: 1-2, 208). Although of no apparent political importance in her own right, her excavators suggest that she was an important cultic centre in the Iron Age, probably due to her position on the slopes of Mount Carmel. The dinos was found in a locus (551) associated with the "public building", by far the largest structure at the site (*ibid.*: 133-4).

Megiddo. Megiddo was a major Israelite city under the United Monarchy, fortified by King Solomon (1 Kings 9.15). Located along a major thoroughfare through the Qishon valley, and acting as the main cross-roads of Israel, Megiddo was of immense strategic importance, a significance underlined by its prophetic centrality at the end of time (Rev. 16.12). It was also politically important, holding the seat of one of the governors of Israel, who was directly answerable to Samaria: a jasper seal inscribed with "*ebed* of Jeroboam" was recovered here, "*ebed*" being the term applied to retainers of the king (Mitchell 1982b: 501). It became the capital of the new Assyrian province of Magiddu after it was attacked in 733/2 BCE (Avi-Yonah and Stern 1977: 831).

As for the context of the sherds, although the exact function of the findspot is debatable, it was clearly an important building.

Tell Hadar. Tell Hadar was situated on the eastern shore of the Sea of Galilee, a fortress town of a king of Geshur, which under David's reign in the early tenth century BCE was an autonomous vassal state of Israel (Kopcke 2002: 112; Kochavi 1989: 3; *idem* 1998: 470), but both just before (under Saul) and just after (under Solomon) seems to have been independent (Aharoni 1969: maps 20 and 23). She lay on an international route to Phoenicia, Galilee, the Gilead and the grain-rich Bashan (Kochavi 1998: 477).

There are no literary references to the site itself, but the excavators have extrapolated from its material assemblage that Tell Hadar was an important settlement, possibly controlling "the entire kingdom of Geshur" (Kochavi 1988-1989: 113).

The dinos was found in a tripartite pillared structure, wherein imports (from the Gilead, upper Galilee and Mediterranean) constituted an unusually high 15% of ceramic finds and wherein household vessels were notably rare/unused (Kochavi 1998: 471, 475). Such structures are now known from many parts of Israel, always on major international trade routes, and many suggestions have been made as to their function (stables, local storehouses, barracks etc). Using a wide range of criteria, Kochavi interprets them as "entrepots" i.e. buildings where traded goods (especially long-distance ones) were stored, measured and dispatched.

Coldstream points out the dinos shape, very rare in Euboea, may be a ceramic adaptation of a handleless bronze cauldron, with all the élite connotations that that implies (1998: 357). Stylistically, the piece could be dated to the early tenth century BCE, but its find stratum has been confidently dated to the eleventh century BCE (Kochavi 1998: 471; Kopcke 2002), thereby threatening to overturn the applecart of early Iron Age Greek chronology.

Samaria. During the period under consideration, Samaria was the capital of the kingdom of Israel, and may have been served by Tell abu Hawam (Riis 1970: 158; *idem* 1991: 2).

By 722/1 BCE, she was conquered, and Samaria became the seat of the Assyrian governor (Avi-Yonah and Stern 1978: 1035). The Samaritan material is mainly pre-LG, suggesting once again that Assyrian domination stemmed the flow of Greek imports to the site. This may have happened *de facto* with the provincialisation of the Hawam region in 734 BCE, which would then be the *terminus ante quem* for the LG material at Samaria too.

Many Samaritan kings had internationalist tendencies. In particular, Jeroboam II, whose reign (782-753 BCE) falls squarely within the SPGIII period of most of the imports, increased those links, especially with the Phoenicians (Mitchell 1982b: 502, 505). Successive kings enjoyed close contacts with the leaders of Tyre (Ahab married Jezebel, the daughter of Ittoba'al of Tyre (1 Kings 16.31)), of Aram-Damascus (1 Kings 20.34) and of Egypt (Mitchell 1982a: 479). Relations with Judah were often close at the élite level, cemented through marriage and name-copying. Thus Jehorem (son of Jehoshaphet of Judah) and Athaliah (daughter of Ahab of Israel) were married (2 Kings 8.18; Mitchell 1982a: 475); and this Jehorem found a namesake in the brother of Ahaziah of Israel (*ibid.*: 481).

This was a period of great material prosperity for the city's élite, giving the prophets much pretext for railing against religious laxity and ostentatious luxury, much of it expressed through feasting. Amos (6.6-17) condemned the unholy *marzeah* (drinking clubs) of the Samaritan élite.

Conclusions. Only one port site with evidence of Greek imports has so far been unearthed in ancient Israelite territory (Tell abu Hawam). All of the inland settlements that received Greek imports were important sites, with the capital of the kingdom receiving the most imports, and, where findspots are known, the imports reached impressive areas of the inland sites.

While most of the imports are likely to have come from Euboea, PSC skyphoi are rare in Israel, forming a smaller proportion of the total imported assemblage in Israel than in any other polity. Instead, much of the Euboean material is

Atticising. There are also few LG sherds in Israel, with Greek imports mainly dating to the SPGIII period.

Judah

No imported Greek Geometric material has so far been found in Judah, despite extensive excavation of all types of sites in that region (Mitchell 1982a: 446-447; Shiloh 1989: 97). Throughout the period, Judah's leaders exercised an insular rule, often forcibly imposing a religious purity that did not sit easily with foreign relations. For example, Phoenician influence is palpably weaker here than in Israel, and Jehoshaphat suppressed Phoenician religion (*ibid.*: 470, 474-475). Nor did Judah have any coastline. Thus she played little part in the international élite networks of the period, a situation which is apparently reflected in the rarity of imported pottery (Shiloh 1989: 104-5).

Philistia

Askalon. Situated on the Via Maris, Askalon was a coastal member of the Pentapolis of Philistia (Dothan 1982: 17), and was renowned in antiquity for its markets (2 Sam 1.20 speaks of the "markets of Ashkelon"). However, the sherd's existence has been questioned (Waldbaum 1994: 97).

Ekron. Ancient Ekron (modern Tell Miqne) was one of the Philistine pentapoleis. The northernmost and furthest from the coast, she dominated the inner coastal plain between Philistia and Judah, overlooking important highways, and may have been served by the port at Askelon (Gitin 1989: 23-24; Niemeier 2001: 16). Although the tenth-eighth centuries BCE witnessed a comparative diminution in her power, she remained for the most part a "semi-independent state" (*ibid.*: 41-43), one which was distinctively Philistine and sufficiently respected by Israel to invoke Amos' wrath (Amos 1.8).

If Waldbaum's attribution of this sherd to Attica is correct (noting that maeanders are an important part of the Atticising repertoire at Lefkandi (e.g. Desborough and Dickinson 1980: 55)), this is the southernmost Attic import in the Levant.

Conclusions. The Philistines occupied an integral "ethno-geographical" coastal strip (Dothan 1982: 16) in southern Palestine, dominated by the five cities of Gaza, Ashdod, Askalon, Ekron and Gath (Joshua 13.2-3). These cities dominated smaller "daughter" settlements (Dothan 1982: 18-19). Reduced to vassal status by Assyria in 734 BCE, each city retained its essential independence, Assyria seems to have been anxious to curb Philistine trade with Phoenicia (Tadmor 1966: 87-88), which would have been a potential source of Greek imports. Philistine sites have not been extensively excavated—indeed, Gath has yet to be identified—so the final total of Greek imports to Philistia may be greater. However, the frequency of Greek imports is clearly waning this far south.

Assyria

Tell Halaf. Situated nearly 400km east of Al Mina on the Western source of the River Khabur, Tell Halaf was, until 808 BCE, independent. Her strategic importance was too great to avoid the acquisitive attentions of Assyria, and she was conquered in that year by Adad-Nirari III (Hawkins 1982: 400). She became an important provincial city, near the heartland of the Assyrian Empire.

Nineveh. Nineveh was a large city in the heart of Assyria, sometime capital of kings (Grayson 1982: 241), and lay at the end of one of the main caravan routes starting at Al Mina (Woolley 1937: 2). Although the temple's original founder is unknown, Adad-Nirari III restored it in 788 BCE (Campbell Thompson and Hutchinson 1929: 137). The Greek pottery and a few bricks commemorating the restoration are the only artefacts found which date to the 10th to 8th centuries BCE.

Other unillustrated Greek imports reported from the temple site were a SM sherd and a Rhodian bird bowl, and a Milesian oinochoe was found in a dump for Ashurbanipal's palace (*ibid.*: 138; Clairmont 1955: 105 no. 56, 108 no. 87).

Conclusions: Assyrians and Greeks. The paucity of Greek finds in the Assyrian heartland should be considered in the context of Assyrian archaeology. The palace sites were first excavated in the nineteenth-century CE and were replete with colossal statues and impressive reliefs attached to monumental edifices. Minor finds tended to get overlooked; Layard has just five references to vases of any description in his report on the Nineveh explorations (1849: 494). The continued importation of Greek imports to Assyrian-controlled Tell Tayinat and Al Mina indicates Assyrian tolerance—indeed appreciation—of Greek ceramics, and the Assyrian conquest of Syria does seem to have had repercussions for the ceramic assemblage, in the disappearance of fine Red Slip forms (Lehmann 1998: 13).

The Assyrian encroachment onto the Levantine littoral has been related to the diminution in the number of sites receiving Greek imports in the LG period (Coldstream 1989: 94), and some have suggested specific Assyrian hostility towards Greeks attempting to trade (e.g. Cook 1962: 65; Boardman 1999a: 46). Certainly, fewer sites received imports in the LG period, during which the Assyrians provincialised most of the coast, than in the preceding SPGIII period. But the evidence—particularly the huge quantity of LG imports to Al Mina—suggests that there was simply a re-orientation to North Syria in the LG period. This region had easy access to the Assyrian heartland and Cyprus, which was itself an Assyrian province by 709 BCE.

Moreover, while direct contact with Greeks may have been of minimal interest to the Assyrians in their heartland, it seems unlikely that, as potential suppliers of goods, they would have been specifically excluded from ports in Assyrian hands. Although the Assyrian Kings continued to enjoy the traditional modes of acquisition of tribute and booty, the dignity of the Assyrian monarchs required a constant supply of the latest luxuries from the West to be displayed in capitals, temples and palaces (Postgate 1979: 199). Indeed, it seems likely that the Assyrian conquest of the Levantine littoral had economic motives (Tadmor 1966: 88; *idem* 1975: 37; Otzen 1979: 255), and the only coastal state as far south as Gaza not to be provincialised was Tyre, the longest-established port, preserved for the material benefits it brought Assyria, via tribute, tolls, and exchange. Even if Ahta (p.12) refers not to Al Mina but to another nearby port, its mention on Tiglath-pileser III's stele demonstrates a hitherto-undocumented Assyrian knowledge of—and covetous interest in—port sites on the Mediterranean coast.

As Helms points out, by the late eighth century, when most of the Levantine littoral as well as Cyprus was under Assyrian control, Greek visitors to virtually any Levantine port would have encountered Assyrian customs agents and administrators (1980: 112).

Babylonia

Babylon. Babylon was the political and religious centre of Babylonia throughout her existence (Oates 1986: 67), and lay at the end of one of the main caravan routes starting at Al Mina (Woolley 1937: 2). During the early centuries of the first millennium BCE Babylonia suffered internal and external pressures (Brinkman 1982: 282-284). A comparative high point was the period of the reigns of Nabu-apla-iddina and of his successor Marduk-zakir-shumi in the ninth century BCE who, respectively, entered and invoked a treaty with the Assyrian monarch Shalmaneser III (858-824 BCE). This treaty was captured for posterity on the throne base of the Assyrian king at Nimrud. Babylonian letters found in the Royal archives at Hamath suggest close trade relations with that state (Parpola 1990).

Deubner suggested an East Greek origin for one of the sherds; the decoration is too nugatory to provenance the other. Certainly, lekythoi are a common MG-LG East Greek form (Coldstream 1968: 262-301). No post-SPGII lekythoi are known in Euboea (Desborough 1980: 315-6).

In addition, Schmidt refers to a continuous sequence of imports from SM to Corinthian (*AA* 1941: col. 792).

Conclusions: Geometric Greek imports in the Levant

As at Al Mina, the majority of Levantine imports are Euboean. Attica is more often a source of inspiration for Euboean potters than of actual imports, which tail off in the LG period.[114] East Greek wares are present in small numbers at Ras el Basit and Tell Sukas. This early concentration of East Greek wares in the north Levant, before their Archaic ubiquity in the region, reflects the interest of the Eastern Greeks in the southern coast of Asia Minor which culminated (in the Archaic period) with the foundations of Phaselis, Soloi, Nagidus and Celendris. There is one possible Corinthian import at Tyre. In sum, with the exception of the Argive import at Tambourit and a possible Argive bowl at Tell Afis, Al Mina receives imports from the same range of Greek Geometric provenances as the rest of the Levant.

We can compare the Greek Geometric pottery from the Levant with that from Al Mina and the Amuq plain (characteristics summarised on p.27ff.):

1. *Greek production*. There is no known Greek production of Greek Geometric pottery at any site.

2. *Imitations*. There are just two possible imitations of Greek wares, one at Ras el Basit, the other at Tell Rachidieh. Both imitate the Greek shape, not the decoration, suggesting that aesthetic appreciation was not the reason for the imports' acceptance. Moreover, there was no unfulfilled market for the imports. The contrast with Italy, where names as well as pots were imported, the shapes imitated, and exposure to both Oriental and Greek imports occasioned a revolution in eating and drinking customs, is very marked (e.g. Rathje 1988; *eadem* 1990).

3. *Kitchenwares*. No Geometric cooking wares have been reported, even from sites where seventh century (East Greek) cooking pots have been found i.e. Askalon, Tell Kabri, Tel Batash and Meʻad Hashavyahu (Waldbaum 1997: 8; Niemeier 2001: 15-6).

4. *Range of shapes*. Imported Euboean pottery at both port sites and central places consists of various types of cups, kraters and amphorae. There are also a significant number of plates (mainly in Phoenicia), three oinochoai and an aryballos. There are also two lekythoi (probably East Greek) and four pyxides (probably Attic, Cycladic and Argive). In terms of absolute numbers, the imports barely exceed the consubstantial limits of the Al Minan range. By contrast, Cypriot and Phoenician imports cover a wide variety of functions. Table 9 shows the relative proportions of individually-catalogued Greek shapes imported in the MPG-LG period to the Levant, excluding the Amuq sites and Al Mina (for whose LG Euboean ceramic complexion see p.26).[115]

By contrast, the range of imported Mycenaean forms is very wide, encompassing around 60 shapes (Leonard 1981: 87). Kraters, alabastra, jars, jugs, flasks, rhyta, cups, mugs, chalices and bowls are all common, as well as some rarer and unidentifiable forms (*ibid.*: 12-136). According to Kilian, the whole range of Mycenaean painted pottery and tableware is present (1990: 459). Moreover, 60% of Mycenaean pots in the Levant were closed ones i.e. containers (Sherratt 1999: 171). Stirrup-jars, likely containers of the perfumed oil or unguents manufactured by the Mycenaeans, are very frequent. This compares to very few containers in the Geometric period, when most pottery must have been imported for its own sake; at this period unguent containers flow in the opposite direction, from east to west (Coldstream 1998a: 354).

5. *Comparison of imports in port and hinterland*. Of all of the polities that received Greek wares outside Unqi, only Hamath and Israel have classic port-hinterland structures. In

---

[114] Attica seems to fade from international associations *ca.* 750 BCE, a period when it has been argued that she was experiencing political *stasis* (Morris 1987).

[115] Many cups and some skyphoi at Ras el Basit are not individually catalogued and so are not included; the actual proportion of drinking wares is probably higher.

Table 9: Morphological distribution of Geometric Greek imports to the Levant

	skyphoi	cups	kotylai	mugs	kraters[116]	amphorae[117]	oinochoai	plates	pyxides	aryballos	lekythoi	
No.	106+	5+	6	1	18	10	3	32	4	1	2	192
%	55	3	3	1	9	5	2	17	2	1	1	

Hamath there is a notable variety of (mainly SPGIII-LG) shapes, including 5 of the 10 amphorae in the Levant. There is no deposition of Greek imports at any site that acted solely as a port.

6. *Distribution of imports in hinterland.* The distribution of Greek Geometric pottery in the Levant outside Al Mina is often dismissed as being of a rather accidental, meaningless character, with sherds being "distributed sporadically" (e.g. Braun 1982: 7). But a much more consistent pattern is emerging: imports are found either at ports (which funnel material inland), or at central places (or sites very closely associated with them), or at sites that are both ports and central places. This distribution pattern suggests that the imports are not randomly distributed, but rather form a coherent pattern of distribution from ports to central places.

The restricted distribution of the imports is noteworthy: excluding the Amuq sites, for which the details are currently too imprecise, just 23 sites have yielded evidence of Greek imports over 350 years, most of them in the period c. 850-c. 750 BCE. By the LG period, when the greatest quantity of imports arrives, the site count is reduced to just nine, of which only one—Al Mina—has a significant quantity. Otherwise, only Ras el Basit and Tyre have more than ten sherds in the LG period. The contrast with the LBA Mycenaean imports to the Levant is very striking. Then, import distribution is diffuse, covering nearly 90 sites, of all types (Leonard 1981: 201-211). This suggests that a much wider range of people had access to the imports.[118] By the Persian period Greek wares are very widely distributed, perhaps appearing on every excavated site (Waldbaum 1997: 5).

As for the contexts of the finds, Geometric imports are often deposited in the central places, which is never the case at the ports. Further, where exact contexts are known, they are often high status ones: 'royal' sanctuaries or temples (Hama, Nineveh and possibly Megiddo), palaces (Hama, Tell Hadar), public buildings (Tell Qiri), élite burials (Tell Rachidieh), and élite zones (Ekron). This suggests that some élite in the Levant, as in Unqi, were aware of and appreciated Greek imports. In the LBA period, imports come from many different contexts— palatial and isolated temples and shrines, official warehouses and domestic storerooms and settlements (Hankey 1993:

104)—some high places, certainly (*eadem* 1981), but also many less elevated findspots, once again suggesting that a wider range of consumers had access to the material.

Overall, there are many similarities between the situation in Al Mina/Unqi and that in the rest of the Levant: there is no production of Greek wares, virtually no imitation of Greek wares, no kitchenwares, and only a small range of shapes is imported—mainly cups, some kraters, fewer amphorae (mainly in north Syria) and, mainly in Phoenicia, plates. The distribution of these imports is very restricted, to ports (where there is no deposition) and central places (where there is some deposition). Some of the findspots are high status ones. The conclusion must be that, as at Al Mina, the imported pottery evidences not residence, but trade.

By contrast, pottery is not the only evidence for Mycenaean contact with the Levant. Kitchenwares, Mycenaean-type loomweights and figurines appear (e.g. Niemeier 2001: 12). Consequently, the possibility of Mycenaeans being resident at some sites has been predicated (though generally rejected) on the basis of a wider range of material evidence than is available for the Geometric period (e.g. Gilmour 1992: 118-119; Kilian 1990: 459).

For the Archaic period, there is the additional evidence of cooking pots at some sites and a few inscriptions to support the idea of Greek (mainly mercenary) residence (e.g. Niemeier 2001; Waldbaum 1997).

Greek Geometric pottery in Cyprus

Over 170 Greek Geometric imports are known, dating from the LPG to SG period, and there are several recent catalogues of the material (e.g. Gjerstad 1977; Wriedt Sørensen 1988). This material largely parallels the imports to the Levant (cf. Crielaard 1999), but does add one important dimension.

Most imports are Euboean although there are a few Cycladic imports to Salamis and elsewhere (Lemos and Hatcher 1991: 206; *idem* 1989: 93; Coldstream 2001: 229). There are also Attic imports, including many in the Royal Tomb I at Salamis, reflecting perhaps the special relationship between Salamis and Athens known at other times (Gjerstad 1977: nos. 28-47 and 49-50; Coldstream 2001: 229).

Using the summarised features of the Greek Geometric pottery at Al Mina and the Amuq (p.27 ff):

[116] Including a dinos, lebes, cauldron and krateriskos.

[117] Including an amphoriskos.

[118] Leonard 1983 detects a hierarchy of findspots, with a few major central places receiving a majority of the goods.

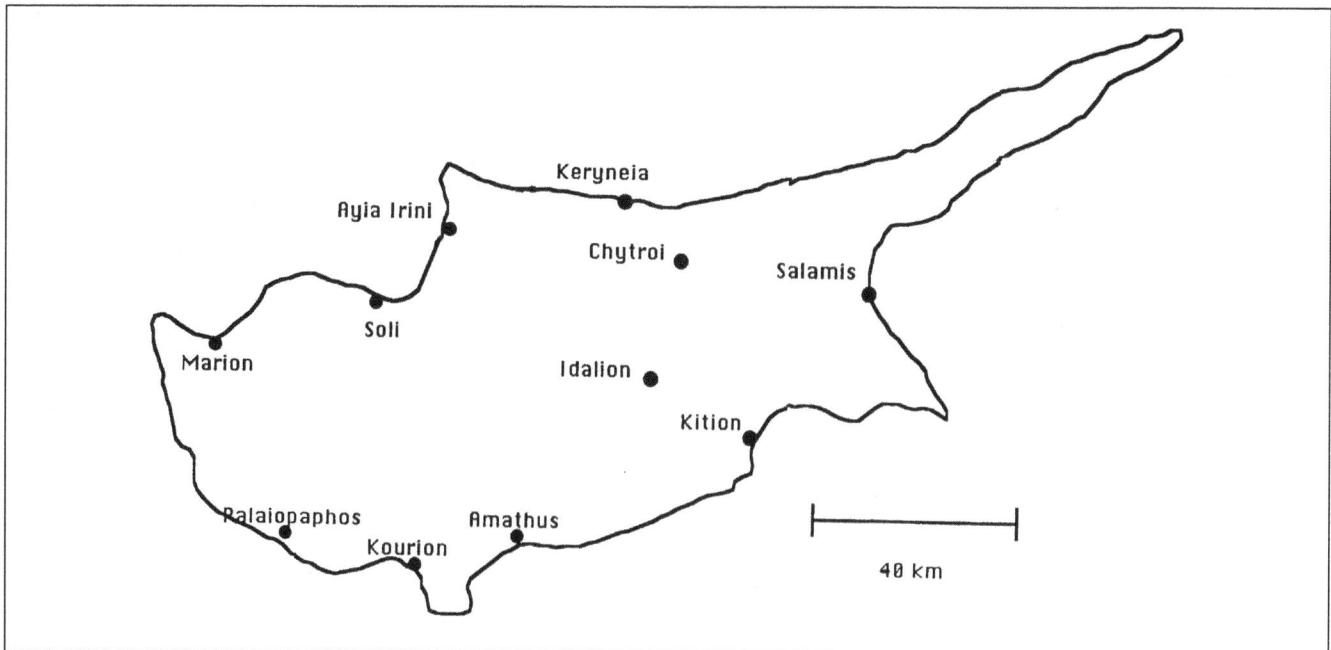

Map 3. Distribution of Greek Geometric pottery in Cyprus

1. *Greek production*. No Greek production of Greek Geometric pottery has been claimed for any site.

2. *Imitations*. In contrast to the rest of the Levant, imitations of Greek wares were commonly produced in Cyprus. PSC skyphoi were the first to be imitated (Catling 1973), but, as for the two Levantine imitations of Greek wares, their form was more appreciated than their decoration, with only one early example bearing the familiar semicircles (Coldstream 1986: 325). The earliest (Phoenician as well as Greek) imitations are limited to coastal Amathus.[119] By the LG period, Greek decoration was also being copied, in some cases so well that the vases have been mistaken for imports (Coldstream 1979: 259).

Significantly, imitations have a quite different distribution from imports, with only a very few of those tombs containing imports also containing imitations (Crielaard 1999a: 275). Further, imitations are mainly found outside the central places in which genuine imports are concentrated. Such a distribution suggests that those denied access to the trading networks controlled by the central places desired to emulate those who did enjoy such access (Rupp 1989: 356). Import-substitution enabled this sub-élite (Sherratt 1999: 185) to ape their economic superiors by acquiring locally-produced imitations.

3. *Kitchenwares*. Although no Greek kitchenwares have been reported from any settlement, so few Iron Age Cyprus settlement sites have been excavated that it would be unwise to read any significance into this.

4. *Range of shapes*. The forms of the Greek Geometric imports are even more positively consubstantial than those on the

Levantine littoral. Indeed, of the 170-odd imports now known, about 130 are drinking wares (i.e. *c*. 76%; cf. 86% at Al Mina). There are a significant number of plates, some kraters, and a few closed forms such as amphorae and oinochoai (Coldstream 1986: 321; *idem* 1988: 42, fig. 1; Crielaard 1999a: 266). The feasting element is most clearly expressed in the 'dinner sets' of Greek imports unearthed not only in Salamis Royal Tomb I, but also in Amathus Tomb 194, and the monumental Kourion grave in which the Cesnola krater and oinochoai were found (Coldstream 1988: 35; *idem* 1994: 79). Rupp cites the presence of vessels for the formal serving and consumption of food and drink as a manifestation of high status in Iron Age Cyprus, noting that such wares would have been used in public consumption rituals (1989: 353-6).

5. *Comparison of imports in port and hinterland*. Most Cypriot sites with Greek Geometric pottery are coastal sites. With the exception of the kingdom of Salamis, only one settlement within each Cypriot kingdom received Greek imports, so it is not possible to detect patterns within polities. But within Cyprus as a whole, the Greek imports are very homogeneous in nature, in terms of provenances and forms.

6. *Distribution of imports in hinterland*. Of the 170-odd mainly MG-LG imports, almost all are from capitals of the LG Cypriot kingdoms (map 3): Salamis (including A. Theodoroi), Amathus, Kition, Soloi, Idalion, Palaeopaphos and Kourion; also Ayia Irini, which was a major sanctuary (Gjerstad 1977; Coldstream 1986: 322; *idem* 1989: 92-3).[120] Significantly, not every capital was so honoured: no Greek Geometric imports have been unearthed at Tammasos, Lapithos and Ledrai. This distribution pattern points strongly to the great interest of importers of Greek pottery in southern Cyprus, to the virtual exclusion of the north. Coldstream

---

[119] Amathus is also the findspot of the earliest Greek and Phoenician imports in Cyprus (Coldstream 1986: 325). Her unusually open nature may be related to the fact that, of all the Cypriot cities, she was dominated neither by Greeks nor Phoenicians, but Eteo-Cypriots.

[120] Note that Coldstream now disregards the unconfirmed finds from Palaekythro and Kazaphani (Boardman 1990b: 182, n. 5).

has argued that the coastal settlements on the south of the island were *en route* to the south Levant, and, via Salamis, to the north Levant too (Coldstream 1989: 92). By contrast, in the LBA period, there is no area (save the more inaccessible parts of the Troodos) where Aegean pottery did not penetrate, and scarcely a tomb or settlement where surface survey has not revealed imported sherds (Sherratt 1999: 170): in Bronze Age Cyprus as in the Bronze Age Levant, it seems that a much wider range of people had access to Greek imports.

As for the context, because of the lack of settlement evidence, all confirmed Greek Geometric imports to Cyprus come from graves or sanctuaries. Yet within the cemeteries themselves there is a distinct pattern of distribution: most large excavated cemeteries have produced no Greek imports (Coldstream 1986: 322; Wriedt Sørensen 1988: 18), and, in the cemeteries that do have some examples, the imports are confined to a few graves. For example at Salamis, all Greek imports come from Royal Tombs 1 and 2. In other words, very few people were buried with Greek imports, and those that were appear to have had a high socio-economic status: all these tombs are regarded, on other grounds, as being the burials of high-status individuals (e.g. Crielaard 1999a: 274). Several scholars have studied the status-messaging of Cypriot tombs. Rupp concluded that there are four significant traits which distinguish élite tombs: tomb design, burial rituals, and two types of import: Phoenician and Greek (1988: 124), which last two factors have also been stressed by Coldstream (1986: 327).

Conclusions

There are many important similarities with the situation in Al Mina/Unqi and in the rest of the Levant: there is no production of Greek wares, no kitchenwares, and only a small range of shapes are present, mainly those effecting eating and especially drinking. The distribution of these imports is restricted to ports and central places, wherin the contexts are sometimes high status.

The main difference is the production of imitations, which by the LG period were rivalling Greek imports in quality, apparently acting as import substitutes for Cypriots who could not access the real thing. In the Levant, Cypriot-produced "Al Mina" ware was apparently accepted on the same terms as the Greek imports; all of the findspots of this ware (Waldbaum 1994: 58-9) also received Greek imports, with the exception of Tell Dor and Tell Ruqheish.[121] Crielaard has

suggested that this points to a degree of "commodization" of the pottery imports (Crielaard 1999a: 282).[122]

Was Al Mina unique?

We can now return to the question of the uniqueness, or otherwise, of Al Mina. Boardman (1990; 1999), Kearsley (1995: 71-3; 1999) and Hodos (2000) argue for the special character of Al Mina, on the basis of the high proportional quantity of Greek imports at the site. The numbers are not without interpretative problems, particularly given that we are only dealing with kept pottery, among which, common sense suggests, Greek imports, outstandingly obvious and unusual for that time and place, could have been disproportionally high (e.g. Waldbaum 1997: 6; Papadopoulos 1997b: 196; though cf. Boardman 1999b: 147).[123] According to Boardman's useful breakdown of the finewares, 47% of diagnostic Geometric pottery was Greek (1999b: 143). In the early levels the proportion seems higher, though Boardman's 93% of all marked pottery in Levels 8-9 being Greek (*ibid.*: 150) could be misleading, since only a minority of sherds (particularly the non-Greek ones) were so marked.[124]

Where, on current evidence, Al Mina certainly distinguishes herself is in absolute quantities. There are about 1500 known Geometric imports at Al Mina (Boardman 1999b: 153). Her hinterland had about 200 known sherds (p.20). For the whole of the rest of the Levant, the figure currently stands at around 190 i.e. taken as a whole, in the Geometric period *c.* 90% of Greek finewares found in the Levant passed through Al Mina, a proportion which is even higher in the LG period to which most Al Mina imports belong. The evidence of the pottery suggests that North Syria was by far the most important Levantine region involved in the maintenance of Greek-Levantine relations, as we might expect for an area whose goods and perhaps ideas and literature were so pivotal in Greece's "Orientalising Revolution".[125]

As regards the Greek pottery, there are compelling similarities in the complexion of the assemblage at Al Mina and her hinterland, and in the rest of the Levant and Cyprus. These similarities suggest that Al Mina, although of special importance in the LG period, was not unique in her character or in her function as a port, funnelling out of and into her hinterland items of trade. It is surely no accident that, even in its unpublished state, the second largest findspot of Greek Geometric pottery in the Levant is Al Mina's hinterland—the Amuq plain.

---

[121] The Geometric sherd found in a late eighth century context at Tell Ruqheish (probably a major commercial headquarters under Assyrian rule) has been identified by Coldstream as a likely Cypriot imitation. Thanks are due to Professors Coldstream and Eliezer Oren for information concerning this sherd and its find-context (sherd published in Qadmoniot 75-76 (1987): 83-91).

[122] According to Kopytoff (1986) "commodification" occurs when a good becomes commonly available and when its history ceases to be relevant.

[123] Woolley's suppression of "redundant" material could well have included the local pottery (1938: 133).

[124] The non-Greek wares are much less well studied than the Greek. Of those pieces that reached England, most is held in the London Institute of Archaeology.

[125] Boardman 2002b: 6 for passage of Syrian goods through Al Mina to Greece.

Chapter 5
Geometric pottery in Greek-Levantine trade

E pur si muove

(And yet it moves)

Galileo (cited Sherratt 1999: 164)

"Items of trade". A simple description, usually, perhaps most sensibly, left at that: self-explanatory (e.g. Graham 1986: 56). The reality behind it is doubtless more complex than we can ever know. As in most fields of human endeavour, particularly cross-cultural trade among culturally diverse partners, there can be no 'one-size-fits-all' explanation for the presence of Geometric Greek imports to the Levant (or of Oriental imports to Greece), or for the wider nature of Greek-East relations. A degree of complexity in the production, distribution and consumption of pottery and other traded goods is to be expected.

Certainly, in periods for which documentary evidence exists, complexity is a key characteristic of trade, involving different (and sometimes the same) people using different modes of exchange, sometimes under the aegis of the state, sometimes in more entrepreneurial modes. In the Early Iron Age, tribute, tolls, conquest, piracy, and "Ionian" slave raids on Eastern soil are all attested as modes of exchange, and are not mutually exclusive (*Od.* 16.425-429 and 14.257-265; Luckenbill 1927: 61, §118; Braun 1982: 14-15).[126] In the eighth century BCE, trade relations between Tyre and Assyrian encompassed onerous tribute, tolls and more commercial trade, albeit on preferential terms (Aubet 2001: 88-94). The Phoenicians, chameleon traders, seem to have adjusted their trading style according to their opportunities, offering a magnificent silver krater to King Thoas of Lemnos (*Il.* 23:740-745), trading silently with Africans (Hdt.4.196), ferrying passengers (*Od.* 13.271-275), slave trafficking (*Il.* 25.744; 15.452-4), and, later, swapping "trinkets" for silver (p.46).[127] The movement of pottery and other, perished, goods may have accompanied any of these, in unknown proportions, over a long period of time. The Geometric pots were probably not the sole mainland Greek import (although, in theory, if ship captains took on goods with lower stowage factors elsewhere, in a tramping pattern, they could be).

Yet the pots did move, and that movement demands explanation(s); a negativist fallacy (Salmon 2000: 245) contributes as little to our understanding of cross-cultural contact as a positivist one.

Value of pottery. In addition to the complexity of trade mechanisms, controversy surrounds the value of pottery in trade. The main opposing views, predicated on Classical Athenian pottery, are those articulated by Boardman (e.g. 1988a; 1988b), who argues on the basis of the price per unit of volume and weight that pottery was a valuable cargo in its own right, and those put forward by Gill (e.g. 1987; 1988; 1989), who posits that pottery was no more than saleable ballast, an index of more valuable goods. The saleable ballast view is principally based on research into the role of pottery in Classical Athens, for which Vickers has argued that an aristocrat would have preferred metallic to ceramic vessels (1985, 1986). It is incontestable that metal has a greater prime value than clay, and worked metal a greater value than worked clay i.e. pots. A wealthy aristocrat seeking to impress his symposion guests may have chosen metal vessels; a king, certainly (according to Athenaeus, the King of Persia would humiliate those who had displeased him by making them drink from mere clay vessels (*Deipnosophists* 11.464)). A less wealthy host would make do with fewer metal vessels, and more clay ones. For even in Classical Athens, the many citizens whose wages averaged 1 *drachma* per day would have regarded the most expensive ceramic vessels, such as the hydriai priced at 3 *drachmai*, as a veritable "'cheap' luxury" (Boardman 1988a: 32), to be rejected in favour of the cheaper coarse wares that litter Greek sites, if not excavation reports.

Moreover, there are functions for which ceramic wares are much more suitable whatever the owner's asset class, such as transporting and storing wine and the consumption of hot substances.[128] The wine jars in the pottery stand behind the

---

[126] For the co-existence of guest friendship and raids see Quiller (1982: 118).

[127] Cf. Curtin 1984: 226 for variety of exchange modes between North American Indians and European traders.

[128] Wine was imported to Assyria in jars, evidently over long distances (Stronach 1995: 180, 193 n. 9).

Assyrian king on a Nimrud ivory (Stronach 1995: 178, fig. 12.2) are likely to have been ceramic. The Rhodian vessels which, when heated, caused wine to be less intoxicating, would have also caused injury if made from metal (Athenaeus *Deipnosophists* 11.464).

Objects can also possess symbolic value. For example, a krater can symbolise the symposion, an élite pastime (Luke 1994b). Assyrian ceramic imports and imitations, limited to shapes for liquid consumption, appeared on the Levantine littoral during the Assyrian period and have been interpreted as objects of prestige, with the periphery of Empire copying Assyrian influence (Lehmann 1998: 19).

Moreover, pottery has a high stowage factor, and itself requires ballast.[129] Further, its breakability renders pottery a less than ideal candidate to act as convenient ballast or indeed as a casual space-filler; much better a heavy substance which would (a) weigh the ship down (b) not require special packaging (cf. Aristophanes *Acharnians* 901-45) and (c) be as marketable at journey's end as it was at the beginning. Many of the substances traditionally used as ballast, such as iron and marble, conformed to all criteria, although they were not necessarily sold. This suggests that, where pottery was taken on board, it was likely to be a cargo in its own right, perhaps, in the case of cheap and cheerful stackable cups, as space-fillers, but also, in the case of more elaborate wares, such as—for our period—the Kourion krater with its eminently breakable oinochoe lid, as more directional goods, assured of a positive reception.

Whatever its domestic worth, there is no implicit reason why pottery should not constitute an *import* of value. In many societies, the ability to acquire imports, which have survived the difficulties and expense of early long-distance (especially maritime) transport, signifies high status, membership of international clubs and successful relations with foreign traders. For example, the élite Swahili class of Lamu actively cultivated close ties, especially marital ones, with foreign merchants to enhance domestic status (Donley 1982: 67). Unlikely goods such as shoes, umbrellas and shell jewellery (ps.6,50) can become desired imports in their own right, signifying status: they are not the *raison d'être* of the relationship, but they come to signify it and to distinguish its beneficiaries from the rest. On the basis of Ezekiel 27—a list of who brings what to sixth century Tyre—Liverani (1991) has proposed an "ideology of imports", built around the huge range of peoples bringing goods to Tyre (no exports are noted). Some of the imports are valuable, such as gold and precious stones, but many are of lesser prime value, such as wheat, honey, horses, sheep etc. Nonetheless, all contributed to Tyre's status at the centre of a trading network, so all are duly noted.

As recent anthropological studies have shown, ascription of value is a culture-specific issue of consumption, with all the social issues that that implies (e.g. Appadurai 1986b; van Wijngaarden 1999: 5). The Iberians who exchanged vast quantities of silver in return for "wares of little worth" did not behave irrationally (Diodorus Siculus 5.35.4; ps.-Aristotle

De Mirabilibus Auscultationibus 135). Silver, of which they had plenty but then lacked the skills to work it, was of negligible value to them. In exchange for it they received what they wanted, which were items of negligible value to the Phoenicians (cf. Gill 1989: 7). One assumes that the same was true of the Libyans who gave gold in exchange for the goods the Phoenicians lay on the beach, unless the Phoenicians were genuinely offering goods they considered equal to the gold (Hdt. 4. 196). The tableau of foolish natives being duped into accepting tit-bits is familiar from the literature on ancient and modern colonialism. The sale of Manhattan to the Dutch by the Lenape Indians for $24/60 Dutch Guilders worth of duffle cloth, kettles, axes, hoes, awls and other "trinkets", is still a cause for wonder. Yet the Indians were able to trade these goods within their own exchange networks as precious imports, and in return sold something over which they had no concept of ownership.[130] These exchanges could certainly be considered exploitative in terms of one party having knowledge not shared by the other (particularly the case of Manhattan, from which the Indians were now, to their amazement, banned). But the incredulous modern equating of gewgaws for valuables is based solely on knowledge of the literate party's domestic value structure.

So there is no *a priori* reason why Geometric Greek pots could not have been a valuable item of a type of trade, used to secure a return trade in desirable goods or services. Indeed, there are practical reasons why some Levantines might be pleased to own a Greek pot, valued for its non-porosity or lustrous paint, and superior to all but the best 'Samaria ware' products (Courbin 1982: 203-4; Coldstream 1989: 92; *idem* 1998: 354-5; Doumet and Kawkabani 1991: 6). Franken (1984: 11) points out that Levantine clays are unsuited for production of the smooth pots provided by the Greeks. So Greek pottery may always have been considered a superior ceramic product compared to the local and even the Cypriot products. Even in the Geometric period, the impressive distribution of Euboean pots, from the Levant to the Far West, the north Aegean to North Africa must, in some part, reflect the readily-perceived quality of the product.

There are also some indications as to the sort(s) of trade that was—and was not—responsible for the import of some of these minimalistly-decorated low prime value goods to choice sites over hundreds of years.

In the first place is the small quantity involved outside Unqi, particularly notable when compared to the masses of Mycenaean or Archaic imports in the East. For example, Tyre has the greatest known quantity of Geometric Greek sherds outside Unqi. Most of these sherds were unearthed during the 1971-2 excavations and soundings, for which no non-Greek material has yet been published, so the total of Greek sherds is disproportionate to the whole assemblage. In order to reach a more realistic evaluation of proportions, the material published by Bikai in 1978 must be used, in which both Greek and non-Greek pottery was catalogued. There are 40 Greek

---

[129] McGrail 1989 discusses stowage factors.

[130] According to Peter Lynch, the net present value of $24 invested at 8% is around $20 trillion. *Manhattan History Tour*, 2000 (http://tlc.discovery.com/tlcpages/newyork/1626.html).

sherds from Stratum XI (A101) (Bikai 1978: pl. XXX, no. 3) to Stratum I. There were 21,038 diagnostic sherds from these levels (*ibid.*: 19), of which the 40 Greek examples constitute 0.19% of the diagnostic ceramic assemblage.[131]

By the sixth century BCE, by contrast, Greek drinking cups were replacing locally produced bowls and Red Slip techniques along the Syrian coast (including at Al Mina), and were ousting hitherto more popular Cypriot imports; by the Achaemenid period, virtually all finewares were Attic imports (Bonatz 1993: 138; Lehmann 1998: 21, 31-32). By this time, Greek pottery was certainly a commodity, although surely not "a serious item of bulk trade" (Boardman 1999b: 153-4) (indeed, given stowage considerations, it could never be so). In the fourteenth-thirteenth centuries BCE too, Greek pottery has been described as reaching a mass market (Sherratt 1999: 187).

Secondly, the reluctance to fill gaps in the Levantine ceramic repertoire with superior products suggests a lack of commercial drive in the Geometric period; all the imports fitted into the existing context of Levantine wares (see further p.53) In particular, there was no attempt to supply forms which did not relate to eating or, especially, drinking. In the Mycenaean period, by contrast, imported open forms complemented the shortcomings of the local ceramic repertoire (Leonard 1981: 100), and in Italy Greek Geometric imports seem to have made their own market. With a few exceptions (p.56), there was no attempt to enhance the Geometric wares' attractiveness by varying the decoration. The basic PSC skyphos was circulating for hundreds of years.

Lastly, when the imports reached the central places, they were often deposited.

Turning to the positive indications concerning the nature of the trade:

1. The imports have a restricted distribution, centred on ports and central places, suggesting that they were not yet commodities, unlike in the preceding and succeeding periods.

2. Intra-site, the contexts of some of the imports are impressive.

3. When deposited, it is often in loci that could be classified as élite. These depositions indicate that (a) the imports were valued: they weren't simply indexes of other imports (although they could be that too) and (b) they were valued by élites.

4. The forms of the imports are consistently related to feasting i.e. they weren't just valued as imports *per* se (like the Whydasian umbrellas and shoes), but they had some inherent meaning. Feasting was their "appropriate social context" (Morris 1986: 8). As such, they could be classified as luxury imports, goods whose principal use is social/rhetorical, restricted (as their distribution and context seems to indicate)

to the élite, and requiring specialised knowledge in their use (Appadurai 1986a: 38).

As Sherratt (1999: 185) points out, there is élite and élite—local, regional and inter-regional. There is no evidence that Assyrian kings supped from clay vases imported from Greece. But, as we have seen, there is evidence to suggest that the end-consumers of these imports belonged to a higher social-economic status than the norm. In north Syria, it has been suggested that the finest Red Slip was destined for the rulers' courts (Lehmann 1998: 13).

The involvement of the élite and the imports' social contexts are linked in the ostentatious consubstantiality used in the ancient world to underscore the high status of the participants and to lubricate the wheels of diplomacy. "Consubstantiality" refers to the ritual sharing of food and especially drink which, consciously or otherwise, strengthens the bonds between participants.[132]

Sharing food and drink was an effective diplomatic mechanism because it provided for the establishment of lasting bonds between participants, especially those who rarely saw each other. Commensality—sharing the same table—has been analysed as a rite of incorporation between those who were previously strangers (van Gennep 1960: 29). As Pitt-Rivers graphically puts it "blood, saliva, semen, milk, meat, fruit, vegetables or beer can make consubstantial those who are related through no womb, vagina or breast" (1973: 93). In other words, sharing substances effects the simulation of kinship, the closest and most permanent bond of all.

The role of exclusive feasting as a high-status activity within the relevant polities is explored, then some possible rituals of Iron Age diplomacy.

Feasting in Early Iron Age Greece and the Levant

Greece

Whatever the historicity of the Homeric Epics, the evidence pertaining to the social *mores* governing feasting rituals is both internally coherent and is consistent with what is known of later historical periods. In Homeric Greece, only kings indulged in the elaborate feasting and the consubstantiality offered most conspicuously by the krater (Luke 1994b: 24). Indeed, feasting was one of the defining characteristics of an aristocrat. As King Agamemnon said to his Cretan counterpart Idomeneus:

> "I honour you above all the Danaans of the fleet horses, whether in war or in some other work, or in the feast when the Argive nobles mix the gleaming wine of the elders in the bowl"
>
> (*Il.* 4.257-260)

In the Geometric period, aristocratic burials, particularly in Athens and at Lefkandi, were distinguished by the huge

---

[131] Similarly, Gilboa 1989: 217 argues that the small numbers of Cypro-Geometric imports to Palestine argue against them being the result of commercial ventures.

[132] Pitt-Rivers (1973: 92-94) for use of "consubstantiality" to describe "the universal notion that possession of a common substance is the basis of a mystical bond".

sympotic vessels placed upon graves (Coldstream 1983: 204), and in the spit-firedog combination immortalized by Achilles (*Il.* 9.212-214).

North Syria

Ugarit in north Syria is the likely origin of the *marza'u*, an exclusive mens' club, possibly of hereditary membership, which entailed heavy drinking sessions (Burkert 1991: 9; Carter 1997: 76).

Syro-Hittite kings of the early first millennium BCE repeatedly had themselves represented at feast on monumental reliefs placed in prominent locations, such as orthostats on palace entrances (Dentzer 1982: 35-44). Occasionally, these feasting scenes were associated with other identifiably kingly activities, such as hunting or war-mongering.

Phoenicia

For the Phoenicians, evidence for feasting rituals, as for so many other aspects of their culture, comes mainly from their overseas *diaspora*. One exception is the sarcophagus of King Ahiram of Byblos, which was dedicated by his son Ittobaal in the tenth century BCE (Pritchard 1969: 661). The chosen relief on one side depicts King Ahiram enthroned at (funerary) banquet.

Overseas in the Geometric period, particularly in the Princely Tombs of Italy, Phoenician sympotic vessels (cups, bowls and plates) have been unearthed along with other Oriental *keimelia*, testifying to Phoenician familiarity with such forms (Rathje 1990: 281-282). In Homer, the gift of a krater to king Thoas of Lemos (*Il.* 23.740-745), and the receipt by Menelaus of a krater from the king of Sidon (*Od.* 4.613-619; 15.111-119) illustrate epic Phoenician involvement in high-level exchange of sympotic wares. Late inscriptions in the Piraeus and Marseilles/Carthage demonstrate the existence of a Phoenician version of the *marzeah* (Barstad 1984: 130-131; Carter 1997: 78, 99).

Israel

The Old Testament provides important evidence for the nature of Israelite feasting rituals. Foremost among these is the *marzeah*, which the Septuagint translator renders as '*thiasos*', that is, a combination of cult and eating (Barnett 1985: 2-3; Burkert 1991: 9; Carter 1997: 78-9). The most famous *mrzh* is that disparaged by Amos (6.4-7) and enjoyed by the "men of mark" of Samaria. The format of the *marzeah*, with its reclining, dining, music making and anointing is very reminiscent of the aristocratic Greek banquet. Although religious in derivation, the social and political aspects expressed in the Samaritan version were apparently dominant by this time, doubtless the immediate cause of Amos' wrath.

The summit of Jeroboam's Samaria has yielded a cache of *ostraka*, recording the receipt of wine and oil by officials and members of the royal court on behalf of the palace (Mitchell 1982b: 507-8).

Philistia

In Philistia, drinking rituals close to those of the *symposion* can be recognised (Burkert 1991: 15-16); although the family of Samson's bride from Timnath is not explicitly stated to be wealthy, the provision of a seven-day feast for thirty male guests would support such an inference.

Assyria

Assyrian palatial reliefs illustrate many activities undertaken by the king, particularly dining, hunting and warfare (usually alone). Perhaps the starkest visual juxtaposition of royal dominion and feasting is depicted on the relief of Assurbanipal at Nineveh (mid-seventh century B.C.E). The perfect confection of a royal 'high tea' enjoyed by the king and his consort is somewhat jarred by the severed head of the latest vanquished foe, King Te-umman of Elam, hanging from a nearby tree: war and feast, the two principal activities of the powerful (plate 3). It is possible that this was a form of the *marzeah* already met in Syrian, Phoenician and Israelite cultures (Barnett 1985: 2-3).

The Nimrud wine lists indicate that in Assyria, as in Babylonia and Samaria, varying quantities of wine were used to reward palace officials, the quantity increasing according to rank (Mallowan 1972: xiv; Stronach 1995: 177).

Moreover, as the krater was a symbol of power in Greece, so the bed/couch used at Oriental feasts may have had a similar symbolism.[133] Assyrian kings repeatedly demanded couches from the leaders of conquered polities as tribute, a potent symbol of political submission if beds were part of the paraphernalia of power.[134]

Babylonia

Evidence for Babylonian culture in the early first millennium BCE is very limited, with little extant archaeological or documentary material. Nonetheless, there are a few indications that feasting was a component of power. For example, as in Assyria and Samaria, wine was issued to administrative officials in varying quantities according to rank (Oates 1986: 190).

Cyprus

Evaluation of the role of feasting depends on mortuary deposits, which indicate that ritual feasting was an important part of the self-expression of the élite, with high-status tombs containing various combinations of dining sets, tripod-stands and roasting spits. For example, the Homeric combination of spits and firedogs is found in the Royal Tomb 79 at Salamis, in a built tomb at Patriki near Salamis, and in the Warrior's

---

[133] Although it is often impossible to distinguish between dining bed and sleeping couches: the bed chamber was an important focus of political power (Dentzer 1982: 67). *Ibid.*: 55, n. 32 has examples of couches demanded of Assyrian foes.

[134] This may explain why, on the Gates of Balawat, the king of Hama reclines on his couch facing the besiegers of his city, shadowed by a figure making a sign of submission.

Plate 3. Banquet of Assurbanipal at Nineveh with the head of King Te-umman of Elam hanging from trees.
ANE 124920. © Copyright The British Museum

grave at Palaeopaphos (Coldstream 1985: 54 and n. 100). Clearly, "in the next world as in this, they (*sc.* aristocrats) were expected to keep a convivial table and a hospitable hearth" (Coldstream 1990: 62), an argument supported by the analysis of the presence in graves of wares serving consumption as an important predictor of high status (Rupp 1989: 355).

Some rituals of Early Iron Age diplomacy

Even in the communication-obsessed age of the Global Village and the Information Superhighway, satisfactory cross-cultural relations between states still depends to some extent on diplomatic relations via embassies and their tireless entertaining. When these are withdrawn, trade becomes difficult and nationals are left unaided. How much more important smoothing diplomatic rituals must have been when travel was difficult and dangerous, and foreign lands truly *terra incognita*.

There is literary testimony to the use of feasting as a diplomatic mechanism by Assyrians in the early first millennium BCE. At the start of his reign in the ninth century BCE, Assurnasirpal II held a great banquet to which envoys of many Levantine states were invited, including Unqi, Khatti, Tyre, Sidon, Gurgum and Melid. When he rebuilt Nineveh he held a massive banquet, to which dignitaries of many regions including Iran, Anatolia and Phoenicia were invited. Even the menu of this feast was recorded for posterity on a royal stele (Hawkins 1982: 389-390; Grayson 1982: 258).

Classicists are familiar with the Homeric guest feast, a ritual meal that was the automatic response to the arrival of a guest (Finley 1999: 125). The evidence from Homer and the Classical period shows that people connected through rituals such as entertainment, communal feasting and hand-clasping were known as *xenoi*. Herman (1989) has drawn out the

significance, rituals, and extent of *xenia*, which he translates as "ritualised friendship", a relationship common to many societies and established by many of the same rituals. Horizontal ties between *xenoi* sponsored safer overseas travel, enhanced the domestic social and political standing of members through the acquisition of imports (and the very fact of having foreign contacts), and facilitated the procurement of wealth and services for *xenoi* (Herman 1989: 74).

In the Bronze Age, terms such as "fraternity", "paternity" and "sonship" were commonly used to describe the relationships of one ruler to another (Munn-Rankin 1956: 76), a tendency which is later articulated in *xenia* (Herman 1989: 18).[135] Bronze Age gift-exchange effected the exchange of valuable goods between rulers, including, to judge from the distribution of imported exotica and the evidence of shipwrecks, Mycenaean ones (Snodgrass 1991: 16-8; Cherry and Knapp 1994: 146-151). The language and form of these relationships was diplomatic, even where their intent and result was the very same procurement of supplies effected by commercial trading.

From all these sources, rituals used to maintain *xenia* relationships could be divided into three stages:

Preliminary. Among devices preliminary to the establishment of relations, the mediator, greetings, oaths, libations, good deeds, *dexia* (pledges, sometimes given material form) and *pista* (token gifts) could all play a part (Herman 1989: 46). These rituals, especially the commensality, the gift-giving, and the handclasps, are common to many known ceremonies for the incorporation of strangers (van Gennep 1960: 28-29).

---

[135] Such fraternal terms are common to many such pseudo-kinship groups (Gennep 1960: 31). In Tonga for example, minor 'titles' present at the Kava drinking party are 'younger brothers' of the 'titles' in the main drinking group: "Our titles are brothers but we are not related" (Bott 1987: 187).

Iconographic attention focused on the *dexia* in its primary meaning of "handshake", which was held to encapsulate the relationship to such an extent that it was used as a visual symbol for the whole process (Herman 1989: 50), and to delineate it verbally (as in the Aeschines citation below). This seems to be true not just of ancient Greeks: Shalmaneser III of Assyria represented his new relationship with the king of Babylon by depicting on his throne base the two rulers shaking hands (*ibid.*: 51, fig. 4).

Initiation. Many preliminary rituals were repeated in the initiation ceremony of guest-friendship, constituents of which included a declaration, oath-taking, feasting, and the exchange of gifts, known as *xénia* or *dora* (Herman 1989: 59-69), which demanded instant reciprocity. This aspect seems to be represented on Shalmeneser's relief by the attendants standing behind their respective kings, bearing gifts. It is most famously recorded in literature by the perverted Glaucos and Diomedes exchange (*Il.* 6.224-236).[136]

Maintenance. The two principal rituals of *xenia* maintenance were feasting and gift-giving. The Homeric guest feast is the classic expression of the former, the presentation of *keimelia* (treasures) of the latter. The Classical Greeks regarded "the table of one's *xenos*" as a sacred bond. When Demosthenes effected the execution of his *xenos* Anaxinos of Oreos, his arch-rival Aeschines was able to rant with righteously justified indignation:

> "you moved to punish with death the same man in whose house you had been entertained at Oreos. The man with whom at the same table you had eaten and drunk and poured libations, the man with whom you had clasped hands in a token of friendship and hospitality"
>
> Aeschines, *Against Ctesiphon* 224

In Homer, *keimelia* are presented to visiting peers, stored (as the Greek word implies), displayed, and then passed to the next visiting aristocrat, as Menelaus passed to Telemachus the krater given to him by the king of Sidon (*Od.* 4.617; 15.117). The continuous circulation of gifts advertised and maintained the membership of the group. As van Gennep (1960: 31) puts it "the movement of objects among persons constituting a defined group creates a continuous social bond", much like commensality.

The *kula* analogy

Hackneyed though citations of the *kula* ring may have become in Classical Archaeology, it remains the case that rituals facilitating the establishment and maintenance of the aristocratic *kula* of the Trobriand Islanders almost exactly parallel all stages of gift-giving inherent to ancient *xenia*. Mauss, basing his famous analysis of the *kula* upon the fieldwork of Bronislaw Malinowski, describes the circulation

of artefacts between élites of the various islands (1990: 23-27).

Preliminary stages of the *kula* are marked by the offering of *pari*, gifts soliciting a more formal relationship, but not sufficient to confirm it (cf. *pista* and *dexia*). Full partnership is marked by the gift and countergift of *vaga* and *yotile* (cf. *xénia/dora*). Once relations are formalised, there is a continuous circulation of the gifts of the *kula*, the *vaygu'a* (shell armbands and necklaces) (cf. circulatory gifts). Alongside these gifts, the likely aim of the initial contacts themselves, were the exchanges of the really useful goods, *gimwali*, the sorts of things that tend not to survive materially, and are felt unworthy of record by Epic writers. Later Greek literature provides examples of both precious and useful goods and services circulating around these networks (Herman 1989: Chapter 4).

The *kula* analogy shows how the élite diplomatic mechanism of gift-giving, beloved of Epic writers and detectable in the material record, can underlie unmentioned, unindexed, trading relations. A modern documented example of this comes from the North American fur trade of the eighteenth century CE, when the actual exchange of traded goods was sandwiched between speechmaking and exchanges of gifts (Curtin 1984: 228).

Participants in ancient *xenia*

While most of the examples of *xenia* for which we possess explicit evidence concern relations between Greeks (Herman 1989: Appendix A and C), there are references to relationships of this nature being forged between Greeks and non-Greeks (e.g. Agesilaos of Sparta with Pharnabazos of Persia's son) (Plutarch *Agesilaos* 13.1-2) (also with Artaxerxes II of Persia, Apollophanes of Cyzicus, *xenoi* in Tegea, Mausolos of Caria, Tachos of Egypt, and Prokles of Phlius)). Moreover, the relationship articulated as *xenia* by the Greeks was not limited to partnerships involving Greeks. For example, Croesus of Lydia and Adrastos of Phrygia were guest-friends (Herodotus 1.43). Huge distances could be traversed via embassies. Cyrus of Persia enjoyed *xenia* with, among many others, a king of India (Xenophon *Cyropaedia* 6.2.1). In fact, Trojans, Lycians (*Il.* 17.150), Lydians, Phrygians, Carians, Persians, Indians, Babylonians, Arabians (Diodorus Siculus 2.24.6), Tyrians (Diodorus Siculus 17.47), Judahites and Benjamites (1 Samuel 18.1-4 and 2 Samuel 1.26), Egyptians, Syrians (Polybius 5.74.4) are all attested as being involved in what the Greeks perceived as guest-friendships (Herman 1989: 166-175).[137]

---

[136] Perverted because Glaucos is apparently swindled in the exchange. Diomedes perverts a ritual of guest-friendship, which is accompanied by all the proper words and gestures, into a Greek triumph over a Trojan foe (van Reden 1985: 26; for another, Polanyian, explanation see Tandy and Neale 1994: 17).

[137] Face-to-face contact seems to have been preferable in the establishment of *xenia*: Xenophon (*Hellenica* 4.1.29) has Apollophanes saying to King Agesilaos of Sparta that he could "bring Pharnabazos to a meeting with him with regard to establishing friendship relations". Similarly, Proxenos of Boiotia, then residing at Cyrus' court in Sardis, writes to Xenophon to invite him to come to seek Cyrus' friendship (Diogenes Laertius 2.49). But it seems that indirect initiation between partners was possible. Envoys could be used: Herodotus (3.39) tells us that Polycrates of Samos had made a treaty of *xenia* with Amasis of Egypt, "sending and receiving from him gifts", and Cyrus and the King of India used embassies to cement their relationship (Xenophon *Cyropaedia* 6.2.1).

In cases where the relationship either is or could be fictional, the point remains that the writers clearly felt that such a relationship would be perceived as plausible by their audiences. And where the rituals surrounding the institution of the relationship survive, they conform to the canonical Greek *xenia*. It therefore seems likely that non-Greeks understood the essential features and meaning of ritualised guest-friendships, that the Greeks were justified in describing these relationships as *xenia*, and that they can be analysed as such.

There are just a few literary references to relations between Greeks and Levantines in the Bronze and early Iron Ages. Most refer to relations between Greeks and "Phoenicians". In Homeric eyes, "Phoenician" could apply not just to those from the settlements which we would identify as metropolitan Phoenician—Tyre, Berytus, Sidon etc.—but to anyone from the Levantine littoral, particularly those involved in trade (e.g. Frankenstein 1979: 288; Morris 1992a: 130; Burkert 1992: 28; Röllig 1992: 93).[138] Gift-giving and the offer of hospitality suggest that King Phaedimos of Sidon and King Menelaus of Sparta were guest-friends *(Od.* 4.617; 15.117). The Phoenicians who gave king Thoas of Lemnos a gift of a krater may also have been soliciting such a relationship *(Il.* 23.740-745).

There are a few references to *xenia* relations between Greeks and other Orientals. King Kinyras of Cyprus presented King Agamemnon with a guest gift of an iron cuirass *(Il.* 11.19-20). In the Bronze Age, the king of Ahhiyawa (Mycenaean Greece?) was addressed as "my brother" in the Tawagalawas Letter (Karavites 1992: 49), and some doubt was cast upon his gift-giving abilities by the king of Hatti (Zaccagnini 1987: 384). It has also been suggested that the lapis objects found in Mycenaean Thebes were a gift from King Tukulti-Ninurta I of Assyria (Porada 1982: 68-70). Peltenburg includes the Aegean in "this international club", and postulates a continuum of gift-giving between the Bronze and Iron Age (1991: 168, 172, n. 4).

The characters Yamani, Phoenix and Aegyptios may also indicate the existence of such relations. "Yamani" ("Ionian") had himself enthroned in Assyrian-controlled Ashdod in Philistia during the reign of Sargon, before fleeing to Egypt and, upon the vengeful Assyrian advance, finding himself being handed back to the Assyrian king by the Egyptian monarch (Luckenbill 1927: 105-106 (§§194-195)). This Yamani has variously been identified as a Greek, a Cypriot, and a Palestinian (e.g. Smith 1942: 100; Austin 1969: 33; Tadmor 1958: 80, n. 217). In the context of *xenia*, another explanation for the name presents itself: it was common practice for ritualised friends to name their sons after their *xenoi*, either using the *xenos'* name or his place of origin (Herman 1989: 19-21) (p.39 has an ancient Israelite/Judahite example). Perhaps this and other characters with similar names in Near Eastern contexts (Niemeier 2001: 17) were the *xenoi* of Greek Ionians, such as the Euboeans. Similarly, the father (Amyntor) of Phoinix (e.g. *Il.* 9.432) may have been the guest-friend of a Phoenician; the father of Aegyptios of Ithaca *(Od.* 2.15) may have enjoyed a similar relationship with an Egyptian (cf. Austin 1968: 24, n. 7).

There is also circumstantial evidence of similarities in the procedure and documentary presentation of feasting which seem to reflect a community of attitudes. For example, reclining at banquet, which had reached Greece by the Archaic period, is attributable to Eastern influence. Certainly the Phoenicians (Rathje 1990: 283), Mesopotamians,[139] and Israelites (Amos 6.4)[140] were all reclining at banquet by the eighth century BCE, and this habit appears to have caught on in Assyria in the seventh century (Dentzer 1982: 51-8). Feasting rituals were similarly ordered in Greek and Near Eastern literature (Lichtenstein 1968). In Akkadian, Ugaritic, Biblical and Homeric accounts of aristocratic feasting, meat preparation invariably precedes wine preparation and consumption *(ibid.*: 24-9), an order embedded in formulaic repetition by Homer (e.g. *Od.* 9.161-2; 10.183-4). Bewailing his absence from Ithaca while in Phaeacia, Odysseus describes the canonical Greek feast *(Od.* 9.1-11). The bread, meat and wine is served to the accompaniment of music. Music was an accompaniment to feasts in Israel (Amos 6.5), north Syria (Dentzer 1982: pl. 8, fig. 53 (Carcemish)), Mesopotamia *(ibid.*: pl. 9, fig. 61), Sumer and Ugarit (Lichtenstein 1968: 30). It is possible that the Eastern lyre itself is a derivation from Greece (Winter 1979: 117, 120), where it was used at feasts *(Od.* 1.153-4).

Linguistic expressions relating to the feast are strikingly congruent in Mesopotamian, Ugaritic and Hebrew literature, and in Homer. For instance, *Od.* 1.149, "they put their hands to the good things lying ready before them", finds precise parallels in the Ugaritic Keret and in Sumerian literature (Lichtenstein 1968: 24, n. 23; Gordon 1962: 254). Individual words relating to the feast were borrowed from the East; the Greek '(w)*oinos*' is related to the Aramaic '*wajn*' and Western Semitic '*jain*' (Burkert 1992: 174, n.2). Words for feasting equipment were evidently shared between Eastern cultures, and then passed onto Greece. For example, analogues of the Israelite '*kos*' ('cup') are known in the Phoenician, Hebrew, Ugaritic, Arabian and Akkadian tongues (Sznycer 1979:91).

[138]The governor of Cypriot Kition, a Phoenician colony, referred to himself as "servant of Hiram, King of the Sidonians". Since a King Hiram was on the Tyrian throne at this time, it seems probable that the Iron Age Phoenicians, whose land was united under the hegemony of Tyre, were known to themselves as Sidonians. There is thus no need to extrapolate a Bronze Age source for this part of the Homeric Epics: the poem is reflecting Iron Age *Levantine* terminology (cf. Culican 1982b: 28). The appellation presumably harked back to an earlier period, when Sidon, now under Tyrian domination, was the primary state (Mitchell 1982a: 448; 1 Kings 16.31). Thus Menelaus *(Od.* 4.613-617; 15.118) may have enjoyed the hospitality not of the king of Sidon, where there is no evidence for any sustained Early Iron Age Greek interest (although there are some Mycenaean connections), but of Tyre, where there is an abundance of such evidence. On a more pragmatic level, Culican (1982b: 28) has suggested that σιδονιη was more 'hexameter-friendly' than any Tyrian adjective.

[139]The change in custom is iconographically illustrated on a bronze situla of the tenth to eighth centuries BCE, upon which the royal couple are represented feasting while seated on individual chairs—which are themselves held aloft by a couch (Dentzer 1982: 47 and pl. 9, fig. 61).

[140]Amos was writing in the time of Uzziah and Jeroboam (Amos 1.1) (i.e. the mid-eighth century BCE). Cf. 1 Kings 13.20 for sitting at banquet in time of Jeroboam.

Finally, much of the terminology and rituals of guest-friendship are universal. In particular, treaty terminology, rooted in ancient Levantine covenant terminology, was communicated to the Greeks (Weinfeld 1973). The otherwise curious Homeric phrase "to cut the oath", for example, has Hebrew, Phoenician and Aramaic parallels. Homer and later Greek writing echo with Levantine terminology, treaty structure and oath ceremonies (Karavites 1992; Faraone 1993).

In the Iron Age as in the Bronze Age, the élites of the Eastern Mediterranean employed common methods of association both within and between polities, among which feasting and gift-giving were essential characteristics.

"What mean these pots?"
(Saltz 1978: ix) (of Greek Geometric pottery in the Levant)

In contrast to the preceding and succeeding periods, Greek Geometric pottery has been mainly found in ports and central places, and was often deposited in elevated findspots. Further, imports were restricted to a few forms effecting feasting, an activity used by élites within and between each of the cultures concerned. In other words, although the complexity of trade and cross-cultural relations militates against subsuming all imports under one model, the imports' distribution and physical and social context suggest that some could have been embedded in the *xenia* relations adumbrated above.

The possibility that some Greek Geometric imports in the Levant could have been gifts has been raised before; Coldstream suggested that the figured kraters found in the Levant, as well as the amphorae in Cretan tombs, were gifts (e.g. 1983: 206; 1989: 93; 1995: 400-1), and Crielaard extended this hypothesis to the humbler vase types, such as skyphoi (1993: 145). Gift-giving is also the basis for the élite relations which Kyrieleis envisages being established between Eastern potentates and Greek nobles disembarking at Al Mina (1988: 57). Certainly, type A ports do tend to sponsor personal, though not necessarily direct, relations between leaders of the territories concerned, leading to the establishment of administered trade and possibly gift exchange.

The distinction of the three stages of *xenia* relations—all of which could involve the donation of feasting vessels—is helpful here.

Initiatory gifts. Herman treats Coldstream's gifted kraters (see above) as this class of gift (1989: 66, n. 74). In the Archaic period, the Spartans sent a bronze krater to Croesus to cement an alliance with him (Herodotus 1.70).

Preliminary gifts. "Objects of little intrinsic value but of immense symbolic significance" (Herman 1989: 50). In the case of the Greek imports, their social context in commensality, an important element in élite self-expression and bonding, would have provided the symbolism. Preliminary gifts need not be of great value to the prospector; indeed, it would be sensible to send "materials of which he (*sc.* the initiator) has plenty more if a ship is lost" (Snodgrass 1991: 18) or if the mission failed.

Circulatory gifts. In Homer, Telemachus' krater is an example of a circulatory gift (*Od.* 4.617; 15.117). The Greek imports are often deposited and thereby withdrawn from circulation: they cannot have constituted circulatory gifts. Destruction (e.g. deliberate deposition) of wealth can indicate the operation of a gift-exchange system (Morris 1986: 8-9).

Overall, where Greek Geometric imports can be characterised as gifts, it seems most appropriate to characterise them as preliminary ones, prospective of the friendship that could effect later exchanges of goods with greater prime value. As preliminary gifts, they are not intended to procure by direct exchange either valuables or really useful goods. There is no sense of the swapping inherent in the old pots for corn theory (described Snodgrass 1980: 128-9, 224; cf. Crielaard 1993: 144 for pots exchanged for Eastern jewellery). Eastern potentates were very unlikely to exchange a ceramic pot, however perfectly crafted, for a consignment of precious metals, textiles, trained slaves or copper ingots. But it could help (perhaps along with other, vanished materials) to promote a relationship that might procure those goods. With pottery appearing in this introductory role, some high-status Levantines might be able to withhold their spittle (cf. Papadopoulos 1997b: 200) long enough to proceed to the next stage of relations with the provider of the pottery, whether Greek, Phoenician or Cypriot.

A preliminary gift of a krater neatly combined the two most important rituals of élite diplomacy—gift-giving and commensality—and complimented the recipient with the implied belief that he could make hostly use of it, with all the social elevation implied. As Ridgway points out, the specialised equipment required for the preparation and consumption of intoxicating liquids plays an important role in the universal obligations of gift exchange (1997: 339).

Of course, most literary, particularly Epic, gifts are vessels of metal, not clay. The Homeric corpus has Telemachus' krater and the gold cup of Bellerophon. King Toi of Hama presented vessels of precious metals to Israel's David (Prausnitz 1966: 178). The Persian kings' gifts to foreign ambassadors were gold and silver vessels (Nylander 1968: 125). By the Archaic period, after several generations of direct access to new metal sources via the Western colonies, Greeks themselves were gifting metal vessels, and metal becomes much more common in Greek lands. Croesus' krater was bronze, and princely Celtic tombs were the final resting places of ornate bronze pieces such as the Vix krater (e.g. Cunliffe 1987: 105). By this time too, Greek pottery in the East was a commodity, imported in vast quantities and even ousting local wares (p.47).

But in the Geometric period, metal goods were travelling westwards, from the Levant to Greece, and the most impressive (extant) objects then produced by Greeks were the elaborate kraters found in the Levantine capitals and the Euboean LG figured wares, mainly kraters, some from the Cesnola school (e.g. Robertson 1940, 7 fig. 3g-h, 3 fig. 1n, 5 fig. 2a; Coldstream 1971: 8-9, nos. 7 and 11, pls 3c and 2d; Descœudres 1978: 10 no. 32). These wares, with their aristocratic allusions such as horses and the Tree of Life, seem to have been manufactured for an Euboean social élite and are widely distributed throughout the Mediterranean, indicating for Coldstream the trading and gift relations of that élite (1994: 77). Indeed, pottery may gain in tradeable value from its lesser prime value, as élites look to more disposable substitutes to use in (for example) mortuary practices, while retaining their metallic counterparts for use in life (Sherratt 1999: 187).

The use of ceramic vessels as gifts in the ancient world is attested: in archaic Etruria, the inscriptions upon the surface of ceramic vessels show that they were presented as gifts (Cristofani 1975: 138-139). In *c.* 700-690 BCE, the Etruscan Hisa Tinnuna may have gifted to his *xenos* at Cuma a local EPC lekythos (Ridgway 1997; *idem* 2000b: 241). King Kotys of Thrace received a gift of fine decorated pottery from his one of his *xenoi* (Plutarch *Moralia* 174D). The inscription on a Geometric ceramic oinochoe found at Aetos on Ithaca alludes to guest-friendship, and may have been a gift from host to travelling *xenos* (Powell 1991: 148-150, no. 45; Robb 1994: 49-51). Even Pharaohs could gift objects of no great prime value: Amasis of Egypt presented to the Samian Heraion two wooden statues of himself, as a mark of his friendship with Polycrates (Hdt. 2.182), a preliminary gift, perhaps?

Where the imports are not likely to be gifts, their overall distribution and physical and social contexrs underline the ability of Levantine élites to control access to imports, which included pots from Greece. The evidence from Cyprus (below) suggests that Greek Geometric pots were treated in the same way as higher prime value imports from other regions. This contrasts sharply with the diffuse distribution of Greek finewares in the preceding and succeeding periods, when the finewares were commodities, available to many.

Import equivalents in Cyprus

It is Cyprus, lying between the Levant and Greece, that best shows the potential equivalence of imported Geometric Greek pottery with prime-value imports from more prosperous regions. For in the princely tombs of Cyprus were deposited fine ceramic vessels from Greece, along with metallic, faience and ivory goods from the East (e.g. Beer 1984), the best (extant) goods that each region offered: import equivalents. At Kourion, for example, the Cesnola krater and oinochoe accompanied a Phoenician silver figured bowl bearing the name of the King of Paphos (Coldstream 1963: 27). This equivalence recurs in Etruria and even in the graves of Lefkandi, where fine Attic pottery mingles with Eastern exotica in high status tombs (Vickers 1989: 51; Coldstream 1995: 401). The apparent metallic references on some of the imports, such as the ribs on Geometric stems, the shape of the Tell Hadar lebes and the Tell Qiri dinos (Coldstream 1983: 206; *idem* 1998: 357), and indeed the metallic sheen of PSC skyphoi, may refer to this recognised equivalence.

Cyprus also shows the potential value of imports, including Greek Geometric pottery, to the recipients: all the central places which received Greek Geometric imports (and whose kingdoms included coastal territory) were situated on the coast, not a requisite location for a central place, and one which is not duplicated in the import-barren north (Rupp 1987:

map 4). This suggests that one crucial aspect of power in the south was the control of imports, a suggestion corroborated by the fact that Greek Geometric imports to Cyprus are at their most frequent during the period which Rupp (1987) argues witnessed the rise of the Cypriot kings i.e. (late) CGIII and especially CA I (cf. Snodgrass 1994b: 169). The most explicit link between the putative nascent kings and Greek (and Phoenician) imports is Royal Tomb I at Salamis which Rupp suggests was a conscious political statement made by the first kings of Salamis (and of Cyprus). That tomb contains a thirty-three piece 'dinner set' composed of Greek pottery vessels. Since the new aristocracy may have been those members of Cypriot society who provided foreigners with goods, the expression of their burgeoning power through the mortuary display and disposal of imports would have been highly appropriate. Greek and Levantine imports can be seen as artefacts that manipulate the achievement of high status rather than just reflect it (Renfrew 1986: 144), the symbols of a foreign élite the display of which (for example, in funerary rites) can, *inter alia*, help achieve superior social rank (Brumfiel and Earle 1987: 3).

Forms of Greek Geometric pottery in the Levant

Each Levantine area which received Greek imports had ceramic forms to correspond broadly to the range of Greek imports: large bowls for kraters, small ones for cups, flat ones for plates, jars for amphorae, and jugs for oinochoai (cf. de Vries (1979: 545) for similar broad comparabilities in the Achaemenid period).

A closer analysis of the Greek Geometric forms imported to the various Levantine areas (summarised in Table 10, below) reveals a differential distribution that can be related to the feasting rituals of each area. Each major form of sympotic Greek import is considered, within the cultures which are known to have received it (excluding Philistia, Assyria and Babylonia where so few imports have been found).

Table 10: Forms of Greek imports to the Levant

	North Syria	Phoenicia	Israel	Philistia	Assyria	Cyprus
Amphorae	√	√	-	-	-	√
Cups	√	√	√	√	√	√
Kraters	√	√	√	-	-	√
Oinochoai	√	-	-	-	-	√
Plates	√	√	√	-	-	√

Amphorae. Most Greek amphorae in the Levant come from north Syria, which boasts a long history of amphorae forms used in consubstantial rituals (Dentzer 1982: 22). Such vessels acted not merely as wine containers in the Greek way, but as amphorae, kraters, oinochoai and cups combined, with the liquid being drunk directly from the jar through tubes. In the third millennium BCE, a "well established iconographic type" was the representation of the royal couple sucking liquid (probably beer) from such a vessel (Burkert 1991: 8).[141] Consubstantiality through imbibing from a communal vessel is part of the iconography of power.[142] Early first millennium Mesopotamian bronze situlae carry representations of bestrawed amphorae at the feasts of princes (Dentzer 1982: 46-47; pl. 10, figs. 64, 66, 69), and the iconographic form appears on two Lyre-Player seals, one from Jerusalem, and one from Rhodes (Boardman 1990a: 8-9, fig. 18 (no. 163) and 13 (no. 87A)) (plate 4). These seals were almost certainly manufactured in north Syria, and were distributed to Greek lands, including Euboea and Pithekoussai.

Plate 4. North Syrian Lyre-Player seal with Lyre-Player sucking liquid from an amphora through a straw. Photo courtesy of Professor John Boardman

Courbin (1993) argues that the four LPG amphorae found at Ras el Basit were originally imported as containers of olive oil. The discovery at Lefkandi of a tenth century amphora inscribed (post-firing) with a trade-mark (Catling 1994) lends credence to the view that commodities were indeed being transported at this time. Euboea was renowned in antiquity for the kind of commodities which could be transported in such amphorae, such as olives, wine, grain and preserved fish (p.57).

In Cyprus, where known imports of Greek amphorae are limited to one (Coldstream 1968: 321), this ritual use of the amphora was introduced from north Syria (Dikaios 1937-1938: 71) and is represented in both the CG III Khrysochou jug and the Hubbard amphora (Vandenbeele 1988: pl. IV). This latter links the eastern iconographic representation with the actual Greek form; indeed the vessel from which the deceased sucks the liquid is an amphora (Dikaios 1937-1938: 60).

---

[141] Dentzer (1982: pl. 1 figs. 1, 3, 5, 7, and 8) illustrates many examples.

[142] In this sense, there is no distinction between this ritual and the Greek *symposion* with which Burkert (1991: 8) contrasts it, characterising the *symposion* as "an egalitarian group" and the amphora scenes as "monarchic". But, between themselves, king and queen are equal, and it is their exclusion of others from sharing their common substance which elevates them, in the same way that the exclusion of others from sharing the krater was a method of élite self-definition and elevation.

No amphorae have been found in Israel, and the shape accounts for just four of the many Greek Geometric imports to Phoenicia. In both these polities, amphorae are rare in domestic and funerary assemblages (Crowfoot *et al.* 1957: figs. 13-33; Bikai 1978).

Cups. The Greek cup was the most frequently imported Geometric Greek form in the Levant. Functionally, cups were present in all of the polities that received Greek Geometric imports, though Levantine cups were usually handleless and round-bottomed (Boardman 2002b) and, as in the Greek world, there were a great variety of shapes and sizes within any one material culture.

In north Syria, a Megiddo ivory (*c.* 1350-1150 B.C.E) indicates a hierarchy of cup sizes, the largest cup resting in the hands of the 'host', faces the other (successively smaller) diners, who are grouped on successively lower seats holding successively smaller cups (Dentzer 1982: pl. 5, fig. 30). Such an association between cups and power had a long pedigree, with cups, emblematic of kingly power, being held aloft by kings on seals of the Ur III period (*ca.* 2100-2000 BCE) (Winter 1986: 265). The Arthurian ease with which king Nestor lifts his full wine cup is a Greek example (*Il.* 11.632-637). Dentzer details the association of cups with power in Persian, Babylonian and Thracian cultures and argues that the cup was a symbol of power in the Bible (1971: 50; 1982: 66).

Phoenician cups were frequently exported westwards in the Iron Age. In Cyprus, the Phoenician term '*ks*' (cup) is inscribed on the bronze bowl from the Teke tomb J at Knossos, in a context of *ca.* 900 BCE (Sznycer 1979).

The best explored Levantine material culture is Old Testament Israel, where the *kos, saf,* and *qubba'at* all acted as cups for wine (Kelso 1948: 19, 27-28, 31). These were of varying shapes and sizes, none of which had an exact Greek equivalent according to the Septuagint translator, who mainly translates them as '*poteria*'.

Cups are a common part of Philistine material culture, many of the native models resembling their Greek counterparts more closely than those of other polities (Dothan 1982: 98-106 ("bowls")).

In many Assyrian scenes of royal dominion unrelated to feasting (such as audiences, homage or the presentation of tribute), the king holds a cup in his hand, surely alluding to his power through feasting (Dentzer 1982: 50), in what Stronach calls the "emblem of successful stewardship" (1995: 177).

The Cypriot ceramic repertoire included cups. The imitation of Greek forms and then of Greek decoration (p.43) shows that the form of the imports was perfectly acceptable.

Kraters. Several Greek kraters were imported to north Syria in the Geometric period. Kraters were a familiar north Syrian Iron Age form, examples having been unearthed at Tell Sukas and Hama (Riis 1948: 57-60; Buhl 1983: 23-27). But iconographically, as one of the Megiddo ivories shows (Dentzer 1982: pl. 5, fig. 28), it is difficult to distinguish amphorae from kraters.[143] Cauldrons may have been used to hold wine mixed with water (Moorey 1980: 192).

The gift of a krater from the king of Sidon to Menelaus suggests that Phoenician aristocrats had a krater-equivalent, as does the Phoenician gift of a krater to King Thoas of Lemnos (*Od.* 4.617; *Il.* 23.740-745). These Homeric kraters have been associated with the Phoenician metal bowls disseminated throughout the Iron Age Mediterranean (Burkert 1992: 16). Iconographical evidence for the actual use of kraters comes from a Phoenician bowl in Cyprus that shows a vessel standing alone in the midst of the banqueters (Dentzer 1982: pl. 18, fig. 101).[144]

At least two Greek kraters, a lebes and a dinos have come to light in Israel. The Greek krater has three possible functional equivalents in the corpus of Iron Age Israelite pottery, in terms of size relative to the remainder of the ceramic corpus: the *aggan*, a 2-4 handled bowl, the *mizraq*, a 4-handled bowl, and the *sefel*. Several scholars have proposed that the *aggan* was "in a way" the precursor of the imported Greek krater (Honeyman 1939: 79; Kelso 1948: 16; Buhl 1983: 126), and the evidence from the Old Testament supports this claim: the Septuagint translator of The Song of Songs (Solomon) renders *aggan* as 'κρατηρ' (*ibid.*). Of the other candidates, the metal *mizraq* had a specifically cultic purpose (Barstad 1984: 127, n. 5). But it was used at the Homeric-style Samaritan feast berated by Amos and so, in ceramic form (as the finest Israelite ceramic product) (Kelso 1948: 13-24) may have been an analogue of the Greek krater. The *sefel* was a luxurious two-handled banqueting bowl, which Prausnitz suggests was the model for the development of the krater in the east, being a parallel of the Greek krater (1966: 186).

It is possible that the wine held by the functional equivalent of the Greek krater was mixed not with water, in the Greek way, but with spices, to which repeated reference is made in the Old Testament (Burkert 1991: 19). The belief in the non-aqueous nature of Old Testament wine stems from Isaiah 1.22, which includes "wine mixed with water" in the litany of criticisms which the prophet levels against profligate Judah, suggesting that he regarded it as a new, perhaps foreign-influenced, practice. So the Greek krater could have been easily assimilated into the existing feasting paraphernalia of Israel. Indeed, Kopcke (2002: 113-4) suggests that the unique shape of the handleless Tell Hadar dinos shows that a Greek potter understood and wished to satisfy eastern preferences. This would be the first post-Mycenaean sign of "market-orientated production", with Greek producers and exporters specifically seeking to please an Oriental market.

Figure 16. Image from the Kaloriziki amphora. Dikaios 1937-8: 71, fig. 6. Reproduced with permission of the British School at Athens

Whether Cyprus had kraters prior to the first Greek imports is contentious. The argument revolves around the classification of the shape in question as an amphora or a krater (or amphoroid krater). For example, the Kaloriziki vessel is dubbed an "amphora" by Dikaios (1937-1938: 71). The illustration on the vase (figure 16) consists of a figure holding a jug over a vessel of the same shape as the one on which it is painted. Its representation is clearly reminiscent of the oinochoe-krater combination known from Greek lands. So Cyprus had vessels which held liquid from which other vessels were filled: 'kraters', in the parlance of Greek ceramics. The acceptance of imported kraters is much more explicable in these circumstances than if we accept that no vessels which functioned as kraters existed prior to the arrival of Greek imports (cf. Demetriou 1989: 21). Certainly, the imports were used in the Greek way: the new kings of Salamis included them among their 'dinner sets' in tombs (Royal Tombs 1 and 2, Gjerstad 1977: 25). At Amathus too, the Greek krater formed part of dinner sets, in Tombs 321, and in T. NW 194 1 (Coldstream 1986: 326).

Oinochoai. Oinochoai are a very rare imported shape on the Levantine littoral. Ignoring Cyprus, just three Greek oinochoai have been unearthed in the Levant outside Al Mina, all at Ras el Basit. Although jugs were certainly a common part of the ceramic assemblage of every Levantine culture, contemporary iconographic representations of the vessels being used to pour liquid from one container to another are rare. Such a rarity suggests that in this capacity oinochoai/jugs had little place in the rituals of Iron Age Levantine banquets, which would explain the low frequency of Greek imports. In the Achaemenid period, Attic oinochoai were a comparatively rare import, leading Keith de Vries to postulate that Orientals generally preferred to have their cups filled individually from the krater, or to use rhyta (1977: 545). Indeed, one of the Megiddo ivories (Dentzer 1982: pl. 5, fig. 28) shows each alternative simultaneously, with a drinking cup being carried from an amphora/krater to the banqueters, while the animal heads represented on top of the container may be rhyta (Barnett 1985: 47). No oinochoai/jugs are evident. Reliefs from Khorsabad shows attendants using small situlae to draw wine from a cauldron (Stronach 1995: 180, fig. 12.3).

Cyprus, where at least seven imported oinochoai have been found, seems to have been more receptive to the potential uses of oinochoai. For example, a number of jugs are represented on the banquet scene of the Hubbard amphora,

---

[143] The Mycenaean amphoroid krater, the prototype for the Greek krater, died out in PG Greece, but continued development in the Eastern Mediterranean. Prausnitz (1966) traces the development of the shape in the East.

[144] Phoenician kraters, as all Oriental ones, were amphora-shaped (e.g. Bikai 1978: 32 and n. 65) but, although Markoe calls the vessel in this scene an "amphora" (1985: 175), its position in the centre of the action, plus the presence of an amphora on the table, suggests that it was being used as a krater.

on the Kaloriziki amphora (figure 16), the Khrysochou jug, a bichrome IV pedestalled krater (*c.* 700 BCE) and a spouted jug of the same ware (Gjerstad 1948: figs. XXII, 1, XXXV, 8).

Plates. The plate is a dispensable part of Euboean sympotic equipment: only a handful of plates are known from the island, and it is probable that the skyphos was used for eating as well as for drinking (Howe 1958: 49, n.24; Popham *et al.* 1989: 18; Coldstream 1998a: 354).

Tyre has so far produced over 20 examples, and Basit, Tell Rachidieh and Samaria one apiece. Thus the vast majority of Euboean plates have come to light in Phoenician lands. In contrast to the situation in Euboea, plates were an integral part of Phoenician material culture: between 37% and 67% of the total diagnostic ceramic assemblage from Strata XI-I at Tyre are plates (Bikai 1978: 27, Table 4), consistently a far greater proportion than any other single shape (*ibid.*: 58, Table 14). The best quality local plate was of Samarian ware, whose slip was non-porous, to which the well-slipped Greek plate would have been considered a worthy alternative (Courbin 1982: 204; Coldstream 1989: 92; *idem* 1998: 355).

This was also the case in Cyprus, whose 'princely' tombs (such as the Royal Tomb 1 at Salamis, and Tomb 194 at Amathus) have many imported plates, and where the plate was the most common domestic ceramic form in the Early Iron Age (Demetriou 1989: 42).

Conclusions

There was no random acceptance of available forms: amphorae are concentrated in the region with the most entrenched ritual use for them; cups are found everywhere, corresponding to their native ubiquity; kraters can be functionally paralleled wherever they are found; oinochoai are mainly restricted to Cyprus, where, unlike the rest of the Levant, their use as pourers at feasts is iconographically attested; and plates are found mainly in the region which has most local use for them, despite their rarity at home.

A similar differential distribution of pottery shapes occurred in the Achaemenid period, for which de Vries noted that "the types of shapes (*sc.* of Greek imports)...seem admirably to match Eastern needs" (1977: 545). As he further pointed out, this match is another nail in the coffin of the 'pots mean people' equation: not only did the range of Greek Geometric imports in the East not match those known from any Euboean domestic comparandum, they also neatly conformed to Eastern ceramic ranges.

It seems that those who supplied the East with pottery knew Eastern preferences, and, in the case of the plates so uncommon in the Euboean homeland, were able to communicate these preferences to the potters who manufactured them: Coldstream's "hint of Euboean market research" (1994: 47). Pure market forces are often cited to explain such import 'fits', such as that of the Levanto-Helladic shapes, produced in the Argolid in the fourteenth-thirteenth centuries BCE (e.g. Sherratt 1982; *eadem* 1999: 187-8; van Wijngaarden 1999: 7). But knowledge of others' customs,

particularly feasting customs, is also to be expected of *xenia* partners. As Peltenburg notes of Bronze Age gift-relations, "the system required of the participants detailed knowledge of the customs of their partners" (1991: 168) or, in Murray's words, the system required "a cultural relationship (*sc.* between Athens and Knossos) that made these gifts useful or symbolically important" (in Coldstream 1983: 107). As well as the forms of the imports, such symbolism is present on the three LG imports to Cyprus that carry the Oriental Tree of Life scene with heraldic animals. Decorated imports to the East are rare, as are depictions of this scene in Greece itself, a coincidence which led Coldstream to suggest that the Euboean donors knew their Cypriot peers' tastes (1994: 84 n. 49).

Although not all the imports need have been used in Eastern feasts, and even then not in ways that Greeks would necessarily recognise as 'correct', they would have been symbolically meaningful to their recipients as vessels related to the feast. The contrast with the situation in the West, where the importation of Geometric Greek forms seems to have occasioned a revolution not just in vase forms, but also in vase names (Rathje 1990: 280), could not be stronger.

The end of the line: Euboea

In the Mycenaean period, most mainland Greek pottery found in the East hailed from the Argolid. In the Archaic and Classical periods, East Greece, Corinth and Attica were the major sources of pottery. In the Geometric period it is Euboea, with a quantitatively minor contribution from Attica (and some of the 'Attic' material is reflected in the Attic repertoire at Lefkandi) (Popham 1994: 27-28). This predominance, plus the extraordinary discoveries at Eretria and especially Lefkandi, led initially to a somewhat uncritical promotion of Euboean activity in both exporting Euboean goods (visibly, only the pottery), and in importing Oriental goods.

Many have criticised this perceived Euboean "prejudice" in Early Iron Age East-Greek relations (e.g. Martelli 1988: 111; Morris 1992b: xiv; Papadopoulos 1997b). It is undeniable that contact with the East influenced all aspects of Greek society with a profundity we are only beginning to comprehend, particularly since much of the influence lay outside the material sphere (e.g. Burkert 1992; Morris 1992a; West 1997). Within that sphere, the visible inward transmission of Oriental artefacts and techniques to Greece is very much more impressive than the visible reverse transmission of small quantities of fineware (Snodgrass 1994a: 3). The pivotal role played by the Eastern Mediterranean in the emergence of the Greeks from the 'Dark Ages' is plain (Coldstream 1989: 90). It is also the case that in any dealings with Levantines the Euboeans would have found culturally more advanced partners, some of whom belonged to sea-faring cultures, most famously the Phoenicians.

In particular, the role of Cyprus is often underestimated in studies of Greek-Levantine relations (Snodgrass 1994a: 4) (as well as Levantine-Far West relations). Its Levantine location, Greek script and mixed population, as well as its insular character, promoted its role as a bridge between cultures, in the Bronze Age, the Iron Age, and the 'Dark Ages', when there is little material evidence for direct Greek-Levantine contact (e.g. Morris 1992a: 127-9; Popham 1994: 33). Al Mina and the Syrian coast lie but *c.* 130 km from northern Cyprus. Cypriot marks on Mycenaean pottery suggest some direct Cypriot involvement in transporting Mycenaean wares to both Cyprus and the Levant (Hirschfeld 1992), and it has been suggested that the Levant received only those Mycenaean imports rejected by the first port-of-call, Cyprus (e.g. Gilmour 1992: 115,118). Certainly, in the Geometric period, as in the Mycenaean, wherever Greek imports are found in the Levant, there too is found Cypriot, and usually in much larger quantities. While this could indicate a role for Cypriots in the importation of Greek Geometric wares (although pottery of a Cypriot style is not necessarily all imported (p.19)), the interesting factor is surely the converse—why is Greek Geometric pottery in the Levant found at so very few places where Cypriot (or, for that matter, Phoenician-style) pottery is found? Nor can the parallel with the Late Bronze Age, when thousands of Mycenaean imports flooded the island, be pressed too far. Although Cyprus, and particularly Amathus on the Tyre route, was probably a staging post on East-West Aegean voyages, Iron Age Greek imports to the island were less numerous and less widely distributed than in the Bronze Age (p.44). They were certainly much less numerous than the quantities reaching Al Mina and the Amuq plain in the Geometric period, suggesting that there was no prior Cypriot selection of imports before ships reached coastal Syria. Further, the sort of luxury Eastern imports that reached Lefkandi do not seem to have been retained on the island in the way one might expect if it had played an active middleman role (Popham 1994: 28; Coldstream 1998a: 356).

Besides Euboea, there are other areas of Greece whose material records indicate contact with the Levant, notably Crete, the Dodecanese and Athens, the source of some imports and the likely home of Oriental craftsmen (e.g. Coldstream 1969; Popham 1994: 22; Snodgrass 1994a: 3).

Nonetheless, there are many indications that Euboea was the first region of mainland Greece to enjoy sustained post-Mycenaean overseas contact with the East:

1. Euboean pottery was the earliest post-Mycenaean Greek pottery imported to the Levant.

2. Euboean pottery was imported in the greatest quantity.

3. Imports from north Syria, Phoenicia and Cyprus appear at Lefkandi earlier than elsewhere in Greek lands, at *c.* 1000 BCE (Popham 1994: 14).

4. The quantity and range of such imports is greater than elsewhere in Greece, encompassing jewellery of gold, glass, amber, rock crystal; bronze and faience vessels; seals, scarabs and pottery (e.g. Popham 1994). Like the Greek pottery in the East, some of the Oriental imports—such as the tens of thousands of faience disc beads—do not have much prime value, and are routinely referred to as "trinkets" (e.g. Braun 1982: 5-6), echoing Homer's *'athurmata'* (*Od.* 15.416). But

some of them, like the grave goods in the Heroon, are spectacular.

5. Euboea betrays the first Greek knowledge of alphabetic script, and may have been the birthplace of early Greek Epic (West 1988; Powell 1991). Euboeo-Phoenician contact may have led to the adaptation of the Greek alphabet from Phoenicians (Ridgway 1994: 42).

6. The Lelantine War between Chalcis and Eretria, fought to control the fertile and clay-rich Lelantine plain, was the first war to involve (Eastern) states from beyond the mainland (Hdt 5.99; Thuc. 1.15.3).

7. "Ionians", among whom Euboeans are numbered, was from an early date Eastern nomenclature for "Greek" (Burkert 1992: 12-3).

For all these indications of early Euboean contact with the East, Snodgrass' sceptical archaeologist could conclude that there is no proof-positive that any Greek stepped beyond the Greek-speaking Aegean between the last major emigration to Cyprus in the eleventh century, and the foundation of Pithekoussai in the eighth (1994: 3). In theory, Levantines (be they Cypriots, Phoenicians or Aramaeans) could have played the major role in carrying whatever and whoever was transported between the two areas. The "initiative", a growing obsession in recent literature (e.g. Coldstream 1994; Crielaard 1996; Papadopoulos 1996: 159; *ibid.* 1997b: 192; *ibid.* 1998; Boardman 2001: 36), could have been Levantine. Residence of Levantines in Greek lands, including Euboea and Euboean Pithekoussai, as craftsmen and traders, *inter alia,* seems likely (e.g. Burkert 1992; Morris 1992a; Popham 1994: 22; Papadopoulos 1997b: 193).

But this strong Oriental infusion does not preclude active Greek involvement in overseas contact, and it seems most improbable that there was no active Euboean involvement at any point in the Geometric period:

1. Whatever resources Euboea offered Levantine visitors, they could probably have obtained them nearer home (Popham 1994: 30). In antiquity, Euboea was known for its grain, olives, vines, fish, horses and cattle (Sackett *et al.* 1966: 34, n.5). Assyrian sources indicate the involvement of Ionians (which could include Euboeans) in slave-raiding (p.21). Iron, copper and purple-producing molluscs could also have been important (Bakhuizen 1976; Morris 1992a: 139-41). The copper "bun" ingots, found off the Euboean coast near Kyme and dating to the middle of the 2nd millennium BCE, indicate that a trade in copper (perhaps recalled in the toponym Chalcis) had long antecedents (Sackett *et al.* 1966: 75-76, 109). Assyria, and so, presumably, its principal suppliers—the Phoenicians—were certainly interested in iron: 160 tons of it was unearthed in Sargon II's palace (Aubet 2001: 82). However, neither iron nor copper is found only in Euboea, nor, indeed, in Greece or the Aegean. Compared to the metal-rich areas of the Taurus and Anatolia (iron and copper), Cyprus (copper), Sardinia/Etruria/Elba (tin, copper, iron, lead) and the Far West (silver, gold, tin), Euboea must have presented

relatively slim pickings. Yet the extraordinary material wealth garnered from Eastern contacts seems out of all proportion to a role as a passive provider of goods available elsewhere.[145]

2. As early as the MPG period, a ceramic *koine* centred on Euboea had spread over the northern Sporades, much of the Cyclades and the Greek mainland from Boeotia to Thessaly (Coldstream 1998a: 355), suggesting early maritime activity.

3. The Euboeans' "venturous spirit" (Popham 1994: 33): a northward expansion to the Chalcidike peninsula may have occurred as early as the twelfth or eleventh centuries BCE (Snodgrass 1994a: 5-6; cf. Papadopoulos 1996), and Euboeans were the first post-Mycenaean Greeks to explore the West. Euboea is ναυςικλειτή (*Hymn. Hom. Ap.* I, 31, 219) (the Phoenicians, too, are famed for their ships: *Od.* 15.415). Crielaard has argued that seafaring (trading, raiding, exploration etc) was an inherent part of the Cypriot and Greek élite lifestyle (1999b: 191).

4. There is a virtual lacuna in Greek imports to the East in the SPGI-II period when Eastern imports to Greece continue unabated (Coldstream 1989: 92),[146] suggesting the existence of at least two separate trading circuits.

5. Euboean imports to the Levant cease around *c.* 700 BCE, when Euboean westward colonisation also ceases.[147] By contrast, Phoenician expansion to the West continues apace. Some have related this withdrawal from external contacts to the Lelantine War, which has been dated to the late eighth century (Boardman 1982b: 754-60).[148] The virtual absence of post-LG Euboean wares in the East, when coupled with an end to active Euboean settlement in the West (Thuc. 6. 3-5; Graham 1982: 97-109), points to an element of both phenomena depending on the active participation of Euboeans.

6. Later Greek authors recalled Euboea as the leading region in early Greek history (Austin (1968: 35-37) and Ridgway (1992: 16-7) have the relevant references).

7. Greek imports are found at very few of the sites where Cypriot and Phoenician imports are common: whoever was importing Cypriot or Phoenician wares to the Levant seems not to have been bringing much Greek.

8. Of the studied diagnostic material from Al Mina, Greek imports greatly outweigh both Phoenician and Cypriot imports in Levels 10-9: whoever was importing the Greek wares to the site seems not to have been bringing much Cypriot or Phoenician.[149]

9. There are some curious gaps in the roster of Greek Geometric imports at Al Mina and the other sites—there are no Cretan wares, for instance, although there were Syrian, Phoenician and Cypriot links with the island from the 9th century onwards (Boardman 2001: 36). Even Attica, where master jewellers from the East are believed to have settled (Coldstream 1995: 398), is comparatively poorly represented among the Al Mina (and wider Levantine) imports. In other words, if Easterners were solely responsible for the presence of Greek Geometric pottery in the East, we have to envisage them consciously selecting pottery from Euboea and consciously ignoring wares from the (in the case of the Phoenicians, very many) other places with which they were in contact. Euboean pottery is technically fine, and, aside from the impressive but few figured wares is, in a minimalist fashion, pleasantly decorated. But this huge over-representation of the ware surely demands another explanation, such as the involvement of Euboeans themselves.[150]

10. The hints of "market research", with Euboean potters being persuaded to produce a shape little coveted at home, but well-used in the Levant—the plate (Coldstream 1998b: 305), bearing the Euboean *leitmotiv* of PSCs.

In sum, the material evidence does not support efforts to entirely exclude from, or entirely credit with, active participation in cross-cultural exchange by any one of the groups whose involvement is suggested by that evidence. Indeed, modern preoccupations with accrediting one or other perceived ethnic or national group with maritime primacy, with all the competitiveness implied (e.g. Winter 1995: 254-5) may reflect contemporary more than ancient concerns. In the case of Homer, so often used to demonstrate Greek anti-Phoenicianism, the landed nobility whose viewpoint is reflected held in contempt professional merchants from all backgrounds (Boardman 2001: 39). Ethnic identity, which many moderns like to regard as comfortably defining, has been shown to be more fluid, dynamic and social in the ancient world than had been previously realised (e.g. Hall 1997), and

[145] Euboea, particularly Chalkis, does share with that other early colonising power, Corinth, an isthmic location, being towns where land and sea communications meet (Bakhuizen 1991: 33-34). Sherratt points to the position of Lefkandi on the Euripos, through which ships could have sailed from the precious metal sources of Eastern Attica to those of Chalidice and Thasos (1999: 181), whither Herodotus (6.47) reports that Phoenicians travelled in search of silver. Assyria did experience a shortage of silver *c.*800 BCE (Aubet 2001: 87), which the Phoenicians may have been anxious to alleviate from all available sources. In Sherratt's view, the metallic-looking Euboean pots were low-cost products 'piggy-backing' on the high-level transfer of valuables through the Euboean gulf. This proposal obviates the need to scratch around for suitable Euboean export material. However, little other Orientalia has been found along the proposed route (Popham 1994: 30), and it does not explain why Euboean interest overseas, East and West, suddenly abated *c.*700 BCE.

[146] The decline in Eastern imports to Lefkandi in the SPGIII period, when Euboean imports reached more Eastern sites than ever, cannot be interpreted in the same way, since the Lefkandi cemeteries, the principal context of the Eastern imports, ceased to be used during this period (Boardman 1990b: 179).

[147] A few SG Euboean wares trickled Eastwards, like (perhaps) the Tell Qiri dinos, and some Corinthianising kotylai at Al Mina (Descœudres 1978: 9-10, nos. 21-24).

[148] Other explanations offered for the cessation of Eastern contacts include the provincialisation of Cyprus in 709 BCE, and a re-orientation of trade routes to East Greece (e.g. Morris 1992a: 148).

[149] A few early non-Greek imports are known (e.g. Kearsley 1999: 116, n. 13).

[150] Boardman 2002 detects a difference in the distribution of Syrian goods westwards that follows not the Phoenician but the Greek sphere of influence.

ancient merchants, much like contemporary ones, may have regarded ethnic origins as irrelevant. On a similarly pragmatic level, Lefkandians—that is, those who inhabited Lefkandi—may have been just as dismayed about neighbouring Chalcidians benefiting from the fruit of overseas contact (and of the Lelantine plain) as they were about Levantines benefiting. Within the Euboean towns themselves, precisely who was benefiting and who was excluded from overseas contact may have been a source of tension (see further below).

But as far as the Greek mainland is concerned, the Euboeans were the first post-Mycenaean internationalists, able to build monumental structures and deposit Eastern exotica at a period when most Greeks were living in much poorer material conditions. From the perspective of Geometric Greece, emphasis on Euboea seems not unreasonable.

The beneficiaries of cross-cultural trade in Geometric Euboea

Whoever the agents were of the East-Greece trade, the distribution of Oriental imports in the cemeteries of Lefkandi clearly indicates the beneficiaries of this trade: virtually all such imports are concentrated in the Toumba cemetery (Higgins 1980: 219; Popham 1987: 76). Crielaard has shown that Orientalia are concentrated in the graves of those who could be characterised as 'élite' (1993: 140-1). The concentration of imports in the graves of the Lefkandian élite suggests that access to them was controlled by that élite, and particularly by those Toumba incumbents connected with the warrior and his consort buried in the MPG Heroon. This couple evidently inspired sufficient loyalty from, or had sufficient control over, their community (and perhaps others (Coldstream 1998a: 355)) not only to be buried with spectacular grave goods, including an antique Babylonian necklace (Popham 1994: 15), but also to be honoured with the first large post-Mycenaean building in Greek lands. The controversy as to the precise function of the structure (arguments summarised Popham (1993b: 99-101)) does not detract from the certainty that huge communal effort must have been dedicated to the honouring of this pair who are readily characterised, in the British psyche at least, as a royal couple. The whole cemetery has been characterised as 'royal' by the excavators (Popham et al. 1982: 247; Popham 1993: 99). Its warrior and horse burials support the hypothesis that this was the burial-ground of the aristocracy: the aristocracies of Eretria and Chalcis were known as *hippeis* (horsemen) and *hippobotai* (horse-breeders) (Popham et al. 1989: 123; Crielaard 1992/3: 236). Horses were prerequisites of such Greek (and Oriental) aristocratic activities as hunting and chariot warfare, and symbolised conspicuous consumption.

Social stratification seems to have emerged in LPG Lefkandi, with high status being expressed through elaborate burial rites and the deposition of Oriental imports. The inception of contacts with the East virtually coincides with the first evidence for social stratification in burial rites: the first Eastern imports to Lefkandi date to around 1000 BCE, the Heroon to around 950 BCE (Popham 1994: 14). The two events are chronologically, and may also be causally, linked: the honour of renewed contacts with the East (and the imports and

technological know-how they provided) would have enhanced the status of those who enjoyed such contacts. However trinket-like some of these imports may have been judged by the Phoenicians themselves, by Homer in more waspish mood, and by modern scholarship (p.57), it seems that the Orientalia, deposited as they were in wealthy graves, were valued by the Euboeans. Indeed, Crielaard suggests that they too were embedded in gift relations (1993: 142-143).

Warfare, internal power and external trade at SPGII Lefkandi are linked by Tomb no. 79 from the Toumba cemetery. The high status of the incumbent is suggested by the bronze cauldron in which the cremated remains were contained, reminiscent of the male buried in the Heroon. Warrior status is intimated by the iron objects: a 'killed' sword, spearheads, arrowheads and knives. An interest in trade is indicated by a possible weighing balance, stone weights, and an antique North Syrian cylinder seal (Popham and Lemos 1995). The Near Eastern connection is echoed in the Phoenician and Cypriot jugs, the likely boat-shaped earrings (*ibid.*, n. 7) and may be alluded to in the collection of six PSC plates: rare in their Euboean homeland, they were a popular form in the east. The debate over whether the deceased was ethnically Euboean (as Popham and Lemos have it), or Oriental (as Papadopoulos 1997b: 192) does not detract from the force of the equation between high status and Levantine contacts in SPG Lefkandi.

It seems that, within Euboea, the aristocracy controlled contacts with the East; at the very least, they controlled the fruits of that contact: the imports. Part of this control may have come via inter-marriage; Coldstream raises the possibility of the Heroon "queen" having Near Eastern kinship (1998: 355-7). Elite inter-marriage as a diplomatic mechanism is well-documented in the East. The emergence of social stratification, some permanence of élite political control (as in the long-lived Heroon-respecting Toumba cemetery), competition for basic resources (such as the Lelantine plain and the labour required to construct the Heroon) and increased demand for goods (such as Orientalia) are among the variables often linked to intensification in production and exchange (Knapp and Cherry 1994: 125).

Crielaard has argued that Euboean colonial expansion was controlled by the aristocracy (1993). Although the élite graves of Pithekoussai have yet to be found, the mortuary evidence from Cuma indicates the involvement of the élite in the colonial West (Ridgway 1992: 277; Coldstream 1998b: 309). One can certainly imagine a scenario whereby social stratification and the consequential differential access to basic resources, such as the Lelantine plain, benefited some elements of society to the extent that others, excluded by real and perceived injustices (Snodgrass 1994a: 2), felt compelled to establish themselves in foreign lands—one of the 'push' factors of the old 'causes of Greek colonisation' debate (e.g. Gwynn 1918).

Conclusions

Some contacts between the Greece and the Levant seem to have survived the calamities that befell the Mycenaean and much of the Levantine world around 1200 BCE. They are detectable in poetry, rituals, myth and archaeology, particularly in Cyprus and Crete (Morris 1992a: *passim, esp.* 110-124), although material evidence is slim between (by conventional dates) *c.*1200-*c.*1000 BCE. Levantine sites with Greek (?Argive and Euboean) imports which may date to the 11th century are Tell Afis and Tell Hadar. In addition, Babylon and Nineveh have reported SM finds. Eastern imports were percolating through to Lefkandi by 1000 BCE, and by the tenth century, Greek imports are reaching more Levantine sites. Euboea is beginning to enter the pan-Mediterranean networks of communication and trade. Crielaard casts Cyprus as a major force in maintaining an aristocratic Mediterranean-wide exchange system through the eleventh and tenth centuries BCE (1999b), and its intermediary role in ushering Greeks back into these networks may have been crucial.

But it is not until the SPGIII period (850-750 BCE) that the widest distribution of Greek imports to the Levant occurs, and not until the LG period (750-700 BCE) that the greatest quantity of imports occurs. By this time north Syria and particularly Al Mina are the most important findspots; the re-orientation of trade to the north Levant is probably related to the Assyrian provincialisation of that region in 738 BCE, as the Assyrians put imports arriving by sea on a more reliable footing, closer to the Assyrian heartland.

After the disappearance of the Euboeans and their pottery from the Eastern scene, Greek (mainly East Greek, then Corinthian and Athenian) pottery enjoys a much wider distribution and is proportionally more important at the sites where it is found. By this time, the imports are certainly commodities, imported *per se* and appreciated by a wide range of consumers as equal, and often superior, to the local ceramics. In the Geometric period, although the imports may well have been considered superior to some local products, their restricted distribution does not support the idea of their commodification at this early date, and they seem to have been part of an exchange network centred around central places, wherein most control over cross-cultural contacts was exercised.

Appendix

The many ceramic characters of Pithekoussai

Ceramics often form the major published class of evidence for Classical sites, particularly those with necropoleis or sanctuaries replete with finewares.

This Appendix aims to demonstrate, using a site which has a wide range of LG ceramic data from a wide range of contexts, how much context can affect data and, hence, 'historical' interpretation.

Finewares

Finewares have been the traditional focus of scholarly attention. The archaeologist's penchant for excavating and publishing them has often been translated, via both the positivist fallacy (Snodgrass 1980: 126) and the history of the study of Greek pottery (e.g. Vickers 1985: 122-6; 1985/6) into the historian's obsession with them, using finewares as evidence for many issues. As Pucci put it "the real battle between historians and archaeologists are fought over the economic significance of tablewares, not containers" (1983: 109). Economic links between sites have been postulated on the basis of fineware imports (e.g. Villard 1960), and tastes and patterns of production adjudged on the basis of the differential distribution of fineware forms (e.g. Boardman 1979; Osborne 1996).

The necropolis

The source of most of the fineware material at many sites. Table 11 shows the distribution of LG finewares from the Pithekoussai necropolis, by provenance and by form.[151]

Historical interpretation: the cosmopolitan emporion. Pithekoussai imports wares from all over the Mediterranean, including Rhodes (whence the KW material), Phoenicia, north Syria, and, in Greece, Corinth. Given this wealth of foreign contacts, it is perhaps not surprising that Pithekoussai

surrendered links with her mother country from a very early stage (fewer than 2% of pots come from Euboea). Despite Euboea's early interest in the Eastern Mediterranaean, and Pithekoussai's close proximity to areas of Phoenician activity (in Sardinia, for example), there is little contact with the East. The exception is the KW aryballoi, probably produced on Rhodes by Phoenicians or Cypriots.

The very high proportion of Corinthian wares may point to the existence of an *enoikismos* at the site.[152]

As for forms, aryballoi (which account for virtually all the KW imports) are by far the most commonly deposited shape, followed by oinochoai. Evidently mortuary rites centred around pouring wine and unguents. The colonists seem to have transported their motherland's dislike of plates. It is not so suprising that Pithekoussai shuns both kraters and amphorae; the canonical symposion was not transported to this site since it was an *emporion*, and not a full *apoikia*. This suggests that the settlers were not members of the Euboean aristocracy.

The necropolis sporadici

Pithekoussai has a second mortuary fineware assemblage: the '*sporadici*', clusters of burnt sherds, mainly of high quality (some from the Cesnola workshop) and including a number of kraters. Both these factors contrast with the ceramic depositions in the graves, and the *sporadici* have been associated with the cremations of the otherwise-invisible Pithekoussan aristocracy (Ridgway 1992: 50-1; Coldstream 1994: 82-3).

The forms and provenances of the *sporadici* are set out in Table 12 below.[153]

---

[151] Data from Ridgway 1982. Diminutives included in parent category, unless otherwise stated. Pieces dated to LGII-MPC have been equally divided; where this would have resulted in a half piece, the full piece has been included in LGII.

[152] Neeft has argued for the presence of resident Corinthian potters (1987: 59-65, 309).

[153] From Ridgway 1982. I have not included those sporadici listed under later periods although, since this appears to have been an early rite (idem 1992: 50), there are very few definitely later ones.

Table 11: Provenances and forms of LG finewares from the Pithekoussan necropolis

	Local	Euboean	Corinthian	Rhodian	KW[154]	Oriental	Phoenician	AM[155]	?	Imported ?	Total	%
krater	2	2	0	0	0	0	0	0	0	0	4	1
oinochoe	115	2	30	0	0	0	0	1	4	2	154	25
brocca	9	0	0	0	0	0	0	2	0	0	11	2
brocchetta	4	0	0	0	0	0	0	6	0	0	10	2
skyphos	26	0	15	0	0	0	0	0	0	0	41	7
kotyle	11	0	28	1	0	0	0	0	0	0	40	6
kyathos	0	0	4	0	0	0	0	0	0	0	4	1
kantharos	11	0	19	0	0	0	0	0	0	2	32	5
tazza	5	0	0	0	0	0	0	0	0	0	5	1
pyxis	1	0	2	0	0	0	0	0	0	0	3	0
coppetta	0	0	0	0	0	0	0	0	1	1	2	0
lekythos	20	2	0	0	2	0	3[156]	0	0	1	28	4
conical lekythos	23	0	1	0	0	0	0	5	0	1	30	5
scodella	9	0	0	0	0	0	0	0	0	0	9	1
plate	3	0	0	0	0	0	0	0	0	0	3	0
aryballos	77	5	70	0	80	8	0	0	0	0	240	39
poppatoio	2	0	0	0	0	0	1	0	0	0	3	0
hapax legomena	3	0	0	0	0	0	0	1	0	0	4	1
Total	321	11	169	1	82	8	4	15	5	7	623	
%	52	2	27	0	13	1	1	2	1	1		

Table 12: Provenances and forms of LG sporadici finewares from the Pithekoussan necropolis

	Local	Euboean	Corinthian	KW	Italian	Total	%
krater	8	2	0	0	0	10	12
skyphos	8	0	2	0	0	10	12
kotyle	20	1	9	0	0	30	35
kyathos	3	0	1	0	0	4	5
kantharos	1	0	0	0	0	1	1
pyxis	2	0	0	0	0	2	2
coppetta	1	0	0	0	0	1	1
lekythos	1	0	0	1	0	2	2
conical lekythos	15	0	5	0	0	20	24
aryballos	3	0	1	0	0	4	5
hapax legomena	0	0	0	0	1	1	1
Total	62	3	18	1	1	85	0
%	73	4	21	1	1		

[154] Kreis-und-Wellenband ("spaghetti-flasks"). Counted separately from Rhodian because, although probably produced on that island, its producers are likely to be Phoenician or Cypriot (Coldstream 1969; cf. Boardman 1994).

[155] Argive Monochrome.

[156] Probably Carthaginian (Ridgway 1999: 305).

Historical interpretation: the independent apoikia. From the scatter of sherds so far found, it is emerging that Pithekoussai was an insular site, with little overseas contact (only two sherds come from beyond the Corinthian or Euboean world). The vast majority of wares in use at the site are local. There does seem to be a special relationship with Corinth, pointing to the existence of a Corinthian enclave.

Most sherds relate to drinking, which must have been the major rite associated with burial.

The high quality of some of the wares, particularly kraters, and the sympotic range of forms, points to the presence of the Euboean élite at the site.

The settlement

The data from the settlement are of a much more general nature than those from the necropolis (Ridgway 1992: 89). Provenances are as follows:

Table 13: Provenances of LG finewares from the settlement at Pithekoussai

Provenances	%
Local	81
Euboean	3
Corinthian	16

There are also minute quantities of AM, Attic, Chiot, Cycladic, Etruscan and Phoenician wares.

The forms of the wares (excluding amphorae and kraters, which are common (Ridgway 1992: 88-9)) are as follows:[157]

Table 14: Functions of LG finewares from the settlement at Pithekoussai

Functions	%
Pourers	34
Drinkers	41
Eaters	25

Historical interpretation: the independent apoikia. From the tens of thousands of sherds found on the acropolis, it is clear that Pithekoussai was a very insular site. The high proportion of Corinthian wares may point to the existence of an *enoikismos*, or at least resident potters from Corinth. Although the Euboean ceramic style remained popular, the absence of imports from Euboea itself suggests that contact with the mother country was suspended from an early period.

This disassociation from the mother country is also suggested by the high proportion of vessels devoted to eating (i.e. plates, bowls and dishes), rare in Euboea itself. Could this be a reflection of older Euboean interest in the East, where plates and dishes are a very common form? Or does it reflect an Eastern presence at the site (Coldstream 1998b: 308): some of the locally-produced wares are based on Phoenician shapes (e.g. Buchner 1982b).

Coarsewares

Until recently such wares were rarely recorded, and are often excluded from consideration. At Pithekoussai "considerable" quantities of coarsewares were found, mainly local, but apparently related to later Etruscan and Italic domestic wares (Ridgway 1992: 89).

Trade amphorae

Trade amphorae, which may have formed the bulk of many ancient cargoes (Parker 1984: 102), are being used with increasing frequency as evidence for economic links between sites, particularly by Roman archaeologists (e.g. Peacock and Williams 1986). There are two contexts for transport amphorae at Pithekoussai—the necropolis and the settlement.

The necropolis

At Pithekoussai transport amphorae were re-used as *enchytrismoi*, containers for the corpses of babies. Ridgway (1982) details their forms as follows:

Table 15: Provenances of LG trade amphorae from the Pithekoussan necropolis

	Local	Euboean	Corinthian	Oriental[158]	Phoenician	Attic	Chiot	?.	Imported ?	Total
Qu.	69	1	2	7	5	5	1	8	15	113
%	61	1	2	6	4	4	1	7	13	

Historical interpretation: apoikia with Eastern contacts. Insofar as she has trading relations with the outside world, Pithekoussai's principal contacts are with the East, with north Syria and Phoenicia accounting for 10% of the amphorae. That such a high proportion of the amphorae deliberately selected for the burial of infants were eastern may point to the existence of a sizeable Levantine *enoikismos* at the site, burying their children in familiar wares. Indeed, even the locally-produced amphorae are seemingly based on Eastern prototypes (Ridgway 1992: 64). It seems that there was little interest in trade relations with Greece itself, particularly with Euboea.

---

[157] The total number of "pourers" is less than that shown in Table 6, since figures in Table 14 include all provenances, Table 6 just Euboean.

[158] Probably Carthaginian (Ridgway 1999: 305).

The settlement

The amphorae from the settlement have been extensively studied by di Sandro (1986),[159] and are represented in Table 16.

Table 16: Provenances of LG trade amphorae from the Pithekoussan settlement

	Local	Euboean	Corinthian	Oriental	Phoenician	Attic	Chiot	?	Total
Qu.	-	1	6	5	18	5	0	3	38
%		3	16	13	47	13	0	8	

Historical interpretation: emporion with Eastern contacts. Trading contacts were very strong with the East, particularly with Phoenicia, which provides almost 50% of the imports; a sizeable Phoenician trading enclave is likely. There were also healthy contacts with Attica and Corinth. By contrast, Pithekoussai seems to have lost contact with Euboea from an early period.

Conclusions

Which of these is the real Pithekoussai? In isolation, none: even without considering other aspects of material culture, the ceramic complexion of a site can differ greatly according to pottery types kept, and their context. Even at Pithekoussai we have no more than 5% of the necropolis material (Ridgway 1998: 301). It is clear that when comparing sites, the same type of pottery from the same context should be used. Rare is the site that bequeaths such universality of data to the archaeologist, and rare the excavator (or publisher) who is able or willing to present all the data in equally detailed format. Nonetheless, there is hope: the Web offers the chance of making data fully available quickly and cheaply.

---

[159] The table includes only those amphorae specifically said to be of LG date in di Sandro's catalogue. Local amphorae are excluded since, although some are catalogued, only the most significant goods (presumably imports) from the settlement dump were saved (Buchner in di Sandro 1986: 20).

Bibliographic Abbreviations

AA	Archäologischer Anzeiger
AAA	Annals of Archaeology and Anthropology.
AAS	Annales archéologiques (arabes) syriennes
AE	Arkhaiologiki Ephimeris
Acta Arch	Acta Archaeologica
AfO	Archiv für Orientforschung
AJ	The Antiquaries Journal
AJA	American Journal of Archaeology
AION (ArchStAnt)	Annali Instituto Orientale, Napoli: dell Archeologia e Storia Antica
AK	Antike Kunst
ANES	Journal of the Ancient Near Eastern Society of Columbia University
AR	Archaeological Reports
AS	Anatolian Studies
BAR I.S.	British Archaeological Reports, International Series
BCH	Bulletin de Correspondance Hellénique
BICS	Bulletin of the Institute of Classical Studies
BASOR	Bulletin of American Schools of Oriental Research
BSA	Annual of the British School at Athens
CAH III.1	Cambridge Ancient History. The Prehistory of the Balkans; and the Middle East and the Aegean world, tenth to eighth centuries B.C (eds Boardman, J.B. Edwards, I.E.S. Hammond, N.G.L. Sollberger, E, 1982). CUP
CAH III.3	Cambridge Ancient History. The Expansion of the Greek World, Eighth to Sixth Centuries B.C. (eds Boardman, J.B. and Hammond, N.G.L. 1982). CUP
CAH IV	Cambridge Ancient History. Persia, Greece and the Western Mediterranean c.525 to 479 B.C. (eds Boardman, J. Hammond, G.L. Lewis, D.M, and Ostwald, M. 1988). CUP
Céramique	La céramique grecque ou de tradition grecque au VIIIe siècle en Italie centrale et méridionale. Cahiers du centre Jean Bérard 3, 1982. Institut Français de Naples.
Contribution	Contribution à l'étude de la société et de la colonisation Eubéennes. Cahiers du centre Jean Bérard 2, 1975. Naples
DdA	Dialoghi di Archeologia

DHA	Dialogues d'histoire ancienne
IEJ	Israel Exploration Journal
JAOS	Journal of the American Oriental Society
JDAI	Jahrbuch des Deutschen Archäologischen Instituts
JHS	Journal of Hellenic Studies
JMA	Journal of Mediterranean Archaeology
JNES	Journal of Near Eastern Studies
NAR	Norwegian Archaeological Review
OpAth	Opuscula Atheniensa
OJA	Oxford Journal of Archaeology
PEQ	Palestine Exploration Quarterly
PP	La Parola del Passato
QDAP	Quarterly of the Department of Antiquities in Palestine
RA	Revue Archéologique
RDAC	Report of the Department of Antiquities, Cyprus
SCE	The Swedish Cyprus Expedition
SIMA	Studies in Mediterranaean Archaeology

Bibliography

Abbey, P. 2000, "Treaty ports & extraterritoriality in 1920s China" [Online], Available: http://www.geocities.com/Vienna/5048/TREATY01.html.

Albenda, B. 1969, "Expressions of Kingship in Assyrian Art" *ANES* 2.1: 41-52.

Andriomenou, A. 1983, "Geometriki kai upogeometriki keramiki ex Eretrias V", *AE*: 161-192.

Appadurai, A. 1986a, "Introduction: commodities and the politics of value" in *ibid.* 1986b (ed.): 3-63.
1986b, *The Social Life of Things. Commodities in cultural perspective.* CUP. Cambridge.

Arnold, R. 1957a, "A Port of Trade: Whydah on the Guinea Coast" in Polanyi *et al.* 1957: 154-176.
1957b, "Separation of Trade and Market: Great Market of Whydah", in Polanyi *et al.* 1957: 177-187.

Aubet, M.E. 2001, The Phoenicians and the West. Politics, Colonies and Trade. CUP.

Austin, M.M. 1968, Relations between Greece and the Levant in the Archaic Age. Ph.D. thesis, Cambridge.

Austin, M.M. and Vidal-Naquet, P. 1980, *Economic and Social History of Ancient Greece: AN INTRODUCTION.* Batsford Academic and Educational Ltd. London.

Avi-Yonah, M. and Stern, E. (eds), 1977, *Encyclopedia of Archaeological Excavations in the Holy Land III, JI - N.* OUP. Oxford.
1978, Encyclopedia of Archaeological Excavations in the Holy Land IV, O - Z. OUP.

Bakhuizen, S.C. 1976, *Chalcis-in-Euboea. Iron and Chalcidians Abroad.* Chalcidian Studies 3. EJ Brill. Leiden.
1991, Euboian colonisation: the non-archaeological evidence", in Fossey, J.M. 1991 (ed.): 25-36.

Balensi, J. 1985, "Revising Tell Abu Hawam", *BASOR* 257: 65-74.

Balmuth, M.S and Tykot, R.H. (eds), 1998, *Sardinian and Aegean chronology: towards the resolution of relative and absolute dating in the Mediterranean: proceedings of the International Colloquium 'Sardinian Stratigraphy and Mediterranean Chronology', Tufts University, Medford, Massachusetts, March 17-19, 1995.* Oxbow. Oxford.

Barnett, R.D. 1940, "The Greek Pottery", *AAA* 26: 98-130.
1975, *A Catalogue of the Nimrud Ivories, with other examples of Ancient Near Eastern Ivories in the British Museum* (first published 1957). The Trustees of the British Museum. British Museum Publications Ltd. London.
1985, "Assurbanipal's Feast", *Eretz Israel* 18: 1-6.

Barstad, H.M. 1984, *The Religious Polemics of Amos. Studies in the Preaching of Amos 2, 7B-8; 4, 1-13; 5, 1-27; 6, 4-7; 8,14.* Supplements to Vetus Testamentum 34. EJ Brill, Leiden.

Beer, C. 1984, "Quelques aspects des contacts de Chypres au VIIIe et VIIe siècles avant nôtre ère", *Opus* 3/2: 253-276.

Ben-Tor, A. and Portugali, Y. 1987, *Tell Qiri: A Village in the Jezreel Valley. Report of the Archaelogical Excavations 1975-1977.* Qedem. Monographs of the Institute of Archaeology 24. The Institute of Archaeology, The Hebrew University of Jerusalem.

Bérard, Cl. 1970, *L'Hérôon à la porte de l'ouest. Eretria III. Fouilles et Recherches.* Éditions Francke Berne. Lausanne.

Bernal, M. 1987, *Black Athena. The Afroasiatic Roots of Classical Civilization. Volume I: The Fabrication of Ancient Greece 1785-1985.* Free Association Books. London.

Biet Arieh, I. 1973, "The western quarters", in Aharoni, Y. 1973 (ed.), *Beer-Sheba I. Excavations at Tel Beer-Sheba, 1969-1971 Seasons.* Tell Aviv, Institute of Archaeology: 31-37.

Bikai, P.M. 1978, *The Pottery of Tyre.* Aris and Phillips Ltd. Warminster.
1987, *The Phoenician Pottery of Cyprus.* A.G. Leventis Foundation. Nicosia.
1990, "*Black Athena* and the Phoenicians", *JMA* 3.1.: 67-75.
1992, "The Phoenicians", Ward, WA and Sharp Joukowsky (eds): 132-141.

Birmingham, J. 1963, "The Chronology of Some Early and Middle Iron Age Cypriot Sites", *AJA* 67: 15-42.

Blackman, D. 2001, "Archaeology in Greece 2000-2001", *AR* 47:1-144.

Blakeway, A. 1932-1933, "Prolegomena to the Study of Greek Commerce with Italy, Sicily and France in the Eighth and Seventh Centuries B.C.", *BSA* 33: 170-208.

Boardman, J. 1952, "Pottery from Eretria", *BSA* 47: 1-48.
1956, "Chian and Naucratite" *BSA* 51: 55-62.
1959, "Greek Potters at Al Mina?" *AS* 9: 163-169.
1965, "Tarsus, Al Mina and Greek Chronology" *JHS* 85: 5-15.

1979, "The Athenian Pottery Trade" *Expedition* 21.4: 33-39.

1980, "The Late Geometric Pottery", with M.J.Price, in Popham M.R. and Sackett L.H. 1980a (eds): 57-80.

1982a, "An Inscribed Sherd from Al Mina", *OJA* 1.3: 365-367.

1982b, "The Islands", CAH III.1: 754-758.

1988a, "Trade in Greek Decorated Pottery", *OJA* 7.1: 27-33.

1988b, "The Trade Figures", *OJA* 7.3: 371-373.

1990a,"The Lyre Player Group of Seals. An Encore", *AA*: 1-17.

1990b, "Al Mina and History", *OJA* 9.2: 169-190.

1994, "Orientalia and Orientals on Ischia", in d'Agostino, B. and Ridgway, D. (eds): 95-100

1996, "Euboeans overseas: a question of identity", in Evely, D. *et al.* (eds): 155-160.

1999a, *The Greeks Overseas. Their Early Colonies and Trade* (fourth edition). Thames and Hudson. London.

1999b, "The Excavated History of Al Mina", in Tsetskhladze, G. *Ancient Greeks, West and East*. Brill: 135-162.

2001 "Aspects of Colonization", *BASOR* 322: 33-42.

2002a (forthcoming), "Greeks and Syria: Pots and People" Snodgrass A.M. and Tsetskhladze G. (eds) *Greek Settlements in the Eastern Mediterranean and the Black Sea*. BAR.

2002b, (forthcoming) "Al Mina: the Study of a Site", in Tsetskhladze, G (ed) *Ancient West and East*. Brill.

Bonatz, D. 1993, "Some considerations on the material culture of coastal Syria in the Iron Age". *EVO* XVI: 123-157.

1998, "Imported Pottery", in Cecchini, S.M. and Mazzoni, S. (eds), *Tell Afis, Siria: scavi sull'acropoli 1988-1992. Ricerche di archeologia del Vicino Oriente*. Pisa: 211-228.

Bott, E. 1987, "The Kava ceremonial as a dream structure", in Douglas, M. 1987 (ed.), *Constructive Drinking. Perspectives on Drink from Anthropology*. CUP and Éditions de la Maisons des Sciences de l'Homme. Cambridge and Paris: 182-204.

Bounni, A. and Lagarce, E and J. and Saliby, N. 1976, "Rapport préliminaire sur la première campagne de fouilles (1975) à Ibn Hani (Syrie)", *Syria* 53: 233-279.

1978, "Rapport préliminaire sur la deuxième campagne de fouilles (1976) à Ibn Hani (Syrie)," *Syria* 55: 233-301.

Braemer, F. 1982, *L'architecture domestique du Levant à l'âge du Fer*. Protohistoire du Levant. Éditions Recherche sur les civilisations. Cahier no. 8. A.D.P.F. Paris.

Braidwood, R.J. 1937, *Mounds in the Plain of Antioch. An Archaeological Survey*. The University of Chicago Oriental Institute Publications 48. The University of Chicago Press. Chicago.

1940, "Report on two sondages on the coast of Syria, south of Tartous" *Syria* 21: 183-221.

Branigan, K. 1981, "Minoan Colonialism," *BSA* 76: 23-35.

1984, "Minoan community colonies in the Aegean?" in Hägg, R. and Marinatos, N. 1984 (eds), *The Minoan Thalassocracy: Myth and Reality. Proceedings of the Third International Symposium at the Swedish Institute in Athens, 31 May-5 June, 1982*. Stockholm: 49-53.

Braun, T.F.R.G. 1982, The Greeks in the Near East", *CAH* III.3: 1-31.

Bresson, A. 1993, "Les cités grecques et leurs *emporia*", in Bresson, A. and Rouillard, P. (eds) 1993: 163-183.

and Rouillard, P. (eds), 1993, *L'emporion*. Publications du centre pierre. Paris.

Brinkman, J.A. 1982, "Babylonia c. 1000-748 B.C.", CAH III.1: 282-313.

Brodie, N.J. and Steele, L. 1986, "Cypriot Black-on-Red: towards a characterisation", *Archaeometry* 3.2: 263-278.

Brumfiel E.M. and Earle, T (eds), 1987, *Specialization, exchange and Complex Societies*. CUP.

Buchner, G. 1966, "Pithekoussai: oldest Greek colony in the West", *Expedition* 8 (summer): 4-12.

1971, "Recent work at Pithekoussai (Ischia) 1965-71," *AR* 17: 63-67.

1975, "Nuovi aspetti e problemi posti dagli scavi di Pitecusa con particolari considerazioni sulle oreficerie di stile orientalizzante antico", *Contribution:* 59-86.

1978, "Testimonianze epigrafiche semitiche dell'viii secolo a.C. a Pithekoussai" *PP* 33: 130-142.

1979, "Early Orientalizing: Aspects of the Euboean Connection", Ridgway, D. and Ridgway, F.R. 1979 (eds): 129-144.

1982a, "Pithekoussai (Ischia)", *Céramique:* 103-107.

1982b, "Die Beziehungen zwischen der euböischen Kolonie Pithekoussai auf der Insel Ischia und dem nordwestsemitischen Mittelmeerraum in der zweiten Hälfte des 8 Jhs.v.Chr.", in Niemeyer, H.G. 1982a (ed.): 277-306.

1983, "Pithekoussai: alcuni aspetti peculiari", *Annuario della Scuola Archeologica di Atene delle Missioni Italiene in Oriente LIX n.s. XLIII (1981), Atti del Convegno Internazionale. Grecia, Italia e Sicilia nell'VIII e VII secolo a.C I. Athens, 15-20 October 1979.* "L'erma" di Bretschneider. Roma: 263-272.

and Boardman, J. 1966, "Seals from Ischia and the Lyre-Player group", *JDAI* 81: 1-62.

Buhl, M-L. 1983, *Sukas VII. The Near Eastern Pottery and Objects of Other Materials from the Upper Strata*. Publications of the Carlsberg Expedition to Phoenicia 9. Copenhagen.

Burghardt, A.F. 1971, "A Hypothesis About Gateway Cities," *Annals of the Association of American Geographers* 61.2: 269-285.

Burkert, W. 1991, "Oriental Symposia: Contrasts and Parallels", in Slater, W.J. 1991 (ed.), *Dining in a Classical Context*. The University of Michigan Press. Ann Arbor: 7-24.

1992, *The Orientalizing Revolution. Near Eastern Influence on Greek Culture in the Early Archaic Age*. Harvard University Press. Cambridge, Massachusetts.

Campbell Thompson, R. and Hamilton, R.W. 1932, "The British Museum Excavations on the Temple of Ishtar at Nineveh, 1930-31", *AAA* 19: 55-116.

and Hutchinson, R.W. 1929, "The Excavations on the Temple of Nabû at Nineveh" *Archaeologia* 79: 103-148;

1931, "The Site of the Palace of Ashurnasirpal at Nineveh, excavated in 1929-30 on behalf of the British Museum", *AAA* 18: 79-112.

and Mallowan, M.E.L. 1933, "The British Museum Excavations at Nineveh, 1931-32", *AAA* 20: 71-186.

Carter, S. 1997, "THIASOS AND MARZEAH. Ancestor Cult in the Age of Homer" in Langdon, S. (ed.) *New Light on a Dark Age. Exploring the Culture of Geometric Greece.* University of Missouri Press. Columbia and London: 72-112.

Casson, L. 1989, *The Periplus Maris Erythraei. Text with Introduction, Translation and Commentary.* Princeton University Press.

Catling, H.W. 1973, "A Pendent Semicircle Skyphos from Cyprus and a Cypriot Imitation", *RDAC*: 179-185.
1993, "The Bronze Amphora and Burial Urn", in Popham, M.R. Calligas P.G. and Sackett, L.H. 1993 (eds): 81-96.
and Catling, E.A. 1980, "Objects in Bronze, Iron and Lead", in Popham M.R. and Sackett L.H. 1980a (eds): 231-264.

Catling, R.W.V. 1990, "Fabric, Technique and Paint" in Popham, M.R. Calligas, P.G. and Sackett, L.H. 1990 (eds): 9-12.
1996, "A tenth-century trade mark from Lefkandi", in Evely, D. *et al.* (eds): 126-132.
and Lemos, I.S.
1990a, "Analysis of the Pottery", in Popham, M.R. Calligas, P.G. and Sackett, L.H. 1990 (eds): 13-90.
1990b, "Conclusions", in *ibid.*: 91-96.
1990c, "Catalogue", in *ibid.*: 97-135.

Chapman, A. 1957, "Port of Trade Enclaves in Aztec and Mayan Civilisations" in Polanyi *et al.* 1957: 114-153.

Cherry, J.F. and Davis, J.L. 1982, "The Cyclades and the Greek Mainland in LC I: The Evidence of the Pottery" *AJA* 86: 333-341.

Ciafardoni, P. 1987, "Tell Afis: un insediamento del ferro nella regione di Idlib", *EVO X.2*: 5-23.

Clairmont, C. 1952, "Griechische Vasen in Baghdad", *Sumer* 8.1: 83-86.
1955, "Greek Pottery from the Near East", *Berytus* 11: 85-141.

Clarke, D.L. 1972, "Models and paradigms in contemporary archaeology", in *ibid.* 1972 (ed.), *Models in Archaeology.* Methuen & Co. London: 1-60.

Coldstream, J.N. 1968, *Greek Geometric Pottery. A Survey of Ten Local Styles and their Chronology.* Methuen and Co. Ltd. London.
1969, "The Phoenicians of Ialysos", *BICS* 16: 1-8.
1971, "The Cesnola Painter: a Change of Address", *BICS* 18: 1-15.
1979, "Geometric Skyphoi in Cyprus", *RDAC*: 255-269.
1977, *Geometric Greece.* Benn. London
1981, "Some peculiarities of the Euboean Geometric figured style", *ASAtene* 49: 241-249.
1982, "Greeks and Phoenicians in the Aegean", in Niemeyer, H.G. 1982a (ed.): 261-272.
1983, "Gift exchange in the eighth century B.C.", in Hägg R. 1983 (ed.): 201-206.
1985, "Archaeology in Cyprus, 1960-1985: The Geometric and Archaic periods", in Karageorghis, V. 1985 (ed.), *Archaeology in Cyprus 1960-1985.* A.G. Leventis Foundation. Nicosia: 47-59.
1986, "Kition and Amathus: Some Reflections on their Westward Links during the Iron Age", in Karageorghis, V. 1986 (ed.), *Acts of the Archaeological International Symposion"Cyprus Between the Orient and the Occident", Nicosia, 8-14 September 1985.* Department of Antiquities, Cyprus: 321-329.
1988, (with a note by P.M. Bikai), "Early Greek Pottery in Tyre and Cyprus: Some Preliminary Comparisons", *RDAC*, Part II: 35-44.
1989, "Early Greek Visitors to Cyprus and the Eastern Mediterranean", in Tatton-Brown, V. 1989 (ed.), *Cyprus and the East Mediterranean in the Iron Age. Proceedings of the Seventh British Museum Classical Colloquium, April 1988.* Trustees of the British Museum. London: 90-96.
1990, "Early Iron Age (Cypro-Geometric). The Rise of the Ancient Kingdoms c.1100-700 BC", in Hunt, D. 1990 (ed.), *Footprints in Cyprus, an illustrated history.* Trigraph. London: 47-64.
1993, "Mixed Marriages at the Frontiers of the Early Greek World", *OJA* 12.1: 89-107.
1994 "Pithekoussai, Cyprus and the Cesnola painter", in d'Agostino B. and Ridgway D. 1994 (eds): 77-86.
1995a, "Euboean Geometric Imports from the Acropolis of Pithekoussai" *BSA* 90: 251-267.
1995b, "The Rich Lady of the Areiopagus and her Contemporaries. A Tribute in Memory of Evelyn Lord Smithson", *Hesperia* 64.5: 391-403.
1996, "Knossos and Lefkandi: The Attic Connections" in Evely D. *et al.* (eds): 133-145.
1998a, "The first exchanges between Euboeans and Phoenicians: who took the initiative?" in Gitin, S. Mazar, A. and Stern, E. (eds): 353-360.
1998b, "Drinking and eating in Euboean Pithekoussai", in Bats, M. and d'Agostino, B. *EUBOICA. L'Eubea e la presenza euboica in Calcidica e in Occidente. Atti del Convegno Internazionale di Napoli 13-16 novembre 1996. Centre Jean Bérard. AION ArchStAnt Quaderno* 12: 303-310.
2001, "Greek Geometric Pottery in Italy and Cyprus: Contrasts and Comparisons", in Bonfante, L. and Karageorghis, V. *Italy and Cyprus in Antiquity 1500-450 BC.* Nicosia.

Collombier A-M. 1987. Céramique grecque et échanges en méditerranée orientale: chypre et la cote syro-phénicienne (fin VIIIe—fin IVe siècles av. J.-C.). *Studia Phoenicia V*: 239-248.

Connor, J.G. 1975, "Ceramics and Artifacts" in Sabloff J.A. and Rathje W.L. 1975a (eds): 114-135.

Cook, J.M. 1951, "A Geometric Amphora and Gold Band", *BSA* 46: 45-49.
1962, *The Greeks in Ionia and The East.* Thames and Hudson. London.

Cook, R.M. 1959, "Die Bedeutung der bemalten Keramik für den griechischen Handel", *JDAI* 74: 114-123.
1972, *Greek Painted Pottery* (first published 1960). Methuen and Co Ltd. London.

Coulton, J. 1993, "The Toumba Building: its architecture" in Popham, M.R. Calligas P.G. and Sackett, L.H. 1993 (eds): 33-70.

Courbin, P. 1957, "Une tombe géometrique d'Argos" *BCH* 81: 322-386.

1975, "Rapport sur la 4ème campagne de fouilles (1974) à Ras el Bassit", *AAS* 25: 59-71.

1976, "Rapport sur la 5ème campagne de fouilles (1975) à Ras El Bassit, *AAS* 26: 63-69.

1977, "Une pyxis géométrique argienne au Liban", *Berytus* 25: 147-157.

1977-8, "Rapport sur la sixième campagne de fouilles à Ras Bassit (Syrie), *AAS* 27-28: 29-40.

1978a, "A-t-on retrouve l'antique Posideion à Ras el Bassit?" *Archeologia* 116 (March): 48-62.

1978b, "La céramique de la Grèce de l'Est à Ras el Bassit", in *Les Céramiques de la Grèce de l'Est et leur diffusion en Occident. Colloques Internationaux du centre national de la recherche scientifique N.569 sciences humaines 6-9 Juillet 1976*. Centre Jean Bérard. Naples: 41-42.

1982, "Une assiette cycladique à Ras el-Bassit" in *Archéologie au Levant. Recueil à la mémoire de Roger SAIDAH*. Collection de la Maison de l'Orient Méditerranéen No.12. Série Archéologique 9: 193-204.

1983a, "Bassit, campagnes 1980-1982", *Syria* 60: 290-292.

1983b, "Bassit", *AAS* 33.2: 119-127.

1986, "Bassit", *Syria* 63: 175-220.

1990a, "Bassit-Posidaion in the Early Iron Age", in Descœudres, J-P. 1990 (ed.): 503-509.

1990b, "Fragments d'amphores protogéometriques grecques à Bassit", in Matthiae, P. and van Loon, M. and Weiss, H. 1990 (eds), *Resurrecting the Past. A Joint Tribute to Adnan Bounni*. Nederlands Historisch-Archeologisch Instituut te Istanbul. Instanbul: 49-64.

1993a, *Fouilles de Bassit. Tombes du Fer*. Éditions Recherche sur les Civilisations. Paris.

1993b, "Fragments d'amphores protogéometriques grecques à Bassit (Syrie)", *Hesperia* 62.1: 95-113.

Crielaard, J.P. 1992/3 "How the West was Won: Euboeans vs. Phoenicians", *Hamburger Beiträge zur Archäologie* 19/20: 235-260.

1993, "The Social Organisation of Euboean Trade with the Eastern Mediterranean during the 10th to 8th Centuries B.C.", *Pharos* I: 139-146.

1999a, "Early Iron Age Greek pottery in Cyprus and North Syria: a consumption-oriented approach" in Crielaard, J.P. *et al* 1999: 261-290.

1999b, "Surfing on the Mediterranean web: Cypriot long-distance communications during the eleventh and tenth centuries BC, in Karageorghis, V. and Stampolidis (eds) *Proceedings of the international symposium 'Eastern Mediterranean: Cyprus-Dodecanese-Crete, 16th-6th c. BC', Rethymnon, May 1997*, Rethymnon: 61-80.

and Stissi, V. and van Wijngaarden, G.J. (eds) 1999, *The Complex Past of Pottery. Production, Circulation and Consumption of Mycenaean and Greek Pottery (sixteenth to early fifth centuries BC. Proceedings of the ARCHON International conference, held in Amsterdam, 8-9 November 1996*. Gieben. Amsterdam

Cristofani, M. 1975, "Il 'dono' nell'Etruria arcaicà", *PP* 30: 132-152.

Crowfoot, J.W. and Crowfoot, G.M. and Kenyon, K.M. 1957, *The Objects from Samaria. Samaria-Sebaste* III. *Reports on the Work of the Joint Expedition in 1931-1933 and of the British Expedition in 1935*. Palestine Exploration Fund. London.

Culican, W. 1982a, "The repertoire of Phoenician pottery", in Niemeyer H.G. 1982a (ed.): 45-82.

1982b, contribution in *ibid.*: 28.

Cunliffe, B. 1987, "Cities, State, and the Transformation of Europe" in Cunliffe, B. (ed.), *Origins. The Roots of European Civilisation*: 81-107.

1988, *Greeks, Romans and Barbarians. Spheres of Interaction*. B.T. Batsford Ltd. London.

Curtin, P.D. 1975, *Economic Change in Precolonial Africa: Senegambia in the Era of the Slave Trade*. The University of Wisconsin Press.

1984, *Cross-cultural trade in world history*. CUP.

d'Agostino, B. and Ridgway, D. 1994 (eds), *APOIKIA: i più antichi insediamenti greci in occidente: funzioni e modi dell'organizzazione politica e sociale: scritti in onore di Giorgio Buchner (A.I.O.N. ns1)*. Naples.

Dalton, G. 1978, "Comments on Ports of Trade in Early Medieval Europe," *NAR* 11: 102-108.

Demetriou, A. 1989, *Cypro-Aegean Relations in the Early Iron Age. SIMA* 83.

Dentzer, J-M. 1971, "Aux origines de l'iconographie du banquet couché", *RA*: 215-258.

1982, *Le motif du banquet couché dans le proche-orient et le monde grec du VIIe au IVe siècle avant J.-C.* Bibliothèque des écoles françaises d'Athenes et de Rome, 246. École française de Rome. Palais Farnese.

Deriu. A. Buchner, G. and Ridgway, D. 1986, "Provenance and Firing Techniques of Geometric Pottery from Pithekoussai: A Mössbauer Investigation", *AION (ArchStAnt)* 8: 99-116.

Desborough, V.R. d'A. 1952, *ProtoGeometric Pottery*. The Clarendon Press. Oxford

1979, "A postscript to an appendix", in Karageorghis *et al.* 1979 (eds), *Studies presented in memory of Porphyrios Dikaios*. Lions club of Nicosia. Nicosia: 119-122.

1980, "The Dark Age Pottery (SM-SPGIII) from Settlement and Cemeteries", in Popham M.R. and Sackett L.H. 1980a (eds): 281-354.

with Dickinson, O.T.P.K. 1980, "The Protogeometric and Sub-Protogeometric Pottery", in Popham M.R. and Sackett L.H. 1980a (eds): 27-56.

Descœudres, J.-P. 1978, "Euboeans in Australia. Some Observations on the Imitations of Corinthian Kotylai Made in Eretria and Found in Al Mina", in *Eretria VI. Fouilles et Recherches*. Éditions Franke Berne. Lausanne: 7-19.

1990, (ed.), *Greek Colonists and Native Populations. Proceedings of the First Australian Congress of Classical Archaeology held in honour of Emeritus Professor A.D. Trendall. Sydney 9-14 July 1985*. Clarendon Press. Oxford.

Deubner, O. 1957, "Die griechischen Scherben von Babylon", in Wetzel, F. Schmidt, E. and Mallwitz, A. 1957 (eds), *Das Babylon der Spätzeit. Ausgrabungen der Deutschen Orient-Gesellschaft in Babylon 8*. Verlag Gebr. Mann. Berlin: 51-58.

de Vries, K. 1977, "Attic Pottery in the Achaemenid Empire", *AJA* 1977: 544-548.

Dikaios, P. 1936-1937, "An Iron Age Painted Amphora in the Cyprus Museum", *BSA* 37: 56-72.

Donley, L.W. 1982, "House Power: Swahili space and symbolic markers" in Hodder, I. (ed.), *Symbolic and Structural Archaeology.* CUP: 63-73.

Dothan, T. 1982, *The Philistines and their material culture.* Yale University Press. New Haven and London.

Doumet, Cl. 1982, "Les tombes IV et V de Rachidieh", *Annales d'Histoire et d'Archéologie* 1: 89-135.
and Kawkabani, I. 1991, "Les tombes de Rachidieh: remarques sur les contacts internationaux et le commerce phenicien au 8ème siècle av. J.-C.", *Communications au 3eme Congrès des Etudes Phéniciennes et Puniques, Tunis, 11-16 Novembre*: 1-14.

Duchêne, H. 1993, "Délos, réalités portuaires et emporion", in Bresson, A. and Rouillard, P. (eds) 1993: 113-125.

Dunbabin, T.J. 1957, *The Greeks and Their Eastern Neighbours. Studies in the Relations between Greece and the Countries of the Near East in the Eighth and Seventh Centuries B.C.* (ed. Boardman, J.). The Society for the Promotion of Hellenic Studies. London.
1968, *The Western Greeks. The History of Sicily and South Italy from the Foundation of the Greek Colonies to 480 B.C.* The Clarendon Press. Oxford.

Dyson, S. 1981, "A Classical Archaeologist's Response to the "New Archaeology"" *BASOR* 242: 7-13.
1993, "From New to New Age Archaeology: Archaeological Theory and Classical Archaeology—A 1990s Perspective", *AJA* 97.2: 195-206.

Edwards, I.E.J. 1982, "Egypt: from the Twenty-second to the Twenty-fourth Dynasty", *CAH* III.1: 534-581.

Elat, M. 1978, "The Economic Relations of the Neo-Assyrian Empire with Egypt", *Journal of the American Oriental Society* 98: 20-34.

Elayi, J. 1987, "Al-Mina sur l'Oronte à l'époque perse", in Lipínski, E. 1987 (ed.), *Phoenicia and The East Mediterranaean in the First Millennium B.C. Proceedings of the Conference held in Leuven from the 14th to the 16th of November 1985. Studia Phoenicia 5.* Orientalia Lovaniensia. Analecta 22. Uitgeverij Peeters. Leuven: 249-266.

Emre, K. 1963, "The pottery of the Assyrian colony period according to the building levels of the Kanis Kârum", *Anatolia* 7: 87-99.

Eph'al, I. and Naveh, J. 1989, "Hazael's Booty Inscriptions" *IEJ* 39.3: 192-202.

Evely, D. et al (eds), 1996, *Minotaur and centaur. Studies in the archaeology of Crete and Euboea presented to M.R. Popham (BAR I.S 638).* Oxford

Fagerström, K. 1988, *Greek Iron Age Architecture. Developments through Changing Times. SIMA 81.* Paul Åströms Förlag. Göteborg.

Faraone, C.A. 1993, "Molten wax, spilt wine and mutilated animals: sympathetic magic in near eastern and early Greek oath ceremonies", *JHS* 113: 60-80.

Figueira, T.J. 1984, "Karl Polanyi and Ancient Trade: The Port of Trade", *The Ancient World* 10.1-2: 15-30.

Finley, M.I. 1962, *"Classical Greece" in Trade and Politics in the Ancient World. Second International Conference of Economic History, Aix-en-Provence, Volume* 1. Montana & Co. Paris, La Haye: 11-35.
1979, *The Bucher-Meyer controversy.* Arno Press. New York.
1999, *The World of Odysseus* (first published 1956). Pimlico. London.

Forrest, W.G.G. 1982, "Central Greece and Thessaly", *CAH* III.3: 286-320.

Fossey, J.M. 1991 (ed.), *Proceedings of the First International Congress on the Hellenic Diaspora from Antiquity to Modern Times 1 (From Antiquity to 1453).* McGill University Monographs in Classical Archaeology and History. Gieben. Amsterdam.

Francis, E.D. and Vickers, M.E. 1983, ""Ivory Tusks" from Al Mina", *OJA* 2: 249-251.
1985, "Greek Geometric Pottery at Hama and its implications for Near Eastern Chronology", *Levant* 17: 131-138.

Franken, H.J. 1984, "Why did attempts to imitate Greek pottery fail in the Near East?" in Brijder H.A.J. 1984 (ed.) *Ancient Greek and Related Pottery. Proceedings of the International Vase Symposium in Amsterdam, 12-15 April 1984.* Allard Pierson Series 5. Amsterdam: 9-11.

Frankenstein, S. 1979, "The Phoenicians in the Far West: A Function of Neo-Assyrian Imperialism", in Larsen, M.T. 1979 (ed.): 263-294.

Frederikson, M. 1979, "The Etruscans in Campania" in Ridgway R. and Ridgway S.R. 1979 (eds): 277-311.

Freidel, D.A. and Sabloff, J.A. 1984, *Cozumel: Late Maya Settlement Patterns.* London.

Fugmann, E. 1958, *Hama II.I. Fouilles et recherches 1931-1938. L'architecture des périodes pré-Hellénistiques.* Copenhagen.

Gale, N.H. 1991 (ed.), *Bronze Age Trade in the Mediterranean. Papers presented at the Conference held at Rewley House, Oxford, in December 1989. SIMA 90.*

Garbini, G. 1978, "Un iscrizione aramaica a Ischia", *PP* 33: 143-150.

Gelb, I.J. 1939, *Hittite Hieroglyphic Monuments.* Oriental Institute Publications 45. Universtity of Chicago Press. Chicago.

Gilboa, A. 1989, New Finds at Tel Dor and the Beginning of Cypro-Geometric Pottery Imports to Palestine", *IEJ* 39: 204-218.

Gill, D.W.J. 1987, "METRU.MENECE: an Etruscan painted inscription on a mid-5th-century BC red-figure cup from Populonia", *Antiquity* 61: 82-87.
1988 "'Trade in Greek decorated pottery'": some corrections", *OJA.* 7.3: 369-70.
1989, Silver Anchors and Cargoes of Oil: Some Observations on Phoenician Trade in the Western Mediterranean" *PBSR*: 1-12.

Gilmour, G. 1992, "Mycenaean IIIA and IIIB pottery in the Levant and Cyprus", *RDAC*: 113-128.

Gitin, S. 1989, "Tell Miqne-Ekron: A Type Site for the Inner Coastal Plain in the Iron Age II Period", *Annual of the American School of Oriental Research* 49.

Gitin, S. Mazar A. and Stern, E. 1998 (eds), *Mediterranean peoples in transition. Thirteenth to early tenth century BCE. Papers of the first international symposium held by the Philip and Muriel Berman Center for Biblical archaeology, Jerusalem, April 1995. In honour of Professor T. Dothan.* Jerusalem.

Gjerstad, E. 1948, *The Swedish Cyprus Expedition IV.2. The Cypro-Geometric, Cypro-Archaic, and Cypro-Classical Periods.* Stockholm.

1974, "The Stratification of Al Mina (Syria) and Its Chronological Evidence," *Acta Archaeologica* 45: 107-123.

1977, "Pottery from various parts of Cyprus", in *ibid.* 1977 (ed.), *Greek Geometric and Archaic Pottery found in Cyprus. Opath* 4 XXVI. Paul Åströms Förlag: 23-59.

Gordon, C.H. 1962, *Before the Bible. The Common Background of Greek and Hebrew Civilisations.* Collins. London.

Graham, A.J. 1982, "The colonial expansion of Greece", *CAH* III.1: 83-162.

1983, *Colony and Mother City in Ancient Greece* (first published 1964). Ares Publishers, Inc. Chicago.

1986, "The Historical Interpretation of Al Mina", *DHA* 12: 51-65.

Grayson, A.K. 1972, *Assyrian Royal Inscriptions. Volume I. From the Beginning to Ashur-resha-ishi I. Records of the Ancient Near East.* Otto Harrassowitz. Wiesbaden.

1976, *Assyrian Royal Inscriptions. Volume II. From Tiglath-Pileser I to Ashur-nasir-apli II. Records of the Ancient Near East.* Otto Harrassowitz. Wiesbaden.

1982, "Assyria: Ashur-dan II to Ashur-Nirari V (934-745 B.C.)," *CAH* III.1: 238-281.

Guzzo Amadasi, M.G. 1977, "Iscrizioni semitiche di nord-ovest in contesti greci e italici (x-vii sec. a.C.)", *DdA* 5.2: 13-27.

Gwynn, A, 1918, "The character of Greek colonisation", *JHS* 38: 88-123.

Hägg, R. 1983 (ed.), *The Greek Renaissance of the Eighth Century B.C. : Tradition and Innovation. Proceedings of the Second International Symposium at the Swedish Institute in Athens, 1-5 June, 1981.* Paul Åströms Förlag. Stockholm.

Haines, R.C. 1971, *Excavations in the Plain of Antioch II. The Structural Remains of the Later Phases. Chatal Hüyük, Tell al-Judaidah, and Tell Ta'yinat. Oriental Institute Publications* 95. The University of Chicago Press.

Hall, J.M. 1997, *Ethnic Identity in Greek Antiquity.* CUP.

Hamilton, R.W. 1932, Review, *JHS* 52: 129-130.

1935, "Excavations at Tell Abu Hawam", *QDAP* 4: 1-69.

Hanfmann, G.M.A. 1956, "On Some Eastern Greek Wares Found at Tarsus", in Weinberg, S.S. 1956 (ed.), *The Aegean and the Near East.* Studies Presented to Hetty Goldman on the Occasion of her seventy-fifth Birthday. J.J Augustin, New York: 165-184.

1963, "The Iron Age Pottery of Tarsus", in Goldman, H. 1963 (ed.), *Excavations at Gözlü Kule, Tarsus. Volume III. The Iron Age: Text.* Princeton University Press: 18-332.

Harrison, T.P. 2001, "Tell Ta'yinat and the Kingdom of Unqi", in Daviau, PMM, Wevers, JM and Weigl, M (eds) *The world of the Aramaeans: Biblical Studies in honour of Paul-Eugène Dion. Journal for the Study of the Old Testament, Supplement Series* 324. Sheffield Academic Press: 115-132.

Hawkins, J.D. 1972-1975, "Hamath", in Edzard, D.O. 1972-1975 (ed.), *Reallexicon de Assyriologie und Vorderasicitischen Archäologie* 4. Walter de Gruyter. Berlin, New York: 67-70.

1974, "Assyrians and Hittites", *IRAQ* 36: 67-83.

1982, "The Neo-Hittite states in Syria and Anatolia", *CAH* III.1: 372-441.

1987-1990, "Luhuti", in Edzard, D.O. 1987-1990 (ed.), *Reallexicon de Assyriologie und Vorderasicitischen Archäologie* 7. Walter de Gruyter. Berlin, New York: 159-161.

Heidel, A. 1946, *The Gilgamesh Epic and Old Testament Parallels.* The University of Chicago Press.

Helms, P.R. 1980, *"Greeks" in the Neo-Assyrian Levant and "Assyria" in Early Greek Writers.* Unpublished Ph.D thesis, University of Pennsylvania.

Herman, G. 1989, *Ritualised Friendship and the Greek City* (first published 1987). CUP.

Herrera, M.D. and Balensi, J. 1986, "More about the Greek Geometric Pottery at Tell Abu Hawam", *Levant* 18: 169-171.

Herscher, E. 1975, "The Imported Pottery", in Pritchard, J.B. (ed.) 1975: 85-96.

Heurtley, W.A. 1935, "Note on Fragments of Two Thessalian Proto-Geometric Vases Found at Tell Abu Hawam", *QDAP* 4: 181.

Higgins, R.A. 1980, "The Jewellery" in Popham M.R. and Sackett L.H. (eds) 1980a: 217-225.

Hind, J.G.F. 1969, *The Greek Colonisation of the Black Sea Area in the Archaic and Classical Periods.* Unpublished Ph.D thesis, Cambridge.

Hirschfeld, N. 1992, "Cypriot marks on Mycenaean pottery" in J.P. Olivier (ed) *Mykenaika. Actes du IXᵉ colloque international sur les texts mycéniens at égéens organisé par le centre de l'Antiquité grecque et romaine de la fondation Hellénique des Recherches Scientifiques et l'Ecole francaise d'Athenes, octobre 1990 (BCH Suppl. XXV):* Athens & Paris 315-19

Hodges, R. 1978a, "Ports of Trade in Early Medieval Europe," *NAR* 11: 97-101.

1978b, "Reply to Comments", *NAR* 11: 114-117.

1982, *Dark Age Economics: The Origins of Towns and Trade A.D. 600-1000.* Duckworth. London.

1988, *Primitive and Peasant Markets.* Basil Blackwell. Oxford.

Hodos, T. 2000, "Kinet Höyük and Al Mina: New Views on Old Relationships" in Tsetskhladze, G.R. Prag, A.J.N.W. and Snodgrass, A.M. (eds): 145-152.

Honeyman, A.M. 1939, "The Pottery Vessels of the Old Testament" *PEQ*: 76-90.

Hood, S. 1951, "Excavations at Tabara el Akrad", *AS* 1: 113-147.

Hrouda, B. 1962, *Tell Halaf IV: Die Kleinfunde aus historischer Zeit* (series ed. M.F. von Oppenheim). Walter de Gruyter & Co. Berlin.

Humphreys, S.C. 1965, "Il commercio in quanto motivo della colonizzazione Greca dell'Italia e della Sicilia," *Rivista Storica Italiana* 72: 421-433.

    1969, "History, Economics and Anthropology: The Work of Karl Polanyi," *History and Theory* 8: 165-212.

    1978, *Anthropology and the Greeks*. Routledge and Kegan Paul. London.

Isserlin, B.S.J. 1973, "Some Common Features in Phoenician/ Punic Town Planning", *Rivista di Studi Fenici* 1.1: 135-152.

    and Plat Taylor, Du J. 1974, *Motya. A Phoenician and Carthaginian City in Sicily. A report of the excavations undertaken during the years 1961-65 on behalf of the University of Leeds, The Institute of Archaeology of London University, and Fairleigh Dickinson University, New Jersey. Volume I. Fieldwork and Excavation.* EJ Brill. Leiden.

James, P. in collaboration with Thorpe I.J. Kokkinos, N. Morkot, R. and Frankish, J. 1991, *Centuries of Darkness. A challenge to the conventional chronology of Old World archaeology*. Jonathon Cape. London.

Johnston, A.W. 1979, *Trademarks on Greek Vases*. Aris and Phillips. Warminster.

    1983, "The extent and use of literacy: the archaeological evidence" in Hägg R. 1983 (ed.): 63-68.

    and Andriomenou, A. 1989, "A geometric graffito from Eretria" *BSA* 84: 217-220.

    and Jones, R.E. 1978, "The 'SOS' Amphora", *BSA* 73: 103-141.

Jones, R.E. 1986, *Greek and Cypriot Pottery. A Review of Scientific Studies*. Fitch Laboratory Occasional Paper 1. The British School at Athens. Athens.

Karageorghis, V. 1963, "Une tombe de guerrier à Palaeopaphos", *BCH* 87: 265-300.

    1968, "Chronique des fouilles et découvertes archéologiques à Chypre en 1967", *BCH* 92: 261-358.

    1982, "Cyprus", *CAH* III.1: 511-533.

Katzenstein, H.J. 1973, *History of Tyre*. The Shocken Institute for Jewish Research of the Jewish Theological Seminary of America. Jerusalem.

Kearsley, R. 1989, *The pendent semi-circle skyphos. A study of its development and chronology and an examination of it as evidence for Euboean activity at Al Mina*. Institute of Classical Studies, Bulletin Supplement 44. London.

    1995, "The Greek Geometric Wares from Al Mina Levels 10-8 and Associated Pottery", *Mediterranean Archaeology* 8: 7-81.

    1999, "Greeks Overseas in the 8th Century BC: Euboeans, Al Mina and Assyrian Imperialism", in Tsetskhladze, G. 1999: 109-134.

Kelso, J.L. 1948, "The Ceramic Vocabulary of the Old Testament", *BASOR Supplementary Studies* 5-6.

Kessler, K. 1975-1976, "Die Anzahl der assyrischen Provinzen des Jahres 738 v. Chr. in Nordsyrien", *Die Welt des Orients* 8.1: 49-63.

Kestemont, G. 1985, "Les phéniciennes en Syrie du Nord" in Lipínski, E. and Gubel, E. 1985 (eds) *Studia Phoenicia III. Phoenicia and its Neighbours. Proceedings of the Colloquium held on the 9th and 10th of December 1983 at the "Vrije Universiteit Brussel" in co-operation with the "Centrum voor Myceense en Archaïsch-Grieshe Cultuur"*. Uitgeverij Peeters. Leuven: 135-149.

Kilian, K. 1990, "Mycenaean colonization: norm and variety" in Descœudres, J.P. (ed.), 1990: 445-467.

Kingsley, S. 2002, "Medieval London mikveh", *Minerva 13.1*: 7.

Klein, J. 1972, "A Greek metalworking quarter—eighth century excavations on Ischia", *Expedition* 14.4 (winter): 34-39.

Kochavi, M. 1988-1989, "Land of Geshur—1988. Tel Hadar", *Excavations and Surveys in Israel* 7-8: 11-112.

    1989, "The Land of Geshur Project: Regional Archaeology of the Southern Golan (1987-1988 seasons), *IEJ* 39: 1-17.

    1991, "The Land of Geshur Project 1989-1990. Tel Hadar", *IEJ* 41: 181-182.

    1992, "Some Connections between the Aegean and the Levant in the Second Millennium BC: A View from the East", in Kopcke, G. and Tokumaru, I. 1992 (eds): 7-15.

    1998, "The eleventh century BCE tripartite pillar building at Tel Hadar" in Gitin, S. Mazar, A. and Stern, E. (eds): 468-478.

Koehl, B. 1985, *Sarepta III: The Imported Bronze and Iron Age Wares from Area II,X*. Publications de l'Université Libanaise Section des Études Archeologiques II. Beirut. Librarie Orientale.

Kopcke, G. 2002, "1000 BCE ? 900 BCE ? A Greek Vase from Lake Galilee", in Ehrenberg, E. ed. *Leaving No Stones Unturned. Essays on the Ancient Near East and Egypt in Honor of Donald P. Hansen*. Eisenbrauns. Winona Lake, Ind.: 109-117.

    and Tokumaru, I. (eds), 1992, *Greece between East and West: 10th-8th Centuries BC. Papers of the Meeting at the Institute of Fine Arts, New York University, March 15-16th, 1990*. Verlag Philipp von Zabern. Mainz.

Kopytoff, I. 1986, "The cultural biography of things: Commoditisation as process" in Appadurai, A. 1986b (ed.): 64-91.

Kantor, H.J. 1962, "A bronze plaque with relief decoration from Tell Tainat", *JNES* 21: 93-117.

Kyrieleis H. 1988, "Ein altorientalischer Pferdeschmuck aus dem Heraion von Samos", *Mitteilungen des Deutschen Archäologischen Instituts, Athenische Abteilung* 103: 37-75.

Larsen, M.T. 1979 (ed.), *Power and Propaganda. A Symposium on Ancient Empires*. Mesopotamia. Copenhagen Studies in Assyriology 7. Akademisk Forlag. Copenhagen.

Layard, A.H. 1849, *Nineveh and Its Remains: with an Account of a Visit to the Chaldean Christians of Kurdistan, and the*

Yezidis or Devil-worshippers; and an Enquiry into the Manners and Arts of the Ancient Assyrians. John Murray. London.

Leonard, A. 1981 "Considerations of Morphological Variation in the Mycenaean Pottery from the South Eastern Mediterranean" *BASOR* 241: 87-101

1983, "The Distribution and Intensity of Mycenaean Commercial Contacts in the South Eastern Mediterranean", *AJA* 93: 242-3.

Leeds, A. 1961, "The Port of Trade in Pre-European India as an Ecological and Evolutionary Type", in Garfield, V.E. 1961 (ed.), *AES Proceedings of the 1961 Annual Spring Meeting of the American Ethnological Society:* 26-48.

Lehmann, G. 1996, *Untersuchungen zur späten Eisenzeit in Syrien und Libanon. Stratigraphie und Keramikformen zwischen ca. 720 bis 300 v. Chr. Altertumskunde des Vorderen Orients.* Bd. 5. Münster. Ugarit-Verlag.

1997, "Al Mina and the East: Syrian and Phoenician Pottery Finds and their Implications", Paper presented at *21ˢᵗ British Museum Classical Colloquium: The Greeks in the East.* December 1997.

1998, "Trends in the Local Pottery Development of the Late Iron Age and Persian Period in Syria and Lebanon, ca. 700 to 300 B.C.", *BASOR* 311: 7-37.

forthcoming, "Al Mina and the East: A Report on Research in Progress", in Villing A. (ed.), The Greeks in the East. Proceedings of the 21st British Museum Classical Colloquium 9th-10th December 1999.

Lemos, I. 1990, *Regional Characteristics in the ProtoGeometric Period and its Implications.* Unpublished D. Phil. dissertation, Oxford.

and Hatcher, H. 1991, "Early Greek vases in Cyprus: Euboea and Attica", *OJA* 10.2: 197-208.

Lichtenstein, M. 1968, "The Banquet Motif in Keret and in Proverbs 9", *ANES* 1: 19-31.

Liddy, D.J. 1996, "A chemical study of decorated Iron Age pottery", in Coldstream, J.N. and Catling, H.W. *Knossos North Cemetery* II. London: 481-514.

Liverani, M. 1991, "The Trade Network of Tyre according to Ezek. 27", in Cogan, M. and Eph'al, I. (eds) *Ah, Assyria...Studies in Assyrian History Presented to H. Tadmor.* Jerusalem: 65-79.

1992, *Studies on the Annals of Ashurnasirpal II 2: Topographical Analysis.* Università di Roma "La Sapienza" Dipartimento de Scienze storiche, archeologiche e antropologiche dell'Antichità. Quaderni di Geografica Storica 4. Roma.

Luckenbill, D.D, 1926, *Ancient Records of Assyria and Babylonia. Volume I. Historical Records of Assyria from the Earliest Times to Sargon.* The University of Chicago Press.

1927, *Ancient Records of Assyria and Babylonia. Volume II. Historical Records of Assyria from Sargon to the End.* The University of Chicago Press.

Luke, J. 1994a, *The nature of Greek contacts with the Levant in the Geometric period (with particular reference to the ceramic evidence).* Ph. D Thesis. Cambridge.

1994b, "The Krater, Krátos and the Polis", *Greece and Rome* xli.1: 23-32.

Lund, J. 1986, *Sukas VIII. The Habitation Quarters.* Publications of the Carlsberg Expedition to Phoenicia 10. Det Kongelige Danske Videnskabernes Selskab. Historisk-filosofiske skrifter 12. Munksgaard. Copenhagen.

Malinowski, B. 1922, *Argonauts of the Western Pacific. An Account of Native Enterprise and Adventure on the Archipelagoes of Melanesia, New Guinea.* Routledge and Kegan Paul Ltd. London.

Mallowan, M.E.L. 1972, "Foreword" in Kinnier Wilson, J.V. *The Nimrud Wine Lists. A study of men and administration at the Assyrian capital in the Eighth Century, B.C.* British School of Archaeology in Iraq.

1966, *Nimrud and its Remains.* Collins. London.

Manhattan History Tour, 2000. Available: http://tlc.discovery.com/tlcpages/newyork/1626.html

Markoe G. 1985, *Phoenician Bronze and Silver Bowls from Cyprus and the Mediterranean.* University of California Publications: Classical Studies 26. University of California Press. California.

Martin, R. 1973, "Rapports entre les structures urbaines et les modes de division et d'exploitation du territoire", in Finley, M.I. 1973 (ed.), *Problèmes de la terre en Grèce ancienne.* Civilisations et Sociétés 33. Mouton et Co. Paris-La Haye: 97-112.

Matthers J. *et al.* 1983, "Black-on-Red Ware in the Levant: A Neutron Activation Analysis Study", *Journal of Archaeological Science* 10: 369-382.

Mauss, M. 1990, *The Gift: The form and reason for exchange in archaic societies.* Translated by W.D. Halls (first published in French, 1925). Routledge. London.

May, H.G. 1935, *Material Remains of the Megiddo Cult.* The University of Chicago. Oriental Institute Publications 26. The University of Chicago Press. Chicago.

1944, review of The Excavation of Tell Beit Mirsim III (W.F. Albright), *Journal of Biblical Literature:* 191-195.

Mazarakis, A.N. 1987, "Geometric Eretria" *AK* 30: 3 -24.

Mazzoni, S. 1987, "Lo scavo dell'edificio del settore D", *EVO* X,2: 25-83.

1991, "Afis", in Weiss H. (ed) 1991: 279.

1995, "Settlement Pattern and the New Urbanization in Syria at the Time of the Assyrian Conquest", in Liverani, M. (ed) *Neo-Assyrian Geography.* Università di Roma "La Sapienza", Dipartimento do Science storiche, archeologiche e antroplogiche dell'Antichità: Quaderni di Geografia 5. Rome: 181-191.

McGrail, S. 1989, "The shipment of traded goods and of ballast in antiquity", *OJA 8.3:* 353-358.

Minns, E.H. 1913, *Scythians and Greeks. A Survey of Ancient History and Archaeology on the North Coast of the Euxine from the Danube to the Caucasus.* CUP. Cambridge.

Mitchell, T.C. 1982a, "Israel and Judah until the revolt of Jehu (931-841 B.C)", *CAH* III.1: 442-487.

1982b, "Israel and Judah from Jehu until the period of Assyrian domination (841-c.750 B.C.), *CAH* III.1: 488-510.

Möller, A. 2001, *Naukratis. Trade in Archaic Greece.* OUP.

Moorey, P.R.S, 1980, "Metal Wine-sets in the Ancient Near East", *Iranica Antiqua* 15: 181-197.

1988, *Cemeteries of the first millennium B.C. at Deve Huyuk, near Carcemish, salvaged by T.E. Lawrence and C. L. Woolley in 1913. BAR I.S.* 57.

Morris, I. 1986, "Gift and Commodity in Archaic Greece", *Man* 21.1 (New Series): 1-17.

1987, *Burial and ancient society: the rise of the Greek city-state.* New Studies in Archaeology. CUP. Cambridge.

Morris, S.P. 1990, "Greece and the Levant", *JMA* 3.1: 57-66.

1992a, *Daidalos and the Origins of Greek Art.* Princeton University Press. Princeton.

1992b, "Greece beyond East and West: Perspectives and Prospects", in Kopcke G. and Tokumaru, I. 1992 (eds): xiii-xviii.

1998, Bearing Greek Gifts: Euboean Pottery on Sardinia", in M.S Balmuth and R.H. Tykot (eds) 1998: 361-362.

Morton, A.D. 1992, *Excavations at Hamwic: Volume I.* CBA Research Report 84.

Muhly, J. 1970, "Homer and the Phoenicians. The Relations between Greece and the Near East in the Late Bronze and Early Iron Ages", *Berytus* 19: 19-64.

Munn-Rankin, J.M. 1956, "Diplomacy in western Asia in the early second millennium B.C.", *IRAQ* 18: 68-110.

Murray, O. 1983, "The Greek Symposion in History", in Gabba, E. 1983 (ed.), *Tria Corda: Scritti in onore di Arnaldo Momigliano.* Edizioni New Press. Como: 257-272.

Neeft, C.W. 1987, *Protocorinthian Subgeometric aryballoi.* Allard Pierson series 7. Amsterdam.

Niemeier W.-D. 1993, "Tel Kabri: Cretan Fresco Painting in a Canaanite Palace", *AJA* 97.2: 32-33.

2001, "Archaic Greeks in the Orient: Textual and Archaeological Evidence", *BASOR* 322: 11-32.

Niemeyer, H-G. 1982a (ed.), *Phönizier im Westen. Die Beiträge des Internationalen Symposiums über "Die Phönizische Expansion im westlichen Mittelmeerraum". Cologne 24-27, April 1979.* Verlag Philipp von Zabern. Mainz am Rhein.

1982b, "Die Phönizische Niederlassung Toscanos: eine Zwischenbilanz" in Niemeyer, H.G. 1982a (ed.): 185-204.

1990, "The Phoenicians in the Mediterranean: A Non-Greek Model for Expansion and Settlement in Antiquity" in Descœudres J.-P. 1990 (ed.): 469-489.

Nylander, C. 1968, "ASSURIA GRAMMATA. Remarks on the 21st Letter of Themistocles", *OpAth* 8: 119-136.

Oates, J. 1986, *Babylon* (first published 1979). Thames and Hudson Ltd. London.

Osborne, R. 1996, "Pots, trade and the Archaic Greek economy", *Antiquity* 70: 31-44.

Otzen, B. 1979, "Israel under the Assyrians" in Larsen, M.T. 1979 (ed.): 251-261.

Özgüc, T. 1964, "The Art and Architecture of Ancient Kanish," *Anatolia* 8: 27-48.

Papadopoulos, J.K. 1996, "Euboians in Macedonia? A Closer Look" in *OJA* 15(2): 151-181.

1997a, "Innovations, imitations and ceramic style: modes of production and mode of disemmination", in Laffineur, R. and Betancourt, Ph. P. *TEXNH. Craftsmen, craftswomen and craftsmanship in the Aegean Bronze Age. Proceedings of the 6th international Aegean conference, Philadelphia, April 1996 (Aegeum* 16), Liege & Austin: 449-462.

1996, "A bucket, by any other name, and an Athenian stranger in Early Iron Age Crete, *Hesperia* 67: 109-123.

1997b, "Phantom Euboians", *JMA* 10.2: 191-219.

1998, "From Macedonia to Sardinia: Problems of Iron Age Aegean Chronology, and Assumptions of Greek Maritime Primacy" in M.S Balmuth and R.H. Tykot (eds) 1998: 362-369.

Parker, A.J. 1984, "Shipwrecks and Ancient Trade in the Mediterranean", *Archaeological Review from Cambridge* 3.2: 99-114.

Parpola, S. 1990, "Appendix 1. A Letter from Marduk-Aplu-Usur of Anah to Rudamu/Urtamis, King of Hamath" in Riis, P.J. and Buhl, M-L. 1990 (eds): 257-265.

Peacock, D.P.S. and Williams, D.F. 1986, *Amphorae and the Roman Economy, an introductory guide.* Longman. New York.

Peltenburg, E. 1991, "Greeting Gifts and Luxury Faience: a Context for Orientalizing Trends in Late Mycenaean Greece", in Gale N.H. 1991 (ed.): 162-179.

Perreault, J.Y. 1993, "Les *emporia* grecs du Levant: mythe ou réalité?" in Bresson, A. and Rouillard, P. 1993 (eds): 59-81.

Pitt-Rivers, J. 1973, "The Kith and the Kin" in Goody, J. 1973 (ed.), *The Character of Kinship.* CUP: 89-105.

Ploug, G. 1973, *Sukas II. The Aegean, Corinthian and Eastern Greek Pottery and Terracottas.* Publications of the Carlsberg Expedition to Phoenicia 2. Det Kongelige Danske Videnskabernes Selskab Historisk-Filosofiske Skrifter 6.2. Munksgaard. Copenhagen.

Polanyi, K. 1963, "Ports of Trade in Early Societies," *Journal of Economic History* 23: 30-45.

and Arensberg, C.R. and Pearson, H.W. 1957, *Trade and Market in the Early Empires; Economies in History and Theory.* The Free Press and the Falcon's Wing Press. Illinois.

Popham, M.R. 1987, "Lefkandi and the Greek Dark Ages", Cunliffe, B. 1987 (ed.), *Origins. The Roots of European Civilisation.* BBC Books. London: 67-80.

1993a, "The Main Excavation of the Building (1981-3)" in Popham, M.R. Calligas P.G. and Sackett, L.H. 1993 (eds): 7-31.

1993b, "The Sequence of Events and Conclusions", in Popham, M.R. Calligas P.G. and Sackett, L.H. 1993 (eds): 97-101.

and Calligas, P.G. and Sackett, L.H. 1989, "Further Excavation of the Toumba Cemetery at Lefkandi, 1984 and 1986, A Preliminary Report", *AR* 35: 117-129.

1990, (eds) *Lefkandi II. The Protogeometric Building at Toumba. Part 1. The Pottery,* by Catling, R.W.V. and Lemos, I.S. BSA. Thames and Hudson.

1993, (eds), *Lefkandi II. The Protogeometric Building at Toumba. Part 2. The Excavation, Architecture and Finds* (with J. Coulton and H.W. Catling). British School of Archaeology at Athens.

and Hatcher, H. and Pollard, A.M. 1980, "Al Mina and Euboea", *BSA* 75: 151-161.

1983, "Euboean Exports to Al Mina, Cyprus and Crete: A Reassessment", *BSA* 78: 281-90.

and Lemos, I.S. 1992, Review of Rosalinde Kearsley: the pendent semi-circle skyphos. *Gnomon* 64: 152-155.

and Sackett, L.H. and Themelis, P.G. 1979 (eds), *Lefkandi I. The Iron Age. The Settlement. The Cemeteries. Plates.* The British School at Athens. Thames and Hudson.

1980a (eds), *Lefkandi I. The Iron Age. The Settlement. The Cemeteries. Text.* The British School at Athens. Thames and Hudson.

1980b, "The Geometric and Protogeometric Settlement", in Popham M.R., Sackett L.H. and Themelis, P.G. 1980a (eds): 11-26.

1980c, "Historical Conclusions", in Popham M.R, Sackett L.H. and Themelis, P.G. 1980a (eds): 355-369.

1980d, "The Other Finds", in Popham M.R, Sackett L.H. and Themelis, P.G. 1980a (eds): 81-97.

1980e, "The Tombs, Pyres and their Contents", in Popham M.R, Sackett L.H. and Themelis, P.G. 1980a (eds): 109-196.

and Touloupa, E, and Sackett, L.H. 1982, "Further Excavation of the Toumba Cemetery at Lefkandi", *BSA* 77: 213-248.

Porada, E. 1981-1982, "The Cylinder Seals Found at Thebes in Boiotia", *AfO* 28: 1-70.

Porláksson, H. 1978, "Comments on Ports of Trade in Early Medieval Europe", *NAR* 11: 112-114.

Postgate, J.N. 1979, "The Economic Structure of the Assyrian Empire", in Larsen, M.T. 1979 (ed.): 193-221.

1992, "The Land of Assur and the yoke of Assur", *World Archaeology* 23.2: 27-263.

Powell, B.B. 1991, *Homer and the Origin of the Greek Alphabet.* CUP. Cambridge.

Prausnitz, M.W. 1966, "A Phoenician Krater from Akhziv", *Oriens Antiquus* 5: 177-188.

Pritchard, J.B. 1954 (ed.), *The Ancient Near East in Pictures Relating to the Old Testament.* Princeton University Press.

1969 (ed.), *Ancient Near Eastern Texts Relating to the Old Testament* (first published 1950). Princeton University Press.

1972, "The Phoenicians in Their Homeland", *Expedition* 14.1: 14-23.

1975, *Sarepta: A Preliminary Report on the Iron Age. Excavations of the University Museum of the University of Pennsylvania, 1970-1972. Museum Monographs* 35. The University Museum. University of Pennsylvania. Philadelpheia.

1978, *Recovering Sarepta, a Phoenician city. Excavations at Sarafand, Lebanon, 1969-1974 by the University Museum of the University of Pennsylvania.* Princeton University Press.

1983, "Sarepta and Phoenician Culture in the West", *Atti del I Congresso Internazionale di Studi Fenici e Punici. Roma 5-10 Novembre 1979.* Volume II. Consiglio Nazionale delle Ricerche. Istituto per la civiltà fenicia e punica (*Studi Fenici e Punici* 2): 521-525.

Pucci, G. 1983, "Pottery and Trade in the Roman Period", in Garnsey, P. Hopkins, K. and Whittaker, C.R. 1979 (eds), *Trade in the Ancient Economy.* Chatto and Hogarth Press. London: 105-117.

Quiller, B. 1981, "The dynamics of Homeric society", *Symbolae Osloenses* 56: 109-155.

Raban, A. 1998, "Near Eastern Harbours: thirteenth-seventh centuries BCE", in Gitin, S. Mazar A. and Stern, E. 1998: 428-438.

Rathje, A. 1984, "I *keimelia* orientalia", *Opus* 3.2: 341-354.

1988, "Manners and Customs in Central Italy in the Orientalising Period: Influences from the Near East", *Acta Hyperborea* 1: 81-90.

1990, "The Adoption of the Homeric Banquet in Central Italy in the Orientalizing Period", in Murray, O. 1990 (ed.), *Sympotica. A Symposium on the Symposion.* The Clarendon Press. Oxford: 279-288.

Rathje, W.L. and Sabloff, J.A. 1972, "A Model of Ports-of-Trade". Unpublished paper presented at the 37th Annual Meeting of the Sociey for American Archaeology, May 5, 1972, Miami.

1973, "Ancient Maya commercial systems: a research design for the island of Cozumel, Mexico", *World Archaeology* 5.1: 221-231.

1975, "Theoretical Background: General Models and Questions", in Sabloff, J.A. and Rathje W.L. 1975a (eds): 6-20.

Reisner, G.A. Fisher, C.S. and Lyon, D.G. 1924, *Harvard Excavations at Samaria 1908-1910.* Harvard University Press. Cambridge.

Renfrew, C. 1975, "Trade as Action at a Distance: Questions of Integration and Communication" in Sabloff, J.A. and Lamberg-Karlovsky, C.C. 1975 (eds), *Ancient Civilisation and Trade.* A School of America Research Book. University of New Mexico Press. Albuquerque: 3-59.

1980, "The Great Tradition versus the Great Divide: Archaeology as Anthropology?", *AJA* 84: 287-298.

1986, "Varna and the emergence of wealth in prehistoric Europe", in Appadurai, A. 1986b (ed.): 141-168.

Revere, R.B. 1957, "'No Man's Coast': Ports of Trade in The Eastern Mediterranean", in Polanyi *et al.* 1957: 38-63.

Richter, G.M.A. 1904-1905, "The Distribution of Attic Vases", *BSA* 11: 224-242.

Ridgway, D. 1973, "The first Western Greeks: Campanian Coasts and Southern Etruria", in Hawkes, C. and Hawkes, S. 1973 (eds), *Greeks, Celts and Romans.* J.M. Dent and Sons Ltd. London: 5-38.

1978, "Composition and Provenance of Western Geometric Pottery: a Prospectus", *Papers in Italian Archaeology (BAR I.S.* 41): 121-128.

1982, "The eighth century pottery at Pithekoussai: an interim report" in *Céramique:* 69-101.

1984, *L'Alba della Magna Grecia.* Archeologia 7. Longanesi & C. Milan.

1988, "The Etruscans", *CAH* IV: 634-675.

1992, *The First Western Greeks* (first published in Italian, 1984). CUP.

1997, "Nestor's Cup and the Etruscans", *OJA* 16: 325-344.

1999, "The Carthiginian Connection: a view from San Montano", in Rolle, R. Schmidt, K. and Docter, R. (eds), *Archäologische Studien in Kontaktzonen der antiken Welt.* Joachim Jungius-Ges.Wiss. Hamburg, 87. Vandenhoeck & Ruprecht. Göttingen: 301-318.

2000a, "The first Western Greeks revisited" in Ridgway, C. Serra Ridgway, F.R. Pearce, M. Herring, E. Whitehouse, R.D. and Wilkins, J.B. (eds) *Ancient Italy in its Mediterranean Setting. Studies in honour of Ellen Macnamara.* Accordia Research Institute, University of London: 179-191.

2000b, "The Orientalizing Phenomenon in Campania: sources and manifestations", *in Akten des Kolloquiums zum Thema: Der Orient und Etrurien. Zum Phänomen des 'Orientalisierens' im westlichen Mittelmeerraum. Tübingen 1997.* Istituti Editoriali e Polografici Internazionali: 233-244.

and Ridgway, F.R, 1979 (eds), *Italy Before the Romans. The Iron Age, Orientalizing and Etruscan Periods.* Academic Press. London.

Riis, P.J. 1948, *Hama II.3. Fouilles et recherches 1931-1938. Les cimetières à crémation.* Copenhagen.

1958-1959, "L'activité de la Mission archéologique danoise sur la côte phénicienne en 1958", *AAS* 8-9: 107-132.

1965, "L'activité de la Mission archéologique danoise sur la côte phénicienne en 1963", *AAS* 15: 57-82.

1970, *Sukas I. The North-Eastern Sanctuary and the First Settling of Greeks in Syria and Palestine.* Publications of the Carlsberg Expedition to Phoenicia 1. Det Kongelige Danske Videnskabernes Selskab Historisk-Filosofiske Skrifter 5.1. Munksgaard: Copenhagen.

1982, "Griechen in Phönizien" in Niemeyer, H.G. 1982a (ed.): 237-255.

1991, "Les problèmes actuals de l'éstablissement pré-hellénistique de Grecs sur la côte phénicienne (lieux, dates, modalités)", *Atti del II Congresso Internazionale di Studi Fenici e Punici I. Roma, 9-14 Novembre 1987.* Consiglio Nazionale delle ricerche. Roma: 203-211.

and Buhl, M-L, 1990, *Les objets de la période dite syro-hittite (Âge du Fer).* København: Nationalmuseen.

Robb, K. 1994, *Literacy and Paideia in ancient Greece.* OUP.

Robertson, M. 1940, "The Excavations at Al Mina, Sueidia, IV. The Early Greek Vases, *JHS* 60: 2-21.

Röllig, W. 1992, "Asia Minor as a Bridge between East and West. The Role of the Phoenicians and Aramaeans in the Transfer of Culture" in Kopcke, G. and Tokumaru, I. 1992 (eds): 93-102.

Rouvier, J. 1896, "Une métropole phéniciènne oubliée; Laodicée de Canaan. *Revue Numismatique* 3 series, Vol 14: 265-282 and 377-396.

Rupp, D. 1987, "Vive le roi: the emergence of the state in Iron Age Cyprus", in *idem* 1987 (ed.), *Western Cyprus: connections. SIMA* 77: 147-169.

1988, "The 'Royal Tombs' at Salamis (Cyprus): Ideological Messages of Power and Authority", *JMA* 1.1: 111-139.

1989, "Puttin' on the Ritz: manifestations of high status in Iron Age Cyprus", in Peltenburg, E. 1989 (ed.), *Early Society in Cyprus.* Edinburgh University Press. Edinburgh: 366-362.

Sabloff, J A, and Friedel D.A. 1975, "A Model of a Pre-Columbian Trading Center" in Sabloff, J.A. and Lamberg-Karlovsky, C.C. 1975 (eds), *Ancient Civilisation and Trade.* A School of America Research Book. University of New Mexico Press. Albuquerque: 369-408.

Sabloff, J A, and Rathje, W.L. 1975a (eds), *A Study of Changing pre-Columbian Commercial Systems. The 1972-1972 Seasons at Cozumel, Mexico. A preliminary report.* Peabody Museum of Archaeology and Ethnology. Harvard University. Cambridge, Massachussets.

1975b, "Cozumel's Place in Yucatean Culture History", in *idem* 1975a (eds): 21-28.

Sackett, L.H. Hankey, V. Howell, P.J. Jacobsen, T.W. and Popham, M.R. 1966, "Prehistoric Euboea: Contributions towards a Survey", *BSA* 61: 33-112.

Sagoma, A.G. 1982, "Levantine storage jars of the 13th to 4th century B.C.", *OpA^th* 14.1: 73-110.

Saidah, R. 1966, "Fouilles de Khaldé. Rapport préliminaire sur la première et deuxième campagnes (1961-2)", *Bulletin de Musée de Beyrouth* 19: 51-90.

1971, "Objets grecs d'époque géométrique découverts récemment sur le littoral libanais (à Khaldé près de Beyrouth)", *AAS* 21: 193-198.

1977, "Une tombe de l'age du fer à Tambourit (région de Sidon)", *Berytus* 25: 135-146.

Salmon, J. 2000, "Pots and Profits", in Tsetskhladze, G.R. Prag, A.J.N.W. and Snodgrass, A.M. (eds): 245-252.

Saltz, D.L. 1978, *Greek Geometric Pottery in the East: The Chronological Implications.* Unpublished Ph.D dissertation, Harvard University.

Sandro, N. di, 1986, "Le anfore arcaiche dallo scarico Gosetti, Pithecusa" *Cahiers des Amphores Archaïques et Classiques 2. Cahiers du centre Jean Bérard* 12. Institut Français de Naples. Naples.

Sapouna-Sakellaraki, E. 1998, "Geometric Kyme: the excavation at Viglatouri, Kyme, on Euboea", in Bats, M. and d'Agostino, B. (eds) 1998, *Euboica. L'Eubea e la presenza euboica in Calcidica e in Occidente. Atti del Convegno Internazionale di Napoli, 1996.* Collection Centre Jean Bérard 16/AION, Quaderno 12. Napoli: 59-104.

Schofield, E. 1983, "The Minoan emigrant", Krzyszkowska, O. and Nixon, L. 1983 (eds), *Minoan Society. Proceedings of the Cambridge Colloquium 1981.* Bristol Classical Press: 293-301.

Sherratt E.S. 1982, Patterns of contact: manufacture and distribution of Mycenaean pottery, 1400-1100 B.C. in Best, J.G.P. & de Vries, N.M.W. (eds) *Interactions and acculturation in the Mediterranean*, II, Amsterdam: 179-195.

1992b, "Immigration and archaeology: some indirect reflections", *Acta Cypria* Part 2: 316-347.

1999, "*E pur si muove*": pots, markets and values in the second millennium Mediterranean" in Crielaard, J.P. *et al.* (eds): 163-211.

and Sherratt, A. 1991, "From Luxuries to Commodities: The Nature of Mediterranean Bronze Age Trading Systems", in Gale N.H. 1991 (ed.): 351-384.

1993, "The growth of the Mediterranean economy in the early first millennium BC", *World Archaeology* 24.3: 361-378.

Shiloh, Y. 1970, "The Four-Room House: its Situation and Function in the Israelite city" *IEJ* 20: 180-190.

1989, "Judah and Jerusalem in the Eighth-Sixth centuries B.C.E.", *Annual of the American School of Oriental Research* 49: 97-105.

Smith, S. 1942, "The Greek Trade at Al Mina: A Footnote to Oriental History", *AJ* 22.2: 87-112.

Smith T.R. 1987, *Mycenaean Trade and Interaction in the West Central Mediterranean, 1600-1000 B.C. BAR I. S.* 371.

Snodgrass, A.M. 1971, *The Dark Age of Greece; an archaeological survey of the eleventh to the eighth centuries B.C.* Edinburgh University Press.
1974, "An historical Homeric society?" *JHS* 94: 114-25.
1980, *Archaic Greece*. J.M. Dent and Sons Ltd. London.
1985, "The New Archaeology and the Classical Archaeologist", *AJA* 89: 31-7.
1986, "Interaction by design: The Greek city state", in Renfrew, C. and Cherry, J. 1986 (eds), *Peer Polity Interaction and Socio-Political Change*: 47-58. CUP.
1991, "Bronze Age Exchange: A Minimalist Position", in Gale N.H. (ed.): 15-20.
1994a "The Growth and standing of the Early Westen Colonies" in Tsetskhladze, G, and De Angelis, F, 1994: 1-10.
1994b, Gains, losses and survivals: what we can infer from the eleventh century BC, in: Karageorghis (ed.), *Proceedings of the international symposium 'Cyprus in the 11th century BC', Nicosia, October 1993*, Nicosia: 167-175.

Steegmuller, F. 1973 (trans. and ed.), *Flaubert in Egypt: A Sensibility on Tour*. Little, Brown & Co. Boston.

Sznycer, M. 1979, "L'inscription phénicienne de Tekke, près de Cnossos", *Kadmos* 18: 89-93.

Sørensen, L.W. 1988, "Greek Pottery from the Geometric to the Archaic period found on Cyprus", *Acta Hyperborea* 1: 12-32.

Steel, L. 1998, The Social Impact of Mycenaean Imported Pottery in Cyprus. *BSA* 93: 285-96.

Stronach, D. 1959, "The development of the fibula in the Near East", in *Iraq* 21: 181-206.
1995, "The Imagery of the Wine Bowl: Wine in Assyria in the Early First Millennium B.C", in McGovern P.E. Fleming, S.J. and Katz, S.H. (eds) *Food and nutrition in history and anthropology v.11*. Amsterdam: Gordon and Breach Publishers: 175-195.

Sukenik, E.L. 1940, "Note on a Pottery Vessel of the Old Testament", *PEQ*: 59-60.

Swift, G.F. Jnr, 1958, *The Pottery of the 'Amq Phases K to O, and Its Historical Relationships*. Unpublished Ph.D dissertation, University of Chicago.

Szentléleky, T. 1969, *Ancient Lamps*. Adolf M. Hakkert. Amsterdam.

Tadmor, H. 1958, "The Campaigns of Sargon II of Assur: A Chronological-Historical Study", *JCS* 12: 77-100.
1966, "Philistia under Assyrian rule" *Biblical Archaeologist* 29: 86-102.
1975, "Assyrian and the West: The Ninth Century and its Aftermath", in Goedicke H. and Roberts, J.J.M. 1975 (eds), *Unity and Diversity. Essays in the History,*

Literature and Religion of the Ancient Near East. The John Hopkins University Press. Baltimore and London: 36-48.
1994, *The inscriptions of Tiglath Pileser III, King of Assyria*. Israel Academy of Science and Humanities. Jerusalem.

Tandy, D. W and Neale, W. C, 1994, "Karl Polanyi's Distinctive Approach to Social Analysis and the Case of Ancient Greece: Ideas, Criticisms, Consequences, in Duncan and Tandy, D.W (eds). *From Political Economy to Anthropology: Situating Economic Life in Past Societies.* Montreal. Black Rose Books: 9-33

Taylor, J. du Plat, 1959, "The Cypriot and Syrian Pottery from Al Mina, Syria," *Iraq* 21: 62-92.

Torrence, R. 1978, "Comments on Ports of Trade in Early Medieval Europe," *NAR* 11: 108-111.

Tsetskhladze, G.R. Prag, A.J.N.W. and Snodgrass, A.M. (eds), 2000, *PERIPLOUS. Papers on Classical Art and Archaeology Presented to Sir John Boardman*. Thames and Hudson.

van Gennep, 1960, *The Rites of Passage* (translated by Vizedom M.B. and Caffee G.L.; first published 1909). Routledge and Kegan Paul. London.

van Wijngaarden, 1999 "An archaeological approach to the concept of value. Mycenaean pottery at Ugarit (Syria), in *Archaeological Dialogues* 1999: 2-23.

von Reden, S. 1995, *Exchange in Ancient Greece*. Duckworth. London.

Vandenabeele, F. 1988, "Kourotrophoi in the Cypriote Terracotta Production from the Early Bronze Age to the Late Archaic Period", *RDAC*: 25-34.

Vickers, M. 1984, "The influence of exotic materials on Attic white-ground pottery", in Brijder, H.A.G. 1984 (ed.), *Ancient Greek and Related Pottery. Proceedings of the International Vase Symposium in Amsterdam, 12-15 April 1984*. Allard Pierson Series 5. Amsterdam: 88-97.
1985, "Artful crafts: The influence of metalwork on Athenian painted pottery", *JHS* 105: 108-128.
1985/6, "Imaginary Etruscans: Changing perceptions of Etruria since the Fifteenth Century", *Hephaistos* 7-8: 153-168.
1986, "Silver, Copper and Ceramics in Ancient Athens", in Vickers, M. 1986 (ed.), *Pots and Pans. A Colloquium on Precious Metals and Ceramics in the Muslim, Chinese and Graeco-Roman Worlds, Oxford 1985*. Oxford Studies in Islamic Art III. OUP: 137-151.
1989, "The Cultural Context of Ancient Greek Ceramics: An Essay in Skeuomorphism", in McGovern, P.E. and Notis, N.D. (eds), *Cross-craft and Cross-cultural Interactions in Ceramics* (Ceramics and Civilization 4; Westerville, Ohio, 1989) 45-64.

Villard, Fr. 1960, *La céramique grecque de Marseille (VIe -IVe siècle). Essai d'histoire économique*. Éditions E. de Boccard. Paris.

Waldbaum, J.C. 1994, "Early Greek Contacts with the Southern Levant, ca. 1000-600 B.C.: The Eastern Perspective", *BASOR* 293: 53-66.

1997, "Greeks *in* the East or Greeks *and* the East? Problems in the Definition and Recognition of Presence", *BASOR* 305: 1-17.

Warren, P.W. 1975, *The Making of the Past. Aegean Civilisations*. Elsevier Phaidon. Lausanne.

Weinfeld, M. 1973, "Covenant Terminology in the Ancient Near East and its Influence on the West", *JAOS* 93.2: 190-199.

Weiss, H. 1991, "Archaeology in Syria", *AJA* 95: 683-740.

Wells, P.S. 1980, *Culture contact and culture change: Early Iron Age central Europe and the Mediterranean World.* CUP.

Wenning, R. 1981, "Griechische Importe in Palästina aus der Zeit vor Alexander d. Gr. Vorbericht über ein Forschungsprojekt", *Boreas. Münstersche Beiträge zur Archäologie* 4: 29-46.
1991, "Nachricten über Griechen in Palästina in der Eisenzeit" in Fossey, J.M. 1991 (ed.): 207-219.

West, M.L. 1988, "The Rise of the Greek Epic", *JHS* 108: 151-172.
1997, *The East Face of Helicon. Western Asiatic Elements in Greek Poetry and Myth*. Clarendon Press. Oxford.

Winter, I.J. 1979, "On the Problems of Karatepe: The Reliefs and their Contexts", *AS* 29: 115-152.
1986, "The King and the Cup: Iconography of the Royal Presentation Scene on Ur III Seals", in Kelly-Buccellati M. 1986 (ed.), in collaboration with Matthiae, P. and Loon, M. van *Insight Through Images. Studies in Honor of Edith Porada*. Bibliotheca Mesopotamica 21. Undena Publications. Malibu: 253-268.
1995, "Homer's Phoenicians: History, Ethnology or Literary Trope? (A perspective on Early Orientalism)" in Carter, J.B. and Morris, S.P (eds).: *The Ages of Homer*. University of Texas Press. Austin: 247-272.

Woolley, C.L. 1937, "Excavations near Antioch in 1936", *AJ* 17.1: 1-15.
1938, "Excavations at Al Mina, Suedia I and II", *JHS* 58: 1-30 and 133-170.
1948, "The Date of Al Mina", *JHS* 68: 148.
1959, *A Forgotten Kingdom. Being a Record of the Results Obtained from the Excavations of Two Mounds Athchana and Al Mina in the Turkish Hatay* (first published 1953). Max Parrish. London.

Wriedt Sørensen, L. 1988 "Greek Pottery found in Cyprus", in *Acta Hyperborea* 1: 12-32

Wright G.E. 1978, "A Characteristic North Israelite House", in Moorey, R. and Parr, P, 1978 (eds), *Archaeology in the Levant. Essays for Kathleen Kenyon*. Aris and Phillips Ltd. Warminster: 149-154.

Yeivin, S. 1962, "Topographic and Ethnic Notes III. Nos. 28-31 in Shoshenk I's list of conquered towns", *Journal of Egyptian Archeology* 48: 75-80.

Yener, A. Edens, C. Harrison, C.P. Verstraete, J. and Wilkinson, T.J. 2000, "The Amuq Valley Regional Project, 1995-1998", *AJA* 104: 163-220.

Yon, M. 1992, "Ugarit: the urban habitat. The Present State of the Archaeological Picture": *BASOR* 286: 19-34

Zaccagnini, C. 1987, "Aspects of ceremonial exchange in the Near East during the late second millennium BC", in Rowlands, M. Larsen, M.T. and Kristiansen, K. 1987 (eds), *Centre and Periphery in the Ancient World*. CUP: 57-65.
1993, "In margine all'*emporion*: modelli di scambio nelle economie del Vicino Oriente antico", in Bresson, A. and Rouillard, P. 1993 (eds): 127-143.

Zadok, R. 1996, "Geographical and Onomastic Remarks on H Tadmor, 'The Inscriptions of Tiglath-Pileser III, King of Assyria', *Nouvelles Assyriologiques Brèves et Utilitaires* 1: 11-13.

Index